D0100119

MOST requested RECIPES

TRUSTED MEDIA BRANDS, INC • MILWAUKEE, WI

362 RECIPES TO WIN YOU RAVES!

Taste of Home readers have created the recipe swap of all recipe swaps! We've pooled more than 360 culinary gems our home cooks have eagerly rated the best of the best—those trusted standbys you can't live without. Now you, too, can enjoy a delicious sampling of these all-time favorites with ***Taste of Home Most Requested Recipes***.

This treasure trove of top reader picks is packed with all the delectable homemade creations you've come to know and love. You'll find everything from easy weeknight dinners to impressive company fare, including appetizers, brunch selections, soups, salads, sides and a scrumptious assortment of cookies and desserts. A bonus chapter, Seasonal Specialties, has memorable treats for year-round entertaining.

Sprinkled throughout the book, you'll find valuable recipe reviews from our TasteofHome.com community. These testimonials share why readers love a particular dish—and why you'll love it, too!

Two at-a-glance icons are a quick way for you to find the most popular recipe features:

FAST FIX These recipes are ready in 30 minutes or less.

(5)INGREDIENTS These recipes require no more than five items (not counting water, oil, salt and pepper) to create a delicious dish.

Each recipe in this collection has been tested by our cooking experts, so you can rest assured it is easy to follow and will taste amazing. You'll also find handy kitchen tips, easy-to-follow instructions, gorgeous photography, and prep and cook times that will allow you to make the most of your time in the kitchen.

With the best-loved recipes featured inside ***Most Requested Recipes***, you're sure to place a winner on the dinner table each and every night.

MOST requested RECIPES

1610 N. 2nd St., Suite 102, Milwaukee WI 53212-3906

International Standard Book Number: 978-1-61765-520-3
International Standard Serial Number: 2166-0522
Component Number: 119200016H

Printed in U.S.A.

1 3 5 7 9 10 8 6 4 2

Pictured on the front cover: Three-Cheese Meatball Mostaccioli (p. 112); Easy Fresh Strawberry Pie (p. 178); Pork and Beef Barbecue (p. 51)
Pictured on the back cover: Pistachio Thumbprints (p. 198); Slow Cooker Lime Chicken Chili (p. 132)

TABLE OF CONTENTS

ARTICHOKE & SPINACH DIP PIZZA, 11

VIETNAMESE PORK LETTUCE WRAPS, 10

HONEY-GARLIC GLAZED MEATBALLS, 20

HOT SPICED CHERRY CIDER, 19

APPETIZERS, SNACKS & BEVERAGES

Who doesn't love to sample different and delicious foods at parties and gatherings? Tantalizing appetizers, pop-in-your-mouth snacks and refreshing sippers are the tastiest way to introduce your guests to fun new flavors. This chapter makes it easy to serve up the most delectable dips and spreads, saucy meatballs, light and flaky puffs, baked wontons, crunchy munchies and other party starters everyone is sure to rave over.

FAST FIX

QUICK WHITE SANGRIA

Using white instead of red wine makes my version of sangria a bit lighter, yet it has the same wonderful sweetness. Frozen fruit allows me to serve this refreshing sipper any time of year.

—SHARON TIPTON CASSELBERRY, FL

START TO FINISH: 15 MIN.
MAKES: 6 SERVINGS

- **¼ cup sugar**
- **¼ cup brandy**
- **1 cup sliced peeled fresh or frozen peaches, thawed**
- **1 cup sliced fresh or frozen sliced strawberries, thawed**
- **1 medium lemon, sliced**
- **1 medium lime, sliced**
- **1 bottle (750 milliliters) dry white wine, chilled**
- **1 can (12 ounces) lemon-lime soda, chilled**
- **Ice cubes**

In a pitcher, mix sugar and brandy until sugar is dissolved. Add remaining ingredients; stir gently to combine. Serve over ice.

MINI MAC & CHEESE BITES

Young relatives were coming for a Christmas party, so I wanted something fun for them to eat. Instead, the adults devoured my mini mac and cheese bites!

—KATHERINE MAINIERO POUGHKEEPSIE, NY

PREP: 35 MIN. • **BAKE:** 10 MIN.
MAKES: 3 DOZEN

- **2 cups uncooked elbow macaroni**
- **1 cup seasoned bread crumbs, divided**
- **2 tablespoons butter**
- **2 tablespoons all-purpose flour**
- **½ teaspoon onion powder**
- **½ teaspoon garlic powder**
- **½ teaspoon seasoned salt**
- **1¾ cups 2% milk**
- **2 cups (8 ounces) shredded sharp cheddar cheese, divided**
- **1 cup (4 ounces) shredded Swiss cheese**
- **¾ cup biscuit/baking mix**
- **2 large eggs, lightly beaten**

1. Preheat oven to 425°. Cook macaroni according to package directions; drain.
2. Meanwhile, sprinkle 1/4 cup bread crumbs into 36 greased mini-muffin cups. In a large saucepan, melt butter over medium heat. Stir in flour and seasonings until smooth; gradually whisk in milk. Bring to a boil, stirring constantly; cook and stir 1-2 minutes or until thickened. Stir in 1 cup cheddar cheese and Swiss cheese until melted.
3. Remove from heat; stir in biscuit mix, eggs and 1/2 cup bread crumbs. Add macaroni; toss to coat. Spoon about 2 tablespoons macaroni mixture into prepared mini-muffin cups; sprinkle with remaining cheddar cheese and bread crumbs.
4. Bake 8-10 minutes or until golden brown. Cool in pans for 5 minutes before serving.

PIZZA ROLLS

This is my husband's famous version of store-bought pizza rolls, and our family loves them. They take some time to make, but they freeze well. So when all the prep work is done, we get to enjoy the fruits of our labor for a long time!
—JULIE GAINES NORMAL, IL

PREP: 50 MIN. • **COOK:** 5 MIN./BATCH
MAKES: 32 ROLLS

- **4 cups (16 ounces) shredded pizza cheese blend or part-skim mozzarella cheese**
- **1 pound bulk Italian sausage, cooked and drained**
- **2 packages (3 ounces each) sliced pepperoni, chopped**
- **1 medium green pepper, finely chopped**
- **1 medium sweet red pepper, finely chopped**
- **1 medium onion, finely chopped**
- **2 jars (14 ounces each) pizza sauce**
- **32 egg roll wrappers**
- **Oil for frying**
- **Additional pizza sauce for dipping, warmed, optional**

1. In a large bowl, combine the cheese, sausage, pepperoni, peppers and onion. Stir in pizza sauce until combined. Place about 1/4 cup filling in the center of each egg roll wrapper. Fold bottom corner over filling; fold sides toward center over filling. Moisten remaining corner with water and roll up tightly to seal.
2. In an electric skillet, heat 1 in. of oil to 375°. Fry pizza rolls for 1-2 minutes on each side or until golden brown. Drain on paper towels. Serve with additional pizza sauce if desired.

TOP TIP

Sweet Italian Sausage vs. Hot Italian Sausage

When a *Taste of Home* recipe calls for Italian sausage, it is referring to sweet Italian sausage. Recipes using hot Italian sausage specifically call for that type of sausage.

5 INGREDIENTS FAST FIX

MUSHROOM BACON BITES

When we have a big cookout, these tasty bites always make an appearance. They're easy to assemble and then brush with prepared barbecue sauce.

—GINA ROESNER ASHLAND, MO

START TO FINISH: 20 MIN. • **MAKES:** 2 DOZEN

24 medium fresh mushrooms
12 bacon strips, halved
1 cup barbecue sauce

1. Wrap each mushroom with a piece of bacon; secure with a toothpick. Thread onto metal or soaked wooden skewers; brush with barbecue sauce.

2. Grill, uncovered, over indirect medium heat for 10-15 minutes or until bacon is crisp and mushrooms are tender, turning and basting occasionally with remaining barbecue sauce.

FAST FIX

DILL BLOODY MARYS

With a nice level of pepper and just enough dill from the pickle, these Bloody Marys are sure to please. Fun garnishes make them like a meal unto themselves!

—JAY FERKOVICH GREEN BAY, WI

START TO FINISH: 10 MIN. • **MAKES:** 2 SERVINGS

1½ cups Clamato juice, chilled
2 tablespoons dill pickle juice
1 tablespoon Worcestershire sauce
¼ teaspoon celery salt
⅛ to ¼ teaspoon pepper
⅛ teaspoon hot pepper sauce
¼ cup vodka, optional
Ice cubes
2 celery ribs
2 pepperoni-flavored meat snack sticks
2 dill pickle spears
2 pitted ripe olives

In a small pitcher, combine the first six ingredients. Stir in vodka if desired. Pour into two glasses filled with ice; garnish with celery, snack sticks, pickles and olives.

STUFFED BREAD APPETIZERS

I recommend doubling the recipe for this tasty appetizer because folks won't be able to stop at just one slice!

—TRACY WESTROM LANSDALE, PA

PREP: 20 MIN. + CHILLING • **MAKES:** ABOUT 2 DOZEN

- **2 packages (one 8 ounces, one 3 ounces) cream cheese, softened**
- **1 cup chopped celery**
- **1 cup (4 ounces) shredded cheddar cheese**
- **½ cup chopped sweet red pepper**
- **½ cup chopped water chestnuts**
- **1 teaspoon garlic salt**
- **1 loaf (26 inches) French bread, halved lengthwise**
- **Mayonnaise**
- **Dried parsley flakes**
- **4 dill pickle spears**
- **4 slices deli ham**

1. In a large bowl, combine the first six ingredients; set aside.

2. Hollow out top and bottom of bread, leaving a ½-in. shell (discard removed bread or save for another use). Spread thin layer of mayonnaise over bread; sprinkle with parsley.

3. Fill each half with cheese mixture. Wrap pickle spears in ham; place lengthwise over cheese mixture on bottom half of loaf. Replace top; press together to seal.

4. Wrap in foil; refrigerate overnight. Just before serving, cut into 1-in. slices.

(5) INGREDIENTS FAST FIX

MINI REUBEN CUPS

Treat your company to this hot and delicious nibble. They're easy to make, and the prebaked wonton wrappers hold all the savory flavors of a classic reuben sandwich.

—GRACE NELTNER LAKESIDE PARK, KY

START TO FINISH: 30 MIN. • **MAKES:** 2 DOZEN

- **24 wonton wrappers**
- **3 packages (2 ounces each) thinly sliced deli corned beef, chopped**
- **⅓ cup sauerkraut, rinsed and well drained**
- **⅓ cup Thousand Island salad dressing**
- **⅔ cup shredded Swiss cheese**

1. Press wonton wrappers into miniature muffin cups coated with cooking spray. Bake at 350° for 6-7 minutes or until lightly browned.

2. Meanwhile, in a small bowl, combine the corned beef, sauerkraut and dressing. Spoon into wonton cups. Sprinkle with cheese.

3. Bake for 8-10 minutes or until filling is heated through. Serve warm.

BLUE CHEESE ONION DIP

I decided to tweak the typical ho-hum onion soup dip you see at every gathering by adding crumbled blue cheese and walnuts for a little crunch. Everyone seems to like the result, because they can't get enough.

—VICKI DESY TUCSON, AZ

PREP: 10 MIN. + CHILLING • **MAKES:** 12 SERVINGS (¼ CUP EACH)

- **2 cups (16 ounces) sour cream**
- **1 cup (4 ounces) crumbled blue cheese**
- **⅔ cup mayonnaise**
- **2 tablespoons onion soup mix**
- **1 garlic clove, minced**
- **⅓ cup chopped walnuts, toasted**
- **Assorted fresh vegetables or potato chips**

In a small bowl, mix the first five ingredients until blended. Refrigerate, covered, at least 2 hours to allow flavors to blend. Just before serving, top with walnuts. Serve with vegetables or chips.

NOTE *To toast nuts, bake in a shallow pan in a 350° oven for 5-10 minutes or cook in a skillet over low heat until lightly browned, stirring occasionally.*

JALAPENO POPPER SPREAD

I've been told by fellow party-goers that this recipe tastes exactly like a jalapeno popper. I like that it can be made without much fuss.

—ARIANE MCALPINE PENTICTON, BC

PREP: 10 MIN. • **BAKE:** 25 MIN.
MAKES: 16 SERVINGS

- **2 packages (8 ounces each) cream cheese, softened**
- **1 cup mayonnaise**
- **½ cup shredded Monterey Jack cheese**
- **¼ cup canned chopped green chilies**
- **¼ cup canned diced jalapeno peppers**
- **1 cup shredded Parmesan cheese**
- **½ cup panko (Japanese) bread crumbs**
- **Sweet red and yellow pepper pieces and corn chips**

In a large bowl, beat the first five ingredients until blended; spread into an ungreased 9-in. pie plate. Sprinkle with the Parmesan cheese; top with the bread crumbs. Bake at 400° for 25-30 minutes or until lightly browned. Serve with peppers and corn chips.

VIETNAMESE PORK LETTUCE WRAPS

Casual, flavorful and low in carbohydrates, these wraps are a perfect low-fuss way to feed a group. Place the ingredients in separate dishes, and let your guests assemble their own wrap, which allows them to personalize each wrap to suit their tastes.

—GRETCHEN BARNES FAIRFAX, VA

PREP: 25 MIN. + STANDING • **COOK:** 10 MIN.
MAKES: 8 SERVINGS

- **½ cup white vinegar**
- **¼ cup sugar**
- **⅛ teaspoon salt**
- **2 medium carrots, julienned**
- **½ medium onion, cut into thin slices**

FILLING

- **1 pound ground pork**
- **1 tablespoon minced fresh gingerroot**
- **1 garlic clove, minced**
- **2 tablespoons reduced-sodium soy sauce**
- **1 tablespoon mirin (sweet rice wine)**
- **¼ teaspoon salt**
- **¼ teaspoon pepper**
- **1 teaspoon fish sauce, optional**

ASSEMBLY

- **8 Bibb lettuce leaves**
- **½ English cucumber, finely chopped**
- **1 small sweet red pepper, finely chopped**
- **3 green onions, chopped**
- **½ cup each coarsely chopped fresh basil, cilantro and mint**
- **1 jalapeno pepper, seeded and finely chopped**
- **¼ cup salted peanuts, chopped**
- **Hoisin sauce**
- **Lime wedges**

1. In a small bowl, mix vinegar, sugar and salt until blended. Stir in carrots and onion; let stand at room temperature 30 minutes.

2. In a large skillet, cook the pork, ginger and garlic over medium heat 6-8 minutes or until pork is no longer pink, breaking up pork into crumbles; drain. Stir in soy sauce, mirin, salt, pepper and, if desired, fish sauce.

3. To serve, drain carrot mixture. Place pork mixture in lettuce leaves; top with cucumber, red pepper, green onions, carrot mixture and herbs. Sprinkle with jalapeno and peanuts; drizzle with hoisin sauce. Squeeze lime juice over tops. Fold lettuce over filling.

FAST FIX

ARTICHOKE & SPINACH DIP PIZZA

I swap garlic oil for regular olive oil when I have it on hand. It adds an extra punch of flavor without overpowering the toppings.
—SHELLY BEVINGTON HERMISTON, OR

START TO FINISH: 20 MIN.
MAKES: 24 PIECES

- **1 prebaked 12-inch pizza crust**
- **1 tablespoon olive oil**
- **1 cup spinach dip**
- **1 cup (4 ounces) shredded part-skim mozzarella cheese**
- **1 jar (7½ ounces) marinated quartered artichoke hearts, drained**
- **½ cup oil-packed sun-dried tomatoes, patted dry and chopped**
- **¼ cup chopped red onion**

1. Preheat oven to 450°. Place crust on an ungreased pizza pan; brush with oil. Spread spinach dip over top. Sprinkle with cheese, artichokes, tomatoes and red onion.
2. Bake 8-10 minutes or until cheese is melted and edges are lightly browned. Cut into squares.

(5) INGREDIENTS FAST FIX

WATERMELON COOLER

Summer means cooling off with a slice of watermelon and a glass of cold lemonade. This recipe combines two favorites in one.
—DARLENE BRENDEN SALEM, OR

START TO FINISH: 10 MIN.
MAKES: 4 SERVINGS

- **2 cups lemonade**
- **3 cups seedless watermelon, coarsely chopped**
- **1 cup crushed ice**

In a blender, combine all ingredients; cover and process until smooth. Pour into chilled glasses; serve immediately.

> "Add a splash of tequila and serve in a hurricane glass to make it a pleaser for the adults."
> **—DRAGONSLAYERSROSEBUD** FROM TASTEOFHOME.COM

FAST FIX

MAPLE CRUNCH POPCORN

For a snack that's sure to bring smiles, try this medley of popcorn and pecans covered in a sweet and buttery coating.
—ELMIRA TROMBETTI PADUCAH, KY

START TO FINISH: 25 MIN.
MAKES: 3½ QUARTS

- **10 cups popped popcorn**
- **1½ cups pecan halves, toasted**
- **1⅓ cups sugar**
- **1 cup butter, cubed**
- **¼ cup maple syrup**
- **¼ cup corn syrup**
- **½ teaspoon salt**
- **1 teaspoon maple flavoring**

1. Place popcorn and pecans in a large bowl; set aside. In a large heavy saucepan, combine the sugar, butter, maple syrup, corn syrup and salt. Cook and stir over medium heat until a candy thermometer reads 300° (hard-crack stage). Remove from the heat; stir in the maple flavoring. Quickly pour over popcorn mixture and mix well.
2. Transfer to baking sheets lined with waxed paper to cool. Break into clusters. Store in airtight containers.

NOTE *We recommend that you test your candy thermometer before each use by bringing water to a boil; the thermometer should read 212°. Adjust your recipe temperature up or down based on your test.*

(5) INGREDIENTS

SLOW COOKER CHEESE DIP

I brought this slightly spicy cheese dip to a gathering with friends and it was a huge hit. The spicy pork sausage provides the zip!

—MARION BARTONE CONNEAUT, OH

PREP: 15 MIN. • **COOK:** 4 HOURS • **MAKES:** 2 QUARTS

- **1 pound ground beef**
- **½ pound bulk spicy pork sausage**
- **2 pounds process cheese (Velveeta), cubed**
- **2 cans (10 ounces each) diced tomatoes and green chilies**
- **Tortilla chips**

1. In a large skillet, cook beef and sausage over medium heat until no longer pink; drain. Transfer to a 3- or 4-qt. slow cooker. Stir in cheese and tomatoes.

2. Cover and cook on low for 4-5 hours or until cheese is melted, stirring occasionally. Serve with tortilla chips.

NOTE *If you're planning to serve Slow Cooker Cheese Dip at a holiday party or family get-together, make it ahead and freeze it. Then all you need to do is thaw and reheat it.*

(5) INGREDIENTS

LEMONADE ICED TEA

I have always loved iced tea with lemon, and this great thirst-quencher just takes it one step further. Lemonade gives the drink a nice color, too. I dress up each glass with a piece of lemon on the rim.

—GAIL BUSS BEVERLY HILLS, FL

PREP: 15 MIN. + CHILLING • **MAKES:** 12 SERVINGS (ABOUT 3 QUARTS)

- **3 quarts water**
- **9 individual tea bags**
- **¾ to 1¼ cups sugar**
- **1 can (12 ounces) frozen lemonade concentrate, thawed**
- **Lemon slices, optional**

In a Dutch oven, bring water to a boil. Remove from the heat; add tea bags. Cover and steep for 5 minutes. Discard tea bags. Stir in sugar and lemonade concentrate. Cover and refrigerate until chilled. Serve over ice. If desired, garnish with lemon slices.

FAST FIX

GARDEN VEGGIE SALSA

My clan loves this salsa. It's made mostly with fresh vegetables from my garden. It's healthy, and you can easily adjust the ingredients to suit your own tastes.

—DAWN GILSON DENMARK, WI

PREP: 20 MIN. • **MAKES:** 6 CUPS

- **3 large tomatoes, chopped**
- **1 cup chopped cucumber**
- **1 medium sweet yellow or red pepper, chopped**
- **¾ cup chopped zucchini**
- **1 small red onion, finely chopped**
- **½ cup chopped fresh cilantro**
- **1 jalapeno pepper, seeded and finely chopped**
- **2 tablespoons olive oil**
- **1 tablespoon white vinegar**
- **¾ teaspoon pepper**
- **½ teaspoon salt**
- **½ teaspoon ground cumin**
- **Tortilla chips**

In a large bowl, combine the first 12 ingredients; toss to combine. Refrigerate, covered, until serving. Serve with tortilla chips.

NOTE *Wear disposable gloves when cutting hot peppers; the oils can burn skin. Avoid touching your face.*

"This Slow Cooker Cheese Dip is amazing! It's a good change of pace from plain cheese dip. I never have any leftovers."

—GMAOF4BABYS FROM TASTEOFHOME.COM

FAST FIX

APPLE SALSA WITH CINNAMON CHIPS

Both my husband and I were raised on farms, and we prefer home cooking to anything processed that comes out of a bag or box. I've served this fresh, colorful treat as an appetizer and as a snack. It's even sweet enough to be a dessert. It's easy to transport, too, if you're going to a potluck or party.

—CAROLYN BRINKMEYER GOLDEN, CO

START TO FINISH: 25 MIN.
MAKES: 4 CUPS SALSA

SALSA

- **2 medium tart apples, chopped**
- **1 cup chopped strawberries**
- **2 medium kiwifruit, peeled and chopped**
- **1 small orange**
- **2 tablespoons brown sugar**
- **2 tablespoons apple jelly, melted**

CHIPS

- **8 flour tortillas (7 or 8 inches)**
- **1 tablespoon water**
- **¼ cup sugar**
- **2 teaspoons ground cinnamon**

1. In a bowl, combine apples, strawberries and kiwi. Grate orange peel to measure 1½ teaspoons; squeeze juice from orange. Add peel and juice to apple mixture. Stir in brown sugar and jelly.

2. For chips, brush tortillas lightly with water. Combine sugar and cinnamon; sprinkle over tortillas. Cut each tortilla into eight wedges. Place in a single layer on ungreased baking sheets.

3. Bake at 400° for 6-8 minutes or until lightly browned. Let cool. Serve chips with salsa.

BUFFALO WING BITES

The Buffalo wing fans in my family were happy to taste test when I invented these snacks. We love them anytime, especially during football games.
—JASEY MCBURNETT ROCK SPRINGS, WY

PREP: 25 MIN. • **BAKE:** 15 MIN.
MAKES: 2 DOZEN (2 CUPS DRESSING)

- **2 tablespoons grated Parmesan cheese**
- **1 envelope ranch salad dressing mix, divided**
- **1 cup mayonnaise**
- **1 cup 2% milk**
- **¼ cup crumbled blue cheese, optional**
- **1¼ cups finely chopped cooked chicken breast**
- **1¼ cups (5 ounces) shredded cheddar-Monterey Jack cheese**
- **¼ cup Buffalo wing sauce**
- **1 tube (13.8 ounces) refrigerated pizza crust**
- **2 tablespoons butter, melted**

1. Preheat oven to 400°. In a small bowl, combine Parmesan cheese and 1 teaspoon dressing mix. In another bowl, mix mayonnaise, milk and remaining dressing mix. If desired, stir in crumbled blue cheese. Refrigerate until serving.
2. In a large bowl, mix chicken, cheddar-Monterey Jack cheese and wing sauce. On a lightly floured surface, unroll pizza crust dough and pat into a 14x12-in. rectangle. Cut into 24 squares.
3. Place 1 rounded tablespoon chicken mixture on the center of each square. Pull corners together to enclose filling; pinch to seal. Place 1 in. apart on greased baking sheets, seam side down. Brush tops with butter; sprinkle with Parmesan cheese mixture.
4. Bake 15-17 minutes or until golden brown. Serve with dressing.

FAST FIX

NUTS AND SEEDS TRAIL MIX

Need an excuse to show off a favorite serving bowl? My party mix combines seeds, nuts, fruit and chocolate. It's one I feel good about sharing with my family.
—KRISTIN RIMKUS SNOHOMISH, WA

START TO FINISH: 5 MIN.
MAKES: 5 CUPS

- **1 cup salted pumpkin seeds or pepitas**
- **1 cup unblanched almonds**
- **1 cup unsalted sunflower kernels**
- **1 cup walnut halves**
- **1 cup dried apricots**
- **1 cup dark chocolate chips**

Place all ingredients in a large bowl; toss to combine. Store trail mix in an airtight container.

“You can eat this by the handful, mix with Greek yogurt or sprinkle over cooked oatmeal. I'm diabetic, and it fits within my eating plan.”
—TEANBL0207
FROM TASTEOFHOME.COM

MAPLE JALAPENOS

Craving something sweet with a little bit of heat? Try these creamy, sweet, hot and savory treats. One bite, and you won't be able to stop!
—**NICOLE LARSON** AMERICAN FORK, UT

PREP: 45 MIN. • **BAKE:** 20 MIN. • **MAKES:** 50 APPETIZERS

- **25 jalapeno peppers**
- **1 package (8 ounces) cream cheese, softened**
- **1 cup (4 ounces) crumbled feta cheese**
- **½ cup maple syrup**
- **½ pound bacon strips, cooked and crumbled**
- **¼ cup packed brown sugar**

1. Cut jalapenos in half lengthwise and remove seeds. Set aside. In a small bowl, beat the cream cheese, feta cheese and syrup until smooth. Spoon into pepper halves.
2. Place in two greased 15x10x1-in. baking pans. Top with bacon and sprinkle with brown sugar. Bake at 350° for 20 minutes for spicy flavor, 30 minutes for medium and 40 minutes for mild.
NOTE *Wear disposable gloves when cutting hot peppers; the oils can burn skin. Avoid touching your face.*

SOUTHWESTERN BEAN DIP

Just by using different types of beans, you can make this dip as spicy as you like it. My family could eat this as a complete meal.
—**JEANNE SHEAR** SABETHA, KS

PREP: 20 MIN. • **BAKE:** 30 MIN. • **MAKES:** ABOUT 9 CUPS

- **2 pounds ground beef**
- **1 tablespoon dried minced onion**
- **1 can (8 ounces) tomato sauce**
- **1 can (16 ounces) kidney beans, rinsed and drained**
- **1 can (16 ounces) chili beans, undrained**
- **4 cups (16 ounces) shredded cheddar cheese**
- **Tortilla chips**

1. In a large skillet, cook beef over medium heat until no longer pink; drain. Transfer to a bowl; add the onion. Mash with a fork until crumbly; set aside.
2. In a blender, process tomato sauce and beans until chunky. Add to beef mixture and mix well. Spoon half into a greased 13x9-in. baking dish; top with half of the cheese. Repeat layers.
3. Bake, uncovered, at 350° for 30 minutes or until cheese is melted. Serve warm with chips.

PARTY CRAB PUFFS

I received this recipe years ago from my grandmother, who taught me to have fun being creative and experimenting in the kitchen. My friends request these little puffs at every gathering.
—**JEAN BEVILACQUA** RHODODENDRON, OR

PREP: 45 MIN. • **BAKE:** 20 MIN./BATCH • **MAKES:** 8 DOZEN

- **1 cup water**
- **½ cup butter, cubed**
- **¼ teaspoon salt**
- **1 cup all-purpose flour**
- **4 large eggs**

FILLING

- **4 hard-cooked large eggs, finely chopped**
- **1 can (6 ounces) lump crabmeat, drained**
- **4 ounces cream cheese, softened**
- **¼ cup mayonnaise**
- **2 tablespoons finely chopped onion**
- **2 tablespoons prepared horseradish, drained**
- **Minced fresh parsley, optional**

1. Preheat oven to 400°. In a large saucepan, bring the water, butter and salt to a boil. Add flour all at once and stir until a smooth ball forms. Remove from heat; let stand 5 minutes. Add eggs, one at a time, beating well after each addition. Continue beating until mixture is smooth and shiny.
2. Drop by teaspoonfuls 2 in. apart onto greased baking sheets. Bake 18-22 minutes or until golden brown. Remove to a wire rack. Immediately split puffs open; remove tops and set aside. Discard soft dough from inside. Cool puffs.
3. In a large bowl, combine filling ingredients. Just before serving, spoon 1 teaspoonful filling into each puff; sprinkle with parsley if desired. Replace tops.

“I've made this same basic puff recipe since the '70s. They're also great with tuna or chicken salad.”

—**EARMARK** FROM TASTEOFHOME.COM

FISH TACO BITES

I think these appetizers are better than full-size fish tacos I've had as an entree. Enjoy the creamy salsa drizzle not only on these bites, but also on other Mexican dishes.

—**CARMELL CHILDS** FERRON, UT

PREP: 30 MIN. • **BAKE:** 20 MIN. • **MAKES:** 3 DOZEN

- **½ cup salsa verde**
- **4 ounces cream cheese, softened**
- **2 tablespoons lime juice, divided**
- **2 tablespoons minced fresh cilantro**
- **1 teaspoon honey**
- **Dash salt**
- **12 frozen breaded fish sticks**
- **1 tablespoon taco seasoning**
- **36 tortilla chip scoops**
- **1½ cups coleslaw mix**
- **¾ cup cubed avocado**
- **¾ cup chopped seeded tomato**
- **Lime wedges and additional minced fresh cilantro**

1. In a blender, combine the salsa verde, cream cheese, 1 tablespoon lime juice, cilantro, honey and salt. Cover and process until smooth; set aside.

2. Place fish sticks on a baking sheet. Bake at 425° for 10 minutes. Sprinkle with half of the taco seasoning. Turn fish sticks over; sprinkle with remaining taco seasoning. Bake 7-9 minutes longer or until crisp.

3. Meanwhile, place tortilla chips on a serving platter. In a small bowl, combine the coleslaw mix, avocado, tomato, remaining lime juice and ½ cup salsa mixture. Spoon mixture into chips.

4. Cut each fish stick into three pieces. Place a fish stick piece in each chip; top each with about ½ teaspoon salsa mixture. Garnish with lime wedges and additional cilantro.

TOP TIP

Cilantro 101

With its slightly sharp flavor, cilantro—also known as Chinese parsley—gives a distinctive taste to Mexican, Latin American and Asian dishes. (The spice coriander comes from the seed of the cilantro plant.) Like all other fresh herbs, cilantro should be used as soon as possible. For short-term storage, immerse the freshly cut stems in a jar or vase filled with about 2 inches of water. Place a large resealable plastic bag over the leaves so they're loosely covered. Refrigerate for several days. Wash just before using.

FAST FIX

CHEESY PIZZA FONDUE

I love cooking and used to sit for hours reading cookbooks from cover to cover. This dip is so easy to make and transport. You won't have to keep it warm long because it'll be gone in a flash.
—JULIE BARWICK MANSFIELD, OH

START TO FINISH: 30 MIN. • **MAKES:** ABOUT 5 CUPS

- **½ pound ground beef**
- **1 medium onion, chopped**
- **2 cans (15 ounces each) pizza sauce**
- **1½ teaspoons dried basil or dried oregano**
- **¼ teaspoon garlic powder**
- **2½ cups (10 ounces) shredded sharp cheddar cheese**
- **1 cup (4 ounces) shredded part-skim mozzarella cheese**
- **Breadsticks, garlic toast and green peppers**

1. In a large saucepan, cook beef and onion over medium heat until meat is no longer pink; drain. Stir in the pizza sauce, basil and garlic powder. Reduce heat to low. Add cheeses; stir until melted.
2. Transfer to a small fondue pot or 1½-qt. slow cooker; keep warm. Serve with breadsticks, garlic toast and green peppers.
NOTE *In addition to breadsticks, serve Cheesy Pizza Fondue with cubes of French or Italian bread.*

(5) INGREDIENTS

HOT SPICED CHERRY CIDER

There's nothing better than coming in from the cold and smelling the aroma of this heartwarming cider that's been simmering in the slow cooker.
—MARLENE WICZEK LITTLE FALLS, MN

PREP: 5 MIN. • **COOK:** 4 HOURS • **MAKES:** 4 QUARTS

- **1 gallon apple cider or juice**
- **2 cinnamon sticks (3 inches)**
- **2 packages (3 ounces each) cherry gelatin**

Place cider in a 6-qt. slow cooker; add cinnamon sticks. Cover and cook on high for 3 hours. Stir in gelatin; cook 1 hour longer. Discard cinnamon sticks before serving.

(5) INGREDIENTS

SUGARED PEANUTS

I tend to make these only for special occasions because I cannot keep my husband and son (and myself!) away from them. They never last long, so you might want to make a double batch.
—POLLY HALL ROCKFORD, MI

PREP: 20 MIN. • **BAKE:** 30 MIN. + COOLING • **MAKES:** 5 CUPS

- **5 cups unsalted peanuts**
- **1 cup sugar**
- **1 cup water**
- **¼ teaspoon salt**

1. In a large heavy saucepan, combine the peanuts, sugar and water. Bring to a boil; cook until syrup has evaporated, about 10 minutes.
2. Spread peanuts in a single layer in a greased 15x10x1-in. baking pan; sprinkle with salt.
3. Bake at 300° for 30-35 minutes or until dry and lightly browned. Cool completely. Store in an airtight container.

CRAWFISH BEIGNETS WITH CAJUN DIPPING SAUCE

Get a taste of the deep South with these slightly spicy beignets. You won't be able to eat just one!

—**DONNA LANCLOS** LAFAYETTE, LA

PREP: 20 MIN. • **COOK:** 5 MIN./BATCH
MAKES: ABOUT 2 DOZEN (¾ CUP SAUCE)

- **1 large egg, beaten**
- **1 pound chopped cooked crawfish tail meat or shrimp**
- **4 green onions, chopped**
- **1½ teaspoons butter, melted**
- **½ teaspoon salt**
- **½ teaspoon cayenne pepper**
- **⅓ cup bread flour**
- **Oil for deep-fat frying**
- **¾ cup mayonnaise**
- **½ cup ketchup**
- **¼ teaspoon prepared horseradish, optional**
- **¼ teaspoon hot pepper sauce**

1. In a large bowl, combine the egg, crawfish, onions, butter, salt and cayenne. Stir in flour until blended.
2. In an electric skillet or deep fryer, heat oil to 375°. Drop tablespoonfuls of batter, a few at a time, into hot oil. Fry until golden brown on both sides. Drain on paper towels.
3. In a small bowl, combine the mayonnaise, ketchup, horseradish if desired and pepper sauce. Serve with beignets.

HONEY-GARLIC GLAZED MEATBALLS

My husband and I raise cattle on our farm here in southwestern Ontario, so it's no surprise that we're fond of these saucy meatballs. I know your family will like them, too.

—**MARION FOSTER** KIRKTON, ON

PREP: 25 MIN. • **BAKE:** 15 MIN.
MAKES: 5½ DOZEN

- **2 large eggs**
- **¾ cup milk**
- **1 cup dry bread crumbs**
- **½ cup finely chopped onion**
- **2 teaspoons salt**
- **2 pounds ground beef**
- **4 garlic cloves, minced**
- **1 tablespoon butter**
- **¾ cup ketchup**
- **½ cup honey**
- **3 tablespoons soy sauce**

1. In a large bowl, combine eggs and milk. Add the bread crumbs, onion and salt. Crumble beef over mixture and mix well. Shape into 1-in. balls. Place on greased racks in shallow baking pans. Bake, uncovered, at 400° for 12-15 minutes or until meat is no longer pink.
2. Meanwhile, in a large saucepan, saute garlic in butter until tender. Stir in the ketchup, honey and soy sauce. Bring to a boil. Reduce heat; cover and simmer for 5 minutes. Drain meatballs; add to sauce. Carefully stir to evenly coat. Cook for 5-10 minutes.

CRISPY BAKED WONTONS

These quick, versatile wontons are great for a savory snack or paired with a bowl of soothing soup on a cold day. I usually make a large batch, freeze half on a floured baking sheet, then store in an airtight container.

—**BRIANNA SHADE** BEAVERTON, OR

PREP: 30 MIN. • **BAKE:** 10 MIN.
MAKES: ABOUT 4 DOZEN

- **½ pound ground pork**
- **½ pound extra-lean ground turkey**
- **1 small onion, chopped**
- **1 can (8 ounces) sliced water chestnuts, drained and chopped**
- **⅓ cup reduced-sodium soy sauce**
- **¼ cup egg substitute**
- **1½ teaspoons ground ginger**
- **1 package (12 ounces) wonton wrappers**
- **Cooking spray**
- **Sweet-and-sour sauce, optional**

1. In a large skillet, cook the pork, turkey and onion over medium heat until meat is no longer pink; drain. Transfer to a large bowl. Stir in the water chestnuts, soy sauce, egg substitute and ginger.

2. Position a wonton wrapper with one point toward you. (Keep the remaining wrappers covered with a damp paper towel until ready to use.) Place 2 heaping teaspoons of filling in the center of wrapper. Fold bottom corner over filling; fold sides toward center over filling. Roll toward the remaining point. Moisten top corner with water; press to seal. Repeat with remaining wrappers and filling.

3. Place on baking sheets coated with cooking spray; lightly coat wontons with additional cooking spray.

4. Bake at 400° for 10-12 minutes or until golden brown, turning once. Serve warm with sweet-and-sour sauce if desired.

FREEZE OPTION *Freeze cooled baked wontons in a freezer container, separating layers with waxed paper. To use, reheat on a baking sheet in a preheated 400° oven until crisp and heated through.*

MARINATED OLIVE & CHEESE RING

We love to make Italian meals into celebrations, and a colorful antipasto always kicks off the party. This one is almost too pretty to eat, especially when sprinkled with pimientos, fresh basil and parsley.
—**PATRICIA HARMON** BADEN, PA

PREP: 25 MIN. + CHILLING • **MAKES:** 16 SERVINGS

- **1 package (8 ounces) cold cream cheese**
- **1 package (10 ounces) sharp white cheddar cheese, cut into ¼-inch slices**
- **⅓ cup pimiento-stuffed olives**
- **⅓ cup pitted Greek olives**
- **¼ cup balsamic vinegar**
- **¼ cup olive oil**
- **1 tablespoon minced fresh parsley**
- **1 tablespoon minced fresh basil or 1 teaspoon dried basil**
- **2 garlic cloves, minced**
- **1 jar (2 ounces) pimiento strips, drained and chopped**
- **Toasted French bread baguette slices**

1. Cut cream cheese lengthwise in half; cut each half into 1/4-in. slices. On a serving plate, arrange cheeses upright in a ring, alternating cheddar and cream cheese slices. Place olives in center.
2. In a small bowl, whisk vinegar, oil, parsley, basil and garlic until blended; drizzle over cheeses and olives. Sprinkle with pimientos. Refrigerate, covered, at least 8 hours or overnight. Serve with baguette slices.

STROMBOLI RING

A friend gave me this party-perfect recipe years ago, and it's so incredibly good. I serve it warm with marinara sauce.
—**BARRIE PEAGLER** SCOTTSDALE, AZ

PREP: 20 MIN. + RISING • **BAKE:** 30 MIN. • **MAKES:** 12 SERVINGS

- **1 pound bulk Italian sausage**
- **1½ cups (6 ounces) shredded Monterey Jack or part-skim mozzarella cheese**
- **2 large eggs, divided use**
- **½ teaspoon Italian seasoning**
- **1 loaf (1 pound) frozen bread dough, thawed**
- **1 tablespoon grated Parmesan cheese**
- **Marinara sauce, warmed, optional**

1. In a large skillet, cook sausage over medium heat until no longer pink; drain. Stir in the Monterey Jack cheese, one egg and Italian seasoning.
2. On a lightly floured surface, roll dough into an 18x6-in. rectangle. Spoon sausage mixture over dough to within 1/2 in. of edges. Roll up jelly-roll style, starting with a long side; pinch seam to seal.
3. Place seam side down on a greased baking sheet; pinch the ends together to form a ring. With scissors, cut from outside edge to two-thirds of the way toward center of ring at 1-in. intervals.
4. Beat remaining egg; brush over dough. Sprinkle with Parmesan cheese. Cover and let rise in a warm place until doubled, about 30 minutes.
5. Bake at 350° for 28-32 minutes or until golden brown. Serve with marinara sauce if desired.

TEXAS TACO PLATTER

When I'm entertaining, this colorful dish is my top menu choice. My friends can't resist the hearty appetizer topped with cheese, lettuce, tomatoes and olives.

—**KATHY YOUNG** WEATHERFORD, TX

PREP: 20 MIN. • **COOK:** 1½ HOURS • **MAKES:** 10-12 SERVINGS

- **2 pounds ground beef**
- **1 large onion, chopped**
- **1 can (14½ ounces) diced tomatoes, undrained**
- **1 can (12 ounces) tomato paste**
- **1 can (15 ounces) tomato puree**
- **2 tablespoons chili powder**
- **1 teaspoon ground cumin**
- **½ teaspoon garlic powder**
- **2 teaspoons salt**
- **2 cans (15 ounces each) Ranch Style beans (pinto beans in seasoned tomato sauce)**
- **1 package (10½ ounces) corn chips**
- **2 cups hot cooked rice**

TOPPINGS

- **2 cups (8 ounces) shredded cheddar cheese**
- **1 medium onion, chopped**
- **1 medium head iceberg lettuce, shredded**
- **3 medium tomatoes, chopped**
- **1 can (2¼ ounces) sliced ripe olives, drained**
- **1 cup picante sauce, optional**

1. In a large skillet or Dutch oven, cook beef and onion over medium heat until meat is no longer pink; drain. Add next seven ingredients; simmer for 1½ hours.

2. Add beans and heat though. On a platter, layer the corn chips, rice, meat mixture, cheese, onion, lettuce, tomatoes and olives. Serve with picante sauce if desired.

TOP TIP

Mexican Menu Ideas

If you're hosting a Mexican-themed party or simply want a south-of-the-border vibe, consider these menu ideas.

- Beverages: lemonade, margaritas, white sangria, wine, beer or coffee with coffee liqueur, sugar, cinnamon and cream.
- Appetizers: quesadillas, nachos, guacamole, chili con queso or black bean soup.
- Side dishes: refried beans, grilled vegetables, Spanish rice or corn custard.
- Desserts: caramelized bananas over ice cream, pineapple with toasted coconut and lime zest, tres leches cake, Mexican flan or mango sorbet.

CRUSTLESS SPINACH QUICHE, 36

CREAMY FROZEN FRUIT CUPS, 26

BLINTZ PANCAKES, 37

BRUNCH PIZZA SQUARES, 43

BREAKFAST & BRUNCH

Morning will be your favorite time of day when you enjoy this eye-opening selection of breakfast delights. Whether you're hosting a crowd for a special occasion brunch or you just want something warm and hearty to get the gang energized for the day, you'll find a delicious sampling of all your rise-and-shine favorites. From to-die-for doughnuts and sweet rolls to incredible egg dishes, fluffy pancakes and other sunny morning classics, these recipes are worth waking up for!

SPINACH QUICHE WITH POTATO CRUST

Although the recipe calls for refrigerated potatoes and frozen spinach, this dish is a smart way to use leftovers. Just sub in 2½ cups mashed potatoes and whatever cooked veggies you have on hand. And instead of bacon, you can use ½ pound of Italian sausage.

—HEATHER KING FROSTBURG, MD

PREP: 25 MIN. • **BAKE:** 55 MIN. + STANDING
MAKES: 8 SERVINGS

- **1 package (24 ounces) refrigerated mashed potatoes**
- **2 tablespoons olive oil, divided**
- **8 ounces sliced fresh mushrooms**
- **2 garlic cloves, minced**
- **5 ounces frozen chopped spinach, thawed and squeezed dry (about ½ cup)**
- **6 bacon strips, cooked and crumbled or ⅓ cup bacon bits**
- **2 teaspoons minced fresh rosemary or ½ teaspoon dried rosemary, crushed**
- **4 large eggs**
- **1 cup 2% milk**
- **¼ teaspoon pepper**
- **1 cup (4 ounces) shredded cheddar cheese**

1. Preheat oven to 350°. Press the mashed potatoes onto the bottom and up the sides of a greased 9-in. deep-dish pie plate. Brush with 1 tablespoon oil. Bake 30 minutes or until edges are golden brown.

2. Meanwhile, in a large skillet, heat remaining oil over medium-high heat. Add mushrooms; cook and stir for 3-4 minutes or until tender. Add garlic; cook 1 minute longer. Remove from the heat. Stir in spinach, bacon and rosemary; spoon over crust. In a small bowl, whisk eggs, milk and pepper until blended; stir in cheese. Pour over mushroom mixture.

3. Bake 25-30 minutes longer or until golden brown and a knife inserted near the center comes out clean. Let stand 10 minutes before cutting.

CREAMY FROZEN FRUIT CUPS

I love to prepare these cool, fluffy fruit cups to give a refreshing boost to a variety of meals. They've been well-received at family gatherings and summer barbecues. Since you make them in advance, there's no last-minute fuss.

—KAREN HATCHER ST. AMANT, LA

PREP: 15 MIN. + FREEZING
MAKES: 1½ DOZEN

- **1 package (8 ounces) cream cheese, softened**
- **½ cup sugar**
- **1 jar (10 ounces) maraschino cherries, drained**
- **1 can (11 ounces) mandarin oranges, drained**
- **1 can (8 ounces) crushed pineapple, drained**
- **½ cup chopped pecans**
- **1 carton (8 ounces) frozen whipped topping, thawed**
- **Fresh mint, optional**

1. In a large bowl, beat the cream cheese and sugar until fluffy. Halve 9 cherries; chop remaining cherries. Set aside halved cherries and 18 orange segments for garnish. Add pineapple, pecans and chopped cherries to cream cheese mixture. Fold in whipped topping and remaining oranges.

2. Line muffin cups with paper or foil liners. Spoon fruit mixture into cups; garnish with reserved cherries and oranges. Freeze until firm. Remove from the freezer 10 minutes before serving. Top with mint if desired.

MEXICAN EGG CASSEROLE

Tomatoes and green chilies give color and zip to this extra-cheesy egg bake. It's a favorite for breakfast or brunch, but it can be enjoyed for lunch or supper, too.
—MARY STEINER WEST BEND, WI

PREP: 15 MIN. • **BAKE:** 45 MIN.
MAKES: 8 SERVINGS

- **½ cup all-purpose flour**
- **1 teaspoon baking powder**
- **12 large eggs, lightly beaten**
- **4 cups (16 ounces) shredded Monterey Jack cheese, divided**
- **2 cups (16 ounces) 4% cottage cheese**
- **2 plum tomatoes, seeded and diced**
- **1 can (4 ounces) chopped green chilies, drained**
- **4 green onions, sliced**
- **½ teaspoon hot pepper sauce**
- **1 teaspoon dried oregano**
- **2 tablespoons minced fresh cilantro**
- **½ teaspoon salt**
- **½ teaspoon pepper**
- **Salsa, optional**

1. In a large bowl, combine flour and baking powder. Add eggs, 3½ cups Monterey Jack cheese, cottage cheese, tomatoes, chilies, onions, hot pepper sauce, oregano, cilantro, salt and pepper. Pour into a greased 13x9-in. baking dish. Sprinkle with remaining Monterey Jack cheese.

2. Bake, uncovered, at 400° for 15 minutes. Reduce heat to 350°; bake 30 minutes longer or until a knife inserted near the center comes out clean. Let stand for 5 minutes before cutting. Serve with salsa if desired.

"This has been on our Christmas morning menu for years. Everybody loves it, especially with a side of salsa and mimosas!"

—WENDYJOFL
FROM TASTEOFHOME.COM

FARMER'S STRATA

Try my hearty casserole for an inexpensive and easy-to-prepare dish. It includes tasty basic ingredients like bacon, cheese and potatoes. You can assemble it ahead and bake it just before folks arrive for your brunch.

—PAT KUETHER WESTMINSTER, CO

PREP: 25 MIN. + CHILLING • **BAKE:** 65 MIN.
MAKES: 16 SERVINGS

- **1 pound sliced bacon, cut into ½-inch pieces**
- **2 cups chopped fully cooked ham**
- **1 small onion, chopped**
- **10 slices white bread, cubed**
- **1 cup cubed cooked potatoes**
- **3 cups (12 ounces) shredded cheddar cheese**
- **8 large eggs**
- **3 cups milk**
- **1 tablespoon Worcestershire sauce**
- **1 teaspoon ground mustard**
- **Dash salt and pepper**

1. In a large skillet, cook bacon over medium heat until crisp; add ham and onion. Cook and stir until onion is tender; drain.

2. In a greased 13x9-in. baking dish, layer half the bread cubes, potatoes and cheese. Top with all of the bacon mixture. Repeat layers of bread, potatoes and cheese.

3. In a large bowl, beat the eggs; add the milk, Worcestershire sauce, mustard, salt and pepper. Pour over all. Cover and chill overnight.

4. Remove from the refrigerator 30 minutes before baking. Preheat oven to 325°. Bake, uncovered, for 65-70 minutes or until a knife inserted near the center comes out clean.

OVERNIGHT BRUNCH CASSEROLE

I love to cook for company, and I host brunches frequently. Standing out from most egg bakes, this casserole combines scrambled eggs and a cheese sauce, and it bakes up into a rich, creamy dish.

—CANDY HESCH MOSINEE, WI

PREP: 30 MIN. + CHILLING
BAKE: 40 MIN. + STANDING
MAKES: 12 SERVINGS

- **3 tablespoons butter, divided**
- **2 tablespoons all-purpose flour**
- **½ teaspoon salt**
- **⅛ teaspoon pepper**
- **2 cups fat-free milk**
- **5 slices reduced-fat process American cheese product, chopped**
- **1½ cups sliced fresh mushrooms**
- **2 green onions, finely chopped**
- **1 cup cubed fully cooked ham**
- **2 cups egg substitute**
- **4 large eggs**

TOPPING

- **3 slices whole wheat bread, cubed**
- **4 teaspoons butter, melted**
- **⅛ teaspoon paprika**

1. In a large saucepan, melt 2 tablespoons butter. Stir in flour, salt and pepper until smooth; gradually add milk. Bring to a boil; cook and stir 2 minutes or until slightly thickened. Stir in cheese until melted. Remove from the heat.

2. In a large nonstick skillet, saute mushrooms and green onions in remaining butter until tender. Add ham; heat through. Whisk the egg substitute and eggs; add to skillet. Cook and stir until eggs are almost set. Stir in cheese sauce.

3. Transfer to a 13x9-in. baking dish coated with cooking spray. Toss bread cubes with butter. Arrange over egg mixture; sprinkle with paprika. Cover and refrigerate overnight.

4. Remove from the refrigerator 30 minutes before baking. Preheat oven to 350°. Bake, uncovered, for 40-45 minutes or until a knife inserted near the center comes out clean. Let stand 10 minutes before cutting.

CRISSCROSS APPLE CROWNS

Wake 'em up on chilly mornings with the tempting aroma of apples and cinnamon wafting through the house. I love making these little buns for breakfast because they're different and easy.

—TERESA MORRIS LAUREL, DE

PREP: 30 MIN. • **BAKE:** 20 MIN.
MAKES: 8 SERVINGS

- **1⅓ cups chopped peeled tart apples**
- **⅓ cup chopped walnuts**
- **⅓ cup raisins**
- **½ cup sugar, divided**
- **2 tablespoons all-purpose flour**
- **2 teaspoons ground cinnamon, divided**
- **Dash salt**
- **1 package (16.3 ounces) large refrigerated flaky biscuits**
- **2 teaspoons butter, melted**

1. In a large microwave-safe bowl, combine the apples, walnuts, raisins, 3 tablespoons sugar, flour, 3/4 teaspoon cinnamon and salt. Microwave on high for 2-3 minutes or until almost tender.

2. Flatten each biscuit into a 5-in. circle. Combine remaining sugar and cinnamon; sprinkle a rounded teaspoonful of sugar mixture over each. Top each with 1/4 cup apple mixture. Bring up edges to enclose mixture; pinch edges to seal.

3. Place seam side down in ungreased muffin cups. Brush tops with butter; sprinkle with the remaining sugar mixture. With a sharp knife, cut an "X" in the top of each.

4. Bake at 350° for 18-22 minutes or until golden brown. Cool for 5 minutes before removing from the pan to a wire rack.

(5) INGREDIENTS FAST FIX

STRAWBERRY BANANA YOGURT SMOOTHIE

Frozen strawberries combine with banana to keep these frosty smoothies extra thick. The recipe is a delightful way to get a substantial dose of nutrients early in the day.

—CHRISTY ADKINS MARTINEZ, GA

START TO FINISH: 5 MIN.
MAKES: 2 SERVINGS

- **½ cup 2% milk**
- **⅓ cup strawberry yogurt**
- **⅓ cup frozen unsweetened strawberries**
- **½ medium firm banana, chopped**
- **4 ice cubes**
- **8 teaspoons sugar**

In a blender, combine all of the ingredients; cover and process for 30-45 seconds or until smooth. Stir if necessary. Pour into chilled glasses; serve immediately.

FRENCH TOAST STICKS

I keep these French toast sticks in the freezer for an instant, filling breakfast. The convenient size makes them an ideal buffet item.

—*TASTE OF HOME* TEST KITCHEN

PREP: 20 MIN. + FREEZING • **BAKE:** 20 MIN.
MAKES: 1½ DOZEN

- **6 slices day-old Texas toast**
- **4 large eggs**
- **1 cup milk**
- **2 tablespoons sugar**
- **1 teaspoon vanilla extract**
- **¼ to ½ teaspoon ground cinnamon**
- **1 cup crushed cornflakes, optional**
- **Confectioners' sugar, optional**
- **Maple syrup**

1. Cut each piece of bread into thirds; place in an ungreased 13x9-in. dish. In a large bowl, whisk the eggs, milk, sugar, vanilla and cinnamon. Pour over bread; soak for 2 minutes, turning once. If desired, coat bread slices with crushed cornflakes on all sides.

2. Place in a greased 15x10x1-in. baking pan. Freeze until firm, about 45 minutes. Transfer to an airtight container or resealable freezer bag and store in the freezer.

TO USE FROZEN FRENCH TOAST STICKS *Place desired number of sticks on a greased baking sheet. Bake at 425° for 8 minutes. Turn; bake 10-12 minutes longer or until golden brown. Sprinkle with confectioners' sugar if desired. Serve with syrup.*

FAST FIX

HUEVOS RANCHEROS WITH TOMATILLO SAUCE

My husband and I visited Cuernavaca, Mexico, where we had huevos rancheros for the first time. He loved it so much that he wanted to try a homemade version when we returned. This is my take on it, which is suited to my family's preference for sunny-side up eggs, but poached or scrambled eggs would also be good.

—CHERYL WOODSON LIBERTY, MO

START TO FINISH: 25 MIN. • **MAKES:** 8 SERVINGS

- **5 tomatillos, husks removed, halved**
- **2 tablespoons coarsely chopped onion**
- **1 to 2 serrano peppers, halved**
- **3 garlic cloves, peeled**
- **1 teaspoon chicken bouillon granules**
- **1 can (15 ounces) Southwestern black beans, undrained**
- **8 large eggs**
- **4 ounces manchego cheese, shredded**
- **8 tostada shells, warmed**
- **½ cup sour cream**
- **Chopped tomato, sliced avocado and minced fresh cilantro, optional**

1. Place the tomatillos, onion, pepper, garlic and bouillon in a food processor. Cover and process until finely chopped; set aside. In a small saucepan, mash beans. Cook on low until heated through, stirring occasionally.

2. Meanwhile, break eggs in batches into a large nonstick skillet coated with cooking spray. Cover and cook over low heat for 5-7 minutes or until eggs are set. Sprinkle with shredded cheese.

3. To serve, spread beans over tostada shells; top with eggs, tomatillo sauce and sour cream. Garnish with tomato, avocado and cilantro if desired.

NOTE *Wear disposable gloves when cutting hot peppers; the oils can burn skin. Avoid touching your face.*

(5) INGREDIENTS FAST FIX

SHEEPHERDER'S BREAKFAST

My sister-in-law always made this delicious breakfast dish when we were camping. Served with toast, juice, and milk or coffee, it's a sure hit with the breakfast crowd. One-dish casseroles like this were a big help while I was raising my nine children, and now I've passed this recipe on to them.

—PAULETTA BUSHNELL ALBANY, OR

START TO FINISH: 30 MIN. • **MAKES:** 8 SERVINGS

- **¾ pound bacon strips, finely chopped**
- **1 medium onion, chopped**
- **1 package (30 ounces) frozen shredded hash brown potatoes, thawed**
- **8 large eggs**
- **½ teaspoon salt**
- **¼ teaspoon pepper**
- **1 cup (4 ounces) shredded cheddar cheese**

1. In a large skillet, cook chopped bacon and onion over medium heat until bacon is crisp. Drain, reserving 1/4 cup drippings in pan.

2. Stir in hash browns. Cook, uncovered, over medium heat 10 minutes or until bottom is golden brown; turn potatoes. With the back of a spoon, make eight evenly spaced wells in potato mixture. Break one egg into each well. Sprinkle with salt and pepper.

3. Cook, covered, on low 10 minutes or until eggs are set and the potatoes are tender. Sprinkle with cheese; let stand until cheese is melted.

SCRAMBLED EGG HASH BROWN CUPS

These cuties pack all your favorite breakfast foods—eggs, hash browns and bacon—into a single-serving-sized cup. Grab one and get mingling.

—TALON DIMARE BULLHEAD CITY, AZ

PREP: 10 MIN. • **BAKE:** 25 MIN. • **MAKES:** 1 DOZEN

- **1 package (20 ounces) refrigerated Southwest-style shredded hash brown potatoes**
- **6 large eggs**
- **½ cup 2% milk**
- **⅛ teaspoon salt**
- **1 tablespoon butter**
- **10 thick-sliced bacon strips, cooked and crumbled**
- **1¼ cups (5 ounces) shredded cheddar-Monterey Jack cheese, divided**

1. Preheat oven to 400°. Divide potatoes among 12 greased muffin cups; press onto bottoms and up sides to form cups. Bake 18-20 minutes or until light golden brown.

2. Meanwhile, in a small bowl, whisk eggs, milk and salt. In a large nonstick skillet, heat butter over medium heat. Pour in egg mixture; cook and stir until eggs are thickened and no liquid egg remains. Stir in bacon and 3/4 cup cheese. Spoon into cups; sprinkle with remaining 1/2 cup cheese.

3. Bake 3-5 minutes or until cheese is melted. Cool 5 minutes before removing from pan.

“I used hot Italian sausage in place of the bacon. I didn't have Southwest-style potatoes on hand, so I sauteed green peppers and onions in butter and added them to the egg mixture. These are wonderful and easy. A definite keeper!”

—KYLEEJ FROM TASTEOFHOME.COM

MUSHROOM SAUSAGE STRATA

This delightful casserole is a filling mainstay for our family's Christmas Day brunch. Being able to assemble the recipe ahead of time is an added bonus.
—**JULIE STERCHI** CAMPBELLSVILLE, KY

PREP: 15 MIN. + CHILLING
BAKE: 35 MIN. + STANDING
MAKES: 8-10 SERVINGS

- **1 pound bulk pork sausage**
- **10 slices whole wheat bread, cubed**
- **1 can (4 ounces) mushroom stems and pieces, drained**
- **½ cup shredded cheddar cheese**
- **½ cup shredded Swiss cheese**
- **6 large eggs, lightly beaten**
- **1 cup 2% milk**
- **1 cup half-and-half cream**
- **1 teaspoon Worcestershire sauce**
- **½ teaspoon pepper**

1. In a large skillet, cook sausage over medium heat until no longer pink; drain. Place bread cubes in a greased 13x9-in. baking dish. Sprinkle with the sausage, mushrooms and cheeses.
2. In a large bowl, whisk remaining ingredients; pour onto ingredients in baking dish. Cover and refrigerate overnight.
3. Remove from the refrigerator 30 minutes before baking. Preheat oven to 350°. Bake, uncovered, for 35-45 minutes or until a knife inserted near the center comes out clean.

FREEZE OPTION *After assembling, cover and freeze strata. To use, partially thaw in refrigerator overnight. Remove from refrigerator 30 minutes before baking. Preheat oven to 350°. Bake strata as directed, increasing time as necessary for a knife inserted near the center to come out clean.*

corner of a pastry or plastic bag; insert a very small round tip. Fill with jelly. Fill each doughnut with about 1 teaspoon jelly. Carefully roll warm doughnuts in sugar. Serve warm.

JOLLY JELLY DOUGHNUTS

Plump and filled with jelly, these sugar-coated doughnuts will disappear as fast as you can churn them out.

—LEE BREMSON KANSAS CITY, MO

PREP: 25 MIN. + RISING • **COOK:** 30 MIN.
MAKES: ABOUT 2½ DOZEN

- **2 packages (¼ ounce each) active dry yeast**
- **2 cups warm milk (110° to 115°)**
- **7 cups all-purpose flour**
- **4 large egg yolks**
- **1 large egg**
- **½ cup sugar**
- **1 teaspoon salt**
- **2 teaspoons grated lemon peel**
- **½ teaspoon vanilla extract**
- **½ cup butter, melted**
- **Oil for deep-fat frying**
- **Red jelly of your choice**
- **Additional sugar**

1. In a large bowl, dissolve yeast in warm milk. Add 2 cups flour; mix well. Let stand in a warm place for 30 minutes. Add egg yolks, egg, sugar, salt, lemon peel and vanilla; mix well. Beat in butter and remaining flour. Do not knead. Cover and let rise in a warm place until doubled, about 45 minutes.

2. Punch dough down. On a lightly floured surface, roll out to ½-in. thickness. Cut with a 2½-in. biscuit cutter. Place on lightly greased baking sheets. Cover and let rise until nearly doubled, about 35 minutes.

3. In a deep-fat fryer or an electric skillet, heat oil to 375°. Fry doughnuts, a few at a time, for 1½-2 minutes on each side or until browned. Drain on paper towels.

4. Cool for 2-3 minutes; cut a small slit with a sharp knife on one side of each doughnut. Cut a small hole in the

FOUR-FRUIT COMPOTE

A beautiful side dish, this compote spotlights winter fruit such as bananas, apples, oranges and pineapple. Of course, it can be made any time of the year, and it's almost guaranteed to bring smiles all around when you serve it.

—DONNA LONG SEARCY, AR

PREP: 15 MIN. + CHILLING
MAKES: 12-16 SERVINGS

- **1 can (20 ounces) pineapple chunks**
- **½ cup sugar**
- **2 tablespoons cornstarch**
- **⅓ cup orange juice**
- **1 tablespoon lemon juice**
- **1 can (11 ounces) mandarin oranges, drained**
- **3 to 4 medium apples, chopped**
- **2 to 3 medium bananas, sliced**

1. Drain pineapple, reserving ¾ cup juice. In a large saucepan, combine sugar and cornstarch. Whisk in the orange, lemon and pineapple juices until smooth. Cook and stir over medium heat until thickened and bubbly; cook and stir 1 minute longer. Remove from the heat; set aside.

2. In a large bowl, combine the fruits. Pour warm sauce over the fruit; stir gently to coat. Cover and refrigerate.

FAST FIX

BANANA BEIGNET BITES

When I was a little girl, my grandmother took me aside one day and taught me how to make her famous banana beignets. Although we made them most often during the holidays, they're fantastic any time of the year.

—AMY DOWNING SOUTH RIDING, VA

START TO FINISH: 30 MIN. • **MAKES:** ABOUT 3 DOZEN

- **¾ cup sugar**
- **¼ cup packed brown sugar**
- **1½ teaspoons ground cinnamon**

BEIGNETS

- **2 cups cake flour**
- **¾ cup sugar**
- **2½ teaspoons baking powder**
- **½ teaspoon ground cinnamon**
- **1 teaspoon salt**
- **1 large egg**
- **1 cup mashed ripe bananas (about 3 medium)**
- **½ cup whole milk**
- **2 tablespoons canola oil**
- **Oil for deep-fat frying**

1. In a small bowl, mix sugars and cinnamon until blended. In a large bowl, whisk the first five beignet ingredients. In another bowl, whisk egg, bananas, milk and 2 tablespoons oil until blended. Add to flour mixture; stir just until moistened.
2. In an electric skillet or deep fryer, heat oil to 375°. Drop tablespoonfuls of batter, a few at a time, into hot oil. Fry about 45-60 seconds on each side or until golden brown. Drain on paper towels. Roll warm beignets in sugar mixture.

CRUSTLESS SPINACH QUICHE

I served this quiche at a church luncheon, and I had to laugh when a gentleman turned to me and said, "This is delicious, and I don't even like broccoli." I replied, "Sir, it isn't broccoli. It's spinach." He quickly answered, "I don't like spinach, either, but this is good!"

—MELINDA CALVERLEY JANESVILLE, WI

PREP: 25 MIN. • **BAKE:** 40 MIN. • **MAKES:** 6-8 SERVINGS

- **1 cup chopped onion**
- **1 cup sliced fresh mushrooms**
- **1 tablespoon vegetable oil**
- **1 package (10 ounces) frozen chopped spinach, thawed and well drained**
- **⅔ cup finely chopped fully cooked ham**
- **5 large eggs**
- **3 cups (12 ounces) shredded Muenster or Monterey Jack cheese**
- **⅛ teaspoon pepper**

In a large skillet, saute onion and mushrooms in oil until tender. Add spinach and ham; cook and stir until the excess moisture is evaporated. Cool slightly. Beat eggs; add cheese and mix well. Stir in spinach mixture and pepper; blend well. Spread evenly into a greased 9-in. pie plate or quiche dish. Bake at 350° for 40-45 minutes or until a knife inserted near the center comes out clean.

BAKED BLUEBERRY-MASCARPONE FRENCH TOAST

This is my go-to recipe when I want something special to serve my guests for a Saturday or Sunday brunch. It never fails. It's especially good in the spring and early summer when fresh-picked blueberries are at their sweetest. The mascarpone cheese makes it over-the-top indulgent!

—PATRICIA QUINN OMAHA, NE

PREP: 15 MIN. + CHILLING
BAKE: 1 HOUR + STANDING
MAKES: 10 SERVINGS

- **8 slices French bread (½ inch thick), cubed (about 4 cups)**
- **2 cups fresh or frozen blueberries**
- **2 cartons (8 ounces each) mascarpone cheese**
- **½ cup confectioners' sugar**
- **10 slices French bread (1 inch thick)**
- **8 large eggs**
- **2 cups half-and-half cream**
- **1 cup whole milk**
- **⅓ cup granulated sugar**
- **1 teaspoon vanilla extract**
- **Additional confectioners' sugar**
- **1 cup sliced almonds, toasted**
- **Additional fresh blueberries, optional**

1. In a greased 13x9-in. baking dish, layer bread cubes and blueberries. In a small bowl, beat mascarpone cheese and confectioners' sugar until smooth; drop by tablespoonfuls over blueberries. Top with bread slices. In a large bowl, whisk eggs, cream, milk, granulated sugar and vanilla; pour over bread. Refrigerate, covered, overnight.
2. Preheat oven to 350°. Remove French toast from refrigerator while oven heats. Bake, covered, 30 minutes. Bake, uncovered, 30-40 minutes longer or until puffed and golden and a knife inserted near the center comes out clean.
3. Let stand 10 minutes before serving. Dust with additional confectioners' sugar; sprinkle with almonds. If desired, serve with additional fresh blueberries.

NOTE *To toast nuts, bake in a shallow pan in a 350° oven for 5-10 minutes or cook in a skillet over low heat until lightly browned, stirring occasionally.*

FAST FIX

BLINTZ PANCAKES

Blending sour cream and cottage cheese—ingredients traditionally associated with the creamy filling in blintzes—into the batter of these pancakes gives them a classic old-fashioned flavor. Top them with berry syrup to turn an ordinary morning into an extraordinary day.

—DIANNA DIGOY SAN DIEGO, CA

START TO FINISH: 30 MIN.
MAKES: 12 PANCAKES

- **1 cup all-purpose flour**
- **1 tablespoon sugar**
- **½ teaspoon salt**
- **1 cup (8 ounces) sour cream**
- **1 cup (8 ounces) 4% cottage cheese**
- **4 large eggs, lightly beaten**
- **Strawberry or blueberry syrup**
- **Sliced fresh strawberries, optional**

1. In a large bowl, combine the flour, sugar and salt. Stir in the sour cream, cottage cheese and eggs until blended.
2. Pour batter by 1/4 cupfuls onto a greased hot griddle in batches; turn when bubbles form on top. Cook until the second side is golden brown. Serve with syrup and, if desired, strawberries.

SOUTHWEST HASH WITH ADOBO-LIME CREMA

If you wake up with a hankering for some south-of-the border flavor, you'll love this bold and zesty specialty. When I have leftover pulled pork on hand, I'll toss it into the hash for some serious yum!
—BROOKE KELLER LEXINGTON, KY

PREP: 20 MIN. • **BAKE:** 25 MIN. • **MAKES:** 4 SERVINGS

- **3 medium sweet potatoes (about 1½ pounds), cubed**
- **1 medium onion, chopped**
- **1 medium sweet red pepper, chopped**
- **1 tablespoon canola oil**
- **1 teaspoon garlic powder**
- **1 teaspoon smoked paprika**
- **¾ teaspoon ground chipotle pepper**
- **½ teaspoon salt**
- **¼ teaspoon pepper**
- **⅔ cup canned black beans, rinsed and drained**
- **4 large eggs**
- **½ cup reduced-fat sour cream**
- **2 tablespoons lime juice**
- **2 teaspoons adobo sauce**
- **½ medium ripe avocado, peeled and sliced, optional**
- **2 tablespoons minced fresh cilantro**

1. Preheat oven to 400°. Place sweet potatoes, onion and red pepper in a 15x10x1-in. baking pan coated with cooking spray. Drizzle with oil; sprinkle with seasonings. Toss to coat. Roast 25-30 minutes or until potatoes are tender, adding beans during the last 10 minutes of cooking time.
2. Place 2-3 in. of water in a large saucepan or skillet with high sides. Bring to a boil; adjust heat to maintain a gentle simmer. Break cold eggs, one at a time, into a small bowl; holding bowl close to surface of water, slip egg into water.
3. Cook, uncovered, 3-5 minutes or until whites are completely set and yolks begin to thicken but are not hard. Using a slotted spoon, lift eggs out of water.
4. In a small bowl, mix sour cream, lime juice and adobo sauce. Serve sweet potato mixture with egg, sour cream mixture and, if desired, avocado. Sprinkle with cilantro.

TOP TIP

Perfect Poached Eggs

When poaching eggs, use the freshest eggs possible. Bring the water to a boil, then reduce it to a simmer before adding the eggs. Break each egg into a shallow cup and gently slide it into the water instead of cracking it directly into the water. Adding 2 tablespoons of vinegar and a dash of salt for each quart of water will help keep the eggs from spreading.

ON-THE-GO BREAKFAST MUFFINS

Family members frequently request that I make these muffins. I usually prepare them on Sunday night so when we're running late on weekday mornings, the kids can grab them to eat on the bus.
—IRENE WAYMAN GRANTSVILLE, UT

PREP: 30 MIN. • **BAKE:** 15 MIN. • **MAKES:** 1½ DOZEN

- **1 pound bulk Italian sausage**
- **7 large eggs, divided use**
- **2 cups all-purpose flour**
- **⅓ cup sugar**
- **3 teaspoons baking powder**
- **½ teaspoon salt**
- **½ cup 2% milk**
- **½ cup canola oil**
- **1 cup (4 ounces) shredded cheddar cheese, divided**

1. Preheat oven to 400°. In a large nonstick skillet, cook sausage over medium heat 6-8 minutes or until no longer pink, breaking into crumbles. Remove with a slotted spoon; drain on paper towels. Wipe skillet clean.
2. In a small bowl, whisk five eggs. Pour into same skillet; cook and stir over medium heat until thickened and no liquid egg remains. Remove from heat.
3. In a large bowl, whisk flour, sugar, baking powder and salt. In another bowl, whisk remaining eggs, milk and oil until blended. Add to flour mixture; stir just until moistened. Fold in ⅔ cup cheese, sausage and scrambled eggs.
4. Fill greased or paper-lined muffin cups three-fourths full. Sprinkle tops with the remaining cheese. Bake for 12-15 minutes or until a toothpick inserted in center comes out clean. Cool 5 minutes before removing from pans to wire racks. Serve warm.
FREEZE OPTION *Freeze cooled muffins in resealable plastic freezer bags. To use, microwave each muffin on high for 45-60 seconds or until heated through.*

CHEESY HASH BROWN EGG CASSEROLE WITH BACON

My husband and sons frequently request this dish, referring to it as "egg pie." The hearty casserole is nice enough for a holiday but is also satisfying enough for a busy weeknight.
—PATRICIA THROLSON BECKER, MINNESOTA

PREP: 20 MIN. • **BAKE:** 35 MIN. • **MAKES:** 8 SERVINGS

- **½ pound sliced bacon, chopped**
- **½ cup chopped onion**
- **½ cup chopped green pepper**
- **12 large eggs, lightly beaten**
- **1 cup 2% milk**
- **1 teaspoon salt**
- **½ teaspoon pepper**
- **¼ teaspoon dill weed**
- **1 package (16 ounces) frozen shredded hash brown potatoes, thawed**
- **1 cup (4 ounces) shredded cheddar cheese**

1. In a large skillet, cook bacon over medium heat until crisp. Remove with a slotted spoon; drain on paper towels. Discard drippings, reserving 2 tablespoons. In the same skillet, saute onion and green pepper in drippings until tender; remove with a slotted spoon.
2. In a large bowl, whisk eggs, milk and seasonings. Stir in the hash browns, cheese, onion mixture and bacon.
3. Transfer to a greased 13x9-in. baking dish. Bake, uncovered, at 350° for 35-45 minutes or until a knife inserted near the center comes out clean.

BREAKFAST BISCUIT CUPS

The first time I made these cups, my husband and his assistant coach came into the kitchen as I pulled the pan from the oven. They devoured the biscuits!

—DEBRA CARLSON
COLUMBUS JUNCTION, IA

PREP: 30 MIN. • **BAKE:** 20 MIN.
MAKES: 8 SERVINGS

- **⅓ pound bulk pork sausage**
- **1 tablespoon all-purpose flour**
- **⅛ teaspoon salt**
- **½ teaspoon pepper, divided**
- **¾ cup plus 1 tablespoon 2% milk, divided**
- **½ cup frozen cubed hash brown potatoes, thawed**
- **1 tablespoon butter**
- **2 large eggs**
- **⅛ teaspoon garlic salt**
- **1 can (16.3 ounces) large refrigerated flaky biscuits**
- **½ cup shredded Colby-Monterey Jack cheese**

1. In a large skillet, cook sausage over medium heat until no longer pink; drain. Stir in the flour, salt and 1/4 teaspoon pepper until blended; gradually add 3/4 cup milk. Bring to a boil; cook and stir for 2 minutes or until thickened. Remove from the heat and set aside.
2. In another large skillet over medium heat, cook potatoes in butter until tender. Whisk the eggs, garlic salt and remaining milk and pepper; add to skillet. Cook and stir until almost set.
3. Press each biscuit onto the bottom and up the sides of eight ungreased muffin cups. Spoon egg mixture, half the cheese, and all the sausage into cups; sprinkle with remaining cheese.
4. Bake at 375° for 18-22 minutes or until golden brown. Cool 5 minutes before removing from pan.

CREAM CHEESE COFFEE CAKE

These impressive loaves really shine at a buffet. Everyone wants a second slice of this treat.

—MARY ANNE MCWHIRTER PEARLAND, TX

PREP: 35 MIN. + RISING
BAKE: 20 MIN. + COOLING
MAKES: 20-24 SERVINGS

- **1 cup (8 ounces) sour cream**
- **½ cup sugar**
- **½ cup butter, cubed**
- **1 teaspoon salt**
- **2 packages (¼ ounce each) active dry yeast**
- **½ cup warm water (110° to 115°)**
- **2 large eggs, lightly beaten**
- **4 cups all-purpose flour**

FILLING

- **2 packages (8 ounces each) cream cheese, softened**
- **¾ cup sugar**
- **1 large egg, lightly beaten**
- **2 teaspoons vanilla extract**
- **⅛ teaspoon salt**

GLAZE

- **2½ cups confectioners' sugar**
- **¼ cup milk**
- **1 teaspoon vanilla extract**
- **Toasted sliced almonds, optional**

1. In a small saucepan, combine the sour cream, sugar, butter and salt. Cook over medium-low heat, stirring constantly, 5-10 minutes or until well blended. Cool to room temperature.
2. In a large bowl, dissolve yeast in warm water. Add sour cream mixture and eggs. Beat until smooth. Gradually stir in flour to form a soft dough (dough will be very soft). Cover dough and refrigerate overnight.
3. Punch dough down. Turn dough onto a floured surface; knead 5-6 times. Divide into fourths. Roll each piece into a 12x8-in. rectangle. In a large bowl, combine filling ingredients until well blended. Spread over each rectangle to within 1 in. of edges.
4. Roll up jelly-roll style, starting with a long side; pinch seams and ends to seal. Place seam side down on greased baking sheets. Cut six X's on top of each loaf. Cover and let rise until nearly doubled, about 1 hour.
5. Preheat oven to 375°. Bake for 20-25 minutes or until golden brown. Remove from pans to wire racks to cool. In a small bowl, combine confectioners' sugar, milk and vanilla; drizzle over warm loaves. Sprinkle with almonds if desired. Store in the refrigerator.

5 INGREDIENTS

BREAKFAST BREAD BOWLS

These bread bowls are so elegant, tasty and simple, you'll wonder why you haven't been making them for years. My wife loves when I make these for her in the morning.

—PATRICK LAVIN JR. BIRDSBORO, PA

PREP: 20 MIN. • **BAKE:** 20 MIN. • **MAKES:** 4 SERVINGS

- **½ cup chopped pancetta**
- **4 crusty hard rolls (4 inches wide)**
- **½ cup finely chopped fresh mushrooms**
- **4 large eggs**
- **⅛ teaspoon salt**
- **⅛ teaspoon pepper**
- **¼ cup shredded Gruyere or fontina cheese**

1. Preheat oven to 350°. In a small skillet, cook pancetta over medium heat until browned, stirring occasionally. Remove with a slotted spoon; drain on paper towels.
2. Meanwhile, cut a thin slice off top of each roll. Hollow out bottom of roll, leaving a ½-in.-thick shell (save removed bread for another use); place shells on an ungreased baking sheet.
3. Add mushrooms and pancetta to bread shells. Carefully break an egg into each; sprinkle eggs with salt and pepper. Sprinkle with cheese. Bake 18-22 minutes or until egg whites are completely set and yolks begin to thicken but are not hard.

FAST FIX

SPICY SCRAMBLED EGG SANDWICHES

When my daughters were young, I'd pile this tasty egg mixture onto toasted English muffins, pour each girl a glass of juice and let them enjoy their breakfast on the patio.

—HELEN VAIL GLENSIDE, PA

START TO FINISH: 30 MIN. • **MAKES:** 4 SERVINGS

- **⅓ cup chopped green pepper**
- **¼ cup chopped onion**
- **3 large eggs**
- **4 large egg whites**
- **1 tablespoon water**
- **¼ teaspoon salt**
- **¼ teaspoon ground mustard**
- **⅛ teaspoon pepper**
- **⅛ teaspoon hot pepper sauce**
- **⅓ cup fresh or frozen corn, thawed**
- **¼ cup real bacon bits**
- **4 English muffins, split and toasted**

1. In a 10-in. skillet coated with cooking spray, cook green pepper and onion over medium heat until tender, about 8 minutes.
2. In a large bowl, whisk the eggs, egg whites, water, salt, mustard, pepper and hot pepper sauce. Pour into skillet. Add corn and bacon; cook and stir until the eggs are completely set. Spoon onto English muffin bottoms; replace tops. Serve sandwiches immediately.

BAKED CHEDDAR EGGS & POTATOES

I love having breakfast for dinner, especially this combo of eggs, potatoes and cheese. It starts in a skillet on the stovetop and then I pop it into the oven to bake.

—NADINE MERHEB TUCSON, AZ

PREP: 20 MIN. • **BAKE:** 10 MIN. • **MAKES:** 4 SERVINGS

- **3 tablespoons butter**
- **1½ pounds red potatoes, chopped**
- **¼ cup minced fresh parsley**
- **2 garlic cloves, minced**
- **¾ teaspoon kosher salt**
- **⅛ teaspoon pepper**
- **8 large eggs**
- **½ cup shredded extra-sharp cheddar cheese**

1. Preheat oven to 400°. In a 10-in. ovenproof skillet, heat butter over medium-high heat. Add potatoes; cook and stir until golden brown and tender. Stir in parsley, garlic, salt and pepper. With back of a spoon, make four wells in the potato mixture; break two eggs into each well.
2. Bake 9-11 minutes or until egg whites are completely set and yolks begin to thicken but are not hard. Sprinkle with cheese; bake 1 minute or until cheese is melted.

RAISIN NUT OATMEAL

There's no better feeling than waking up to a ready-to-eat hot breakfast. The oats, fruits and spices in this homey meal bake together overnight, so the recipe is a keeper for busy cooks.
—VALERIE SAUBER ADELANTO, CALIFORNIA

PREP: 10 MIN. **COOK:** 7 HOURS • **MAKES:** 6 SERVINGS

- **3½ cups fat-free milk**
- **1 large apple, peeled and chopped**
- **¾ cup steel-cut oats**
- **¾ cup raisins**
- **3 tablespoons brown sugar**
- **4½ teaspoons butter, melted**
- **¾ teaspoon ground cinnamon**
- **½ teaspoon salt**
- **¼ cup chopped pecans**

In a 3-qt. slow cooker coated with cooking spray, combine the first eight ingredients. Cover and cook on low for 7-8 hours or until liquid is absorbed. Spoon oatmeal into bowls; sprinkle with pecans.

NOTE *You may substitute 1½ cups quick-cooking oats for the steel-cut oats and increase the fat-free milk to 4½ cups.*

"I tried this recipe with almond milk and it was fabulous. My entire family loved it. So delicious!"
—HON1HON1 FROM TASTEOFHOME.COM

FAST FIX

CHOCOLATE CHIP PANCAKES

Give ordinary pancakes kid-friendly appeal with chocolate chips and a drizzle of cinnamon and honey syrup. This is one of those special Saturday morning favorites the little ones will remember.
—LEEANN HANSEN KAYSVILLE, UT

START TO FINISH: 25 MIN. • **MAKES:** 6 SERVINGS

- **2 cups all-purpose flour**
- **¼ cup sugar**
- **2 tablespoons baking powder**
- **1 teaspoon salt**
- **2 large eggs**
- **1½ cups milk**
- **¼ cup canola oil**
- **½ cup miniature chocolate chips**

CINNAMON HONEY SYRUP

- **1 cup honey**
- **½ cup butter, cubed**
- **1 to 2 teaspoons ground cinnamon**

1. In a large bowl, combine the flour, sugar, baking powder and salt. Combine eggs, milk and oil; add to dry ingredients just until moistened. Fold in chocolate chips.
2. Pour the batter by ¼ cupfuls onto a lightly greased hot griddle. Turn when bubbles form on top; cook until second side is golden brown. Keep warm.
3. Combine the syrup ingredients in a 2-cup microwave-safe bowl. Microwave, uncovered, on high until butter is melted and syrup is hot, stirring occasionally. Serve with pancakes.

(5) INGREDIENTS FAST FIX

BRUNCH PIZZA SQUARES

I love using convenience items, like the crescent rolls in these easy squares. Guests always ask me for the recipe. To hurry along the preparation of this casserole and others like it, I'll brown a few pounds of sausage ahead of time and keep it in the freezer to have on hand at a moment's notice.

—LACHELLE OLIVET PACE, FL

START TO FINISH: 30 MIN. • **MAKES:** 8 SERVINGS

- **1 pound bulk pork sausage**
- **1 tube (8 ounces) refrigerated crescent rolls**
- **4 large eggs**
- **2 tablespoons milk**
- **1/8 teaspoon pepper**
- **3/4 cup shredded cheddar cheese**

1. In a large skillet, crumble sausage and cook over medium heat until no longer pink; drain. Unroll crescent dough onto the bottom and 1/2 in. up the sides of a lightly greased 13x9-in. baking pan; seal seams. Sprinkle with sausage.
2. In a large bowl, beat the eggs, milk and pepper; pour over sausage. Sprinkle with cheese.
3. Bake, uncovered, at 400° for 15 minutes or until a knife inserted in the center comes out clean.

FAST FIX

BREAKFAST PITAS

On hurried mornings, my husband and I enjoy these pita pockets all by themselves for a quick breakfast. When you want a larger meal, serve hash brown potatoes and fruit on the side.

—PEGGY BLATTEL CAPE GIRARDEAU, MO

START TO FINISH: 15 MIN. • **MAKES:** 2 SERVINGS

- **1 cup cubed fully cooked ham**
- **1/3 cup chopped onion**
- **1/3 cup chopped green pepper**
- **2 tablespoons butter**
- **3 large eggs, lightly beaten**
- **1/2 cup shredded cheddar cheese**
- **1/2 teaspoon seasoned salt**
- **1/4 teaspoon pepper**
- **2 pita breads (6 inches), halved and warmed**

In a large skillet, saute the ham, onion and green pepper in butter until tender. Add eggs; cook and stir over medium heat until eggs are almost set. Add the cheese, seasoned salt and pepper. Cook and stir until eggs are completely set. Spoon into pita halves.

POTATO MINESTRONE, 57

BLT WRAPS, 49

GRANDMA'S CHICKEN 'N' DUMPLING SOUP, 58

PORK AND BEEF BARBECUE, 51

SOUPS & SANDWICHES

Whether for lunch, dinner or a snack in between, soups and sandwiches are the perfect mealtime solution when your family craves comfort food at its best. Discover your new favorite steamy pot of homemade goodness when you ladle up any one of these effortless soups. Enjoy a bowl all by itself or pair it with one of our delicious sandwich specialties, each one chock-full of the freshest ingredients. Some mighty good eating is sure to follow.

FAST FIX

OPEN-FACED GRILLED SALMON SANDWICHES

In my family, we love to fish. What better reward from a day of fishing than eating what you just caught? We make salmon several ways, but this one is the absolute family favorite.

—STEPHANIE HANISAK PORT MURRAY, NJ

START TO FINISH: 30 MIN.
MAKES: 4 SERVINGS

- **4 salmon fillets (1 inch thick and 5 ounces each), skin removed**
- **¾ cup mesquite marinade**
- **¼ teaspoon pepper**
- **4 slices sourdough bread (½ inch thick)**
- **¼ cup tartar sauce**
- **4 iceberg lettuce leaves**
- **4 lemon wedges, optional**

1. Place fillets in an 8-in. square dish. Pour marinade over fillets; turn fish to coat. Let stand 15 minutes.
2. Drain salmon, discarding marinade. Sprinkle salmon with the pepper.
3. Moisten a paper towel with cooking oil; using long-handled tongs, rub on grill rack to coat lightly. Grill salmon, covered, over medium heat or broil 4 in. from heat 4-6 minutes on each side or until fish just begins to flake easily with a fork.
4. Grill bread, covered, over medium heat 1-2 minutes on each side or until lightly toasted. Spread with tartar sauce; top with lettuce and salmon. If desired, serve with lemon wedges.

TOP TIP

Skinless Salmon

Peeling the skin from fresh salmon can be difficult, but my method makes it a cinch. Bring 1/2 inch of water to a slow boil in a frying pan. Put the salmon, skin side down, in the water for 1 minute. Carefully remove the salmon from the water, and peel the skin. Gently rinse the fish and proceed with the recipe.

—FREDO C. LOS ANGELES, CA

NORTH PACIFIC CHOWDER

Tender veggies and tarragon add fantastic flavor to this chunky fish chowder. It's truly one of the best I've ever tasted.
—PAM WOOLGAR QUALICUM BEACH, BC

PREP: 15 MIN. • **COOK:** 35 MIN.
MAKES: 9 SERVINGS (2¼ QUARTS)

- **8 bacon strips**
- **1 small onion, chopped**
- **1 celery rib, chopped**
- **1 carton (32 ounces) chicken broth**
- **4 medium red potatoes, cubed**
- **2 tablespoons all-purpose flour**
- **1 pint half-and-half cream**
- **1 pound halibut fillets, cubed**
- **1 tablespoon minced fresh tarragon or 1 teaspoon dried tarragon**
- **½ teaspoon salt**
- **¼ teaspoon pepper**
- **Tarragon sprigs, optional**

1. In a large saucepan over medium heat, cook bacon until crisp. Drain, reserving 1 teaspoon drippings. Crumble bacon and set aside. Saute onion and celery in the drippings. Add broth and potatoes. Bring to a boil. Reduce heat; cover and cook for 15-20 minutes or until potatoes are tender.
2. Combine flour and cream until smooth; gradually stir into soup. Bring to a boil; cook and stir for 2 minutes. Stir in the halibut, tarragon, salt, pepper and crumbled bacon. Reduce heat; simmer, uncovered, for 5-10 minutes or until fish flakes easily with a fork. Garnish with tarragon sprigs if desired.

FAST FIX

ITALIAN STEAK SANDWICHES

My sister came up with these quick sandwiches that are packed with Italian flavor from basil and garlic. Add some carrot sticks or a tomato salad for a fantastic lunch you can make in minutes.
—MARIA REGAKIS SAUGUS, MA

START TO FINISH: 15 MIN.
MAKES: 4 SERVINGS

- **2 tablespoons olive oil**
- **2 garlic cloves, minced**
- **⅛ teaspoon crushed red pepper flakes**
- **½ pound sliced deli roast beef**
- **½ cup beef broth**
- **2 tablespoons red wine or additional beef broth**
- **2 teaspoons dried parsley flakes**
- **2 teaspoons dried basil**
- **¼ teaspoon salt**
- **¼ teaspoon dried oregano**
- **⅛ teaspoon pepper**
- **4 sandwich rolls, split**
- **4 slices provolone cheese**

In a large skillet, heat oil over medium-high heat. Add garlic and pepper flakes; cook and stir 1 minute. Add roast beef, broth, wine and seasonings; heat through. Place beef slices on rolls; drizzle with broth mixture. Top with cheese.
FREEZE OPTION *Freeze cooled meat mixture and juices in freezer container. To use, partially thaw in refrigerator overnight. Heat through in a saucepan, stirring occasionally and adding a little broth if necessary.*

(5) INGREDIENTS FAST FIX

SIMPLE CHICKEN SOUP

I revised a recipe that my family loved so it would be lighter and easier to make. It's a hearty and healthy meal when served with a green salad and fresh bread.

—SUE WEST ALVORD, TX

START TO FINISH: 20 MIN. • **MAKES:** 6 SERVINGS

- **2 cans (14½ ounces each) reduced-sodium chicken broth**
- **1 tablespoon dried minced onion**
- **1 package (16 ounces) frozen mixed vegetables**
- **2 cups cubed cooked chicken breast**
- **2 cans (10¾ ounces each) reduced-fat reduced-sodium condensed cream of chicken soup, undiluted**

In a large saucepan, bring broth and onion to a boil. Reduce heat. Add the vegetables; cover and cook for 6-8 minutes or until crisp-tender. Stir in chicken and soup; heat through.

"This is my favorite soup. I eat it all winter long. The only thing I do differently is add egg noodles."

—DENIBD53 FROM TASTEOFHOME.COM

CHUNKY BEEF & VEGETABLE SOUP

Nothing cures the winter blahs like wonderful soup, including this beefy one I first cooked up on a snowy day. Serve with artisan bread.

—BILLY HENSLEY MOUNT CARMEL, TN

PREP: 25 MIN. • **COOK:** 2¾ HOURS • **MAKES:** 8 SERVINGS (3 QUARTS)

- **1½ pounds beef stew meat, cut into ½-inch pieces**
- **1 teaspoon salt, divided**
- **1 teaspoon salt-free seasoning blend, divided**
- **¾ teaspoon pepper, divided**
- **2 tablespoons olive oil, divided**
- **4 large carrots, sliced**
- **1 large onion, chopped**
- **1 medium sweet red pepper, chopped**
- **1 medium green pepper, chopped**
- **2 garlic cloves, minced**
- **1 cup Burgundy wine or additional reduced-sodium beef broth**
- **4 cups reduced-sodium beef broth**
- **1 can (14½ ounces) diced tomatoes, undrained**
- **2 tablespoons tomato paste**
- **2 tablespoons Worcestershire sauce**
- **1 bay leaf**
- **4 medium potatoes (about 2 pounds), cut into ½-inch cubes**

1. Sprinkle beef with 1/2 teaspoon each salt, seasoning blend and pepper. In a Dutch oven, heat 1 tablespoon oil over medium heat. Brown beef in batches. Remove from pan.

2. In same pan, heat remaining oil over medium heat. Add carrots, onion and peppers; cook and stir until carrots are crisp-tender. Add garlic; cook 1 minute longer.

3. Add wine, stirring to loosen browned bits from pan. Stir in broth, tomatoes, tomato paste, Worcestershire sauce, bay leaf and remaining seasonings. Return beef to pan; bring to a boil. Reduce heat; simmer, covered, 2 hours.

4. Add potatoes; cook 30-40 minutes longer or until beef and potatoes are tender. Skim fat and discard bay leaf.

FAST FIX

BLT WRAPS

My mom used to make these delicious wraps for all of the kids and grandkids on summer days at the lake. Nowadays, we love to pack them along for picnics and days in the park.

—SHELLY BURKS BRIGHTON, MO

START TO FINISH: 15 MIN. • **MAKES:** 8 SERVINGS

- **16 ready-to-serve fully cooked bacon strips, warmed if desired**
- **8 flour tortillas (8 inches), room temperature**
- **4 cups chopped lettuce**
- **2 cups chopped tomatoes (3 small tomatoes)**
- **2 cups (8 ounces) shredded cheddar cheese**
- **½ cup ranch salad dressing**

Place two bacon strips across the center of each tortilla. Top with lettuce, tomatoes and cheese; drizzle with salad dressing. Fold bottom and sides of tortilla over filling and roll up.

TO MAKE AHEAD *Assemble wraps without heating bacon; wrap in plastic wrap and store in refrigerator up to 2 days.*

FAST FIX

DELI BEEF SANDWICHES WITH HORSERADISH MAYONNAISE

Sweet cherry preserves balance the bold horseradish in this hearty sandwich. What a delicious noontime treat!

—GREG FONTENOT THE WOODLANDS, TX

START TO FINISH: 10 MIN. • **MAKES:** 4 SERVINGS

- **½ cup mayonnaise**
- **2 tablespoons cherry preserves**
- **4 teaspoons prepared horseradish**
- **8 slices whole wheat bread**
- **¾ pound sliced deli roast beef**
- **4 lettuce leaves**
- **1 large tomato, thinly sliced**
- **Dash each salt and pepper**

In a small bowl, combine the mayonnaise, preserves and horseradish. Spread 1 tablespoon over each of four bread slices. Layer with roast beef, lettuce and tomato; sprinkle with salt and pepper. Spread remaining mayonnaise mixture over remaining bread; place over top.

FAST FIX

CUBAN PANINI

The Cuban sandwich is a twist on the traditional ham and cheese, usually with ham, Swiss, pickles and condiments, and sometimes, as in this hearty version, smoked turkey.

—JANET SANDERS PINE MOUNTAIN, GA

PREP: 20 MIN. • **COOK:** 5 MIN./BATCH
MAKES: 4 SERVINGS

- **2 garlic cloves, minced**
- **½ teaspoon olive oil**
- **½ cup reduced-fat mayonnaise**
- **8 slices artisan bread**
- **8 thick slices deli smoked turkey**
- **4 slices deli ham**
- **8 slices Swiss cheese**
- **12 dill pickle slices**
- **1 cup fresh baby spinach**

1. In a small skillet, cook and stir garlic in oil over medium-high heat until tender. Cool.
2. Stir garlic into mayonnaise; spread over bread slices. Layer four slices of bread with turkey, ham, cheese, pickles and spinach; close sandwiches.
3. Cook on a panini maker or indoor grill for 2-3 minutes or until browned and the cheese is melted.

EMILY'S BEAN SOUP

Served with thick slices of warm homemade bread, my soup makes a wonderful fall or winter meal. The recipe evolved over the years as I experimented with different ingredients. I often double it and freeze what we don't eat—that way, I can throw some in a pot for a quick meal or if unexpected guests drop by.

—EMILY CHANEY PENOBSCOT, ME

PREP: 25 MIN. + STANDING
COOK: 3 HOURS
MAKES: ABOUT 5½ QUARTS

- **½ cup each dried great northern beans, kidney beans, navy beans, lima beans, butter beans, split green or yellow peas, pinto beans and lentils**
- **Water**
- **1 meaty ham bone**
- **2 teaspoons chicken bouillon granules**
- **1 can (28 ounces) tomatoes with liquid, quartered**
- **1 can (6 ounces) tomato paste**
- **1 large onion, chopped**
- **3 celery ribs, chopped**
- **4 medium carrots, sliced**
- **2 garlic cloves, minced**
- **¼ cup minced chives**
- **3 bay leaves**
- **2 tablespoons dried parsley flakes**
- **1 teaspoon dried thyme**
- **1 teaspoon ground mustard**
- **½ teaspoon cayenne pepper**

1. Wash all beans thoroughly; drain and place in a large saucepan. Add 5 cups of water. Bring to a rapid boil; boil for 2 minutes. Remove from the heat; cover and let stand for 1 hour.
2. Meanwhile, place ham bone and 3 qts. of water in a stockpot. Simmer until beans have stood for 1 hour.
3. Drain beans and add to the ham stock; add remaining ingredients. Simmer for 2-3 hours or until beans are tender. Cut meat from ham bone; discard bone. Add additional water to soup if desired.

PORK AND BEEF BARBECUE

It's the combination of beef stew meat and tender pork that keeps friends and family asking about these tangy sandwiches. Add a lettuce leaf and a tomato slice for a crisp contrast.
—CORBIN DETGEN BUCHANAN, MI

PREP: 15 MIN. • **COOK:** 6 HOURS • **MAKES:** 12 SERVINGS

- **1 can (6 ounces) tomato paste**
- **½ cup packed brown sugar**
- **¼ cup chili powder**
- **¼ cup cider vinegar**
- **2 teaspoons Worcestershire sauce**
- **1 teaspoon salt**
- **1½ pounds beef stew meat, cut into ¾-inch cubes**
- **1½ pounds pork chop suey meat or pork tenderloin, cut into ¾-inch cubes**
- **3 medium green peppers, chopped**
- **2 large onions, chopped**
- **12 sandwich buns, split**
- **Lettuce and tomatoes, optional**

1. In a 5-qt. slow cooker, combine the first six ingredients. Stir in beef, pork, green peppers and onions. Cover and cook on low for 6-8 hours or until meat is tender.

2. Shred meat with two forks. Serve on buns, with lettuce and tomatoes if desired.

FAST FIX

CHEESE-TOPPED SLOPPY JOES

My Aunt Nellie passed along the recipe for these quick-to-fix sandwiches. A busy farm wife, she served them to the harvest crew. Nowadays, we microwave leftovers—and they're delicious.
—MARY DEMPSEY OVERLAND PARK, KS

START TO FINISH: 25 MIN. • **MAKES:** 6 SERVINGS

- **1 pound ground beef**
- **2 celery ribs, chopped**
- **1 tablespoon chopped onion**
- **1 tablespoon all-purpose flour**
- **1 tablespoon brown sugar**
- **½ teaspoon ground mustard**
- **¾ cup ketchup**
- **6 hamburger buns, split**
- **6 slices Swiss cheese**

1. In a large skillet, cook the beef, celery and onion over medium heat until meat is no longer pink; drain. Stir in the flour, brown sugar, mustard and ketchup.
2. Bring to a boil. Reduce heat; simmer, uncovered, for 10 minutes, stirring occasionally. Serve on buns with cheese.

FAST FIX

HONEY-MUSTARD BRATS

Our honey mustard glaze gives every bite of these brats a sweet and punchy flavor. Everyone who tries them agrees they're delicious.
—LILY JULOW LAWRENCEVILLE, GA

START TO FINISH: 25 MIN. • **MAKES:** 4 SERVINGS

- **¼ cup Dijon mustard**
- **¼ cup honey**
- **2 tablespoons mayonnaise**
- **1 teaspoon steak sauce**
- **4 uncooked bratwurst links**
- **4 brat buns, split**

1. In a small bowl, mix mustard, honey, mayonnaise and steak sauce.
2. Grill bratwurst, covered, over medium heat 15-20 minutes or until a thermometer reads 160°, turning occasionally; brush frequently with mustard mixture during the last 5 minutes. Serve on buns.

FAST FIX

30-MINUTE CHILI

A neighbor gave me a pot of this delicious chili, and I had to have the recipe. Pork sausage is a nice change of pace from the ground beef many chili recipes call for.
—JANICE WESTMORELAND BROOKSVILLE, FL

START TO FINISH: 30 MIN. • **MAKES:** 12 SERVINGS (3 QUARTS)

- **1 pound bulk pork sausage**
- **1 large onion, chopped**
- **2 cans (16 ounces each) chili beans, undrained**
- **1 can (28 ounces) crushed tomatoes**
- **3 cups water**
- **1 can (4 ounces) chopped green chilies**
- **1 envelope chili seasoning mix**
- **2 tablespoons sugar**

In a Dutch oven, cook sausage and onion over medium heat 6-8 minutes or until meat is no longer pink, breaking into crumbles; drain. Add remaining ingredients; bring to a boil. Reduce heat; simmer, covered, 20 minutes, stirring often.

TOP TIP

Got Leftover Chili?

Here's a tasty way to use up leftover chili. Warm about 4 cups of chili and pour into a deep-dish pie pan. (If you have a little less than 4 cups, add some drained whole kernel corn.) Prepare a small box of corn bread mix according to package directions and drop batter over the chili. Bake at 375° for 30 minutes or until corn bread is done. Sprinkle with shredded cheddar cheese.
—BARBARA K. FAUCETT, MO

FAST FIX

LASAGNA SOUP

All the traditional flavors of lasagna come together in this heartwarming bowl of comfort.

—**SHERYL OLENICK** DEMAREST, NJ

START TO FINISH: 30 MIN. • **MAKES:** 8 SERVINGS (2¾ QUARTS)

- **1 pound lean ground beef (90% lean)**
- **1 large green pepper, chopped**
- **1 medium onion, chopped**
- **2 garlic cloves, minced**
- **2 cans (14½ ounces each) diced tomatoes, undrained**
- **2 cans (14½ ounces each) reduced-sodium beef broth**
- **1 can (8 ounces) tomato sauce**
- **1 cup frozen corn**
- **¼ cup tomato paste**
- **2 teaspoons Italian seasoning**
- **¼ teaspoon pepper**
- **2½ cups uncooked spiral pasta**
- **½ cup shredded Parmesan cheese**

1. In a large saucepan, cook beef, green pepper and onion over medium heat 6-8 minutes or until meat is no longer pink, breaking up beef into crumbles. Add garlic; cook 1 minute longer. Drain.

2. Stir in tomatoes, broth, tomato sauce, corn, tomato paste, Italian seasoning and pepper. Bring to a boil. Stir in pasta. Return to a boil. Reduce the heat; simmer, covered, for 10-12 minutes or until pasta is tender. Sprinkle with cheese.

FAST FIX

FISH PO'BOYS

Whether you're rich or poor, you'll feel like a million bucks after one big bite into this classic sandwich. Use your favorite brand of frozen breaded fish, and adjust the amount of hot pepper sauce to suit your tastes.

—***TASTE OF HOME*** **TEST KITCHEN**

START TO FINISH: 30 MIN. • **MAKES:** 6 SERVINGS

- **2 packages (11.4 ounces each) frozen crunchy breaded fish fillets**
- **½ cup mayonnaise**
- **1 tablespoon minced fresh parsley**
- **1 tablespoon ketchup**
- **2 teaspoons stone-ground mustard**
- **1 teaspoon horseradish sauce**
- **2 to 4 drops hot pepper sauce**
- **1½ cups deli coleslaw**
- **6 hamburger buns, split**

1. Bake fish fillets according to the package directions. Meanwhile, in a small bowl, combine the mayonnaise, parsley, ketchup, mustard, horseradish sauce and hot pepper sauce until blended.

2. Spoon ¼ cup coleslaw onto the bottom of each bun; top with two pieces of fish. Spread with sauce; replace bun tops.

BLACK BEAN SOUP

Fill your tummy without expanding your waistline with this bean-filled soup. Add lean beef or chicken for extra protein.
—ANGEE OWENS LUFKIN, TX

PREP: 20 MIN. • **COOK:** 25 MIN. • **MAKES:** 8 SERVINGS (2 QUARTS)

- **3 cans (15 ounces each) black beans, rinsed and drained, divided**
- **3 celery ribs with leaves, chopped**
- **1 large onion, chopped**
- **1 medium sweet red pepper, chopped**
- **1 jalapeno pepper, seeded and chopped**
- **2 tablespoons olive oil**
- **4 garlic cloves, minced**
- **2 cans (14½ ounces each) reduced-sodium chicken broth or vegetable broth**
- **1 can (14½ ounces) diced tomatoes with green peppers and onions, undrained**
- **3 teaspoons ground cumin**
- **1½ teaspoons ground coriander**
- **1 teaspoon Louisiana-style hot sauce**
- **¼ teaspoon pepper**
- **1 bay leaf**
- **1 teaspoon lime juice**
- **½ cup reduced-fat sour cream**
- **¼ cup chopped green onions**

1. In a small bowl, mash one can black beans; set aside. In a large saucepan, saute the celery, onion, red pepper and jalapeno in oil until tender. Add garlic; cook 1 minute longer.
2. Stir in the broth, tomatoes, cumin, coriander, hot sauce, pepper, bay leaf, mashed black beans and remaining whole beans. Bring to a boil. Reduce heat; cover and simmer for 15 minutes.
3. Discard bay leaf. Stir in lime juice. Garnish each serving with 1 tablespoon sour cream and 1½ teaspoons green onion.
NOTE *Wear disposable gloves when cutting hot peppers; the oils can burn skin. Avoid touching your face.*

FAST FIX

PIZZA JOES

These Italian-style sloppy joes are an easy twist on the classic. The meat can be prepared early and kept warm until it's time to eat.
—JOANNE SCHLABACH SHREVE, OH

START TO FINISH: 30 MIN. • **MAKES:** 6 SERVINGS

- **1 pound lean ground beef (90% lean)**
- **1 can (15 ounces) pizza sauce**
- **1 teaspoon dried oregano**
- **½ medium onion**
- **½ medium green pepper**
- **1 ounce sliced pepperoni**
- **6 hamburger buns, split**
- **½ cup shredded mozzarella cheese**
- **½ cup sliced fresh mushrooms**

1. In a large skillet over medium heat, cook beef until no longer pink; drain. Stir in pizza sauce and oregano.
2. In a food processor, combine the onion, pepper and pepperoni; cover and process until chopped. Add to beef mixture. Simmer 20-25 minutes or until vegetables are tender. Spoon mixture onto buns. Top with cheese and mushrooms.

CARAMELIZED HAM & SWISS BUNS

My next-door neighbor shared her version of this recipe with me. Assemble the sandwiches in advance and bake them right before company arrives. The combination of poppy seeds, horseradish, ham, cheese and brown sugar is simply delicious!

—**IRIS WEIHEMULLER** BAXTER, MN

PREP: 25 MIN. + CHILLING • **BAKE:** 30 MIN. • **MAKES:** 1 DOZEN

- **1 package (12 ounces) Hawaiian sweet rolls, split**
- **½ cup horseradish sauce**
- **12 slices deli ham**
- **6 slices Swiss cheese, halved**
- **½ cup butter, cubed**
- **2 tablespoons finely chopped onion**
- **2 tablespoons brown sugar**
- **1 tablespoon spicy brown mustard**
- **2 teaspoons poppy seeds**
- **1½ teaspoons Worcestershire sauce**
- **¼ teaspoon garlic powder**

1. Spread roll bottoms with horseradish sauce. Layer with ham and cheese; replace tops. Arrange in a single layer in a greased 9-in. square baking pan.
2. In a small skillet, heat butter over medium-high heat. Add onion; cook and stir 1-2 minutes or until tender. Stir in remaining ingredients. Pour over rolls. Refrigerate, covered, several hours or overnight.
3. Preheat oven to 350°. Bake, covered, 25 minutes. Bake, uncovered, 5-10 minutes longer or until golden brown.

HEARTY LIMA BEAN SOUP

This colorful soup boasts a golden broth dotted with tender vegetables and lima beans. It makes an excellent lunch or first course.

—**BETTY KORCEK** BRIDGMAN, MI

PREP: 20 MIN. + STANDING • **COOK:** 2 HOURS 50 MIN.
MAKES: 14 SERVINGS (3½ QUARTS)

- **1 pound dried lima beans**
- **1 large meaty ham bone or 2 ham hocks**
- **2½ quarts water**
- **5 celery ribs, cut into chunks**
- **5 medium carrots, cut into chunks**
- **1 garlic clove, minced**
- **2 tablespoons butter**
- **2 tablespoons all-purpose flour**
- **2 teaspoons salt**
- **½ teaspoon pepper**
- **Pinch paprika**
- **1 cup cold water**
- **1 can (14½ ounces) stewed tomatoes**

1. Place beans in a Dutch oven; add water to cover by 2 in. Bring to a boil; boil for 2 minutes. Remove from the heat; cover and let stand for 1 hour. Drain beans, discarding liquid; return beans to pan.
2. Add ham bone and 2½ qt. water; bring to a boil. Reduce heat; cover and simmer for 1½ hours.
3. Debone ham and cut meat into chunks; return to pan. Add celery and carrots. Cover and simmer for 1 hour or until beans are tender.
4. In a small skillet, saute garlic in butter for 1 minute. Stir in the flour, salt, pepper and paprika. Add cold water; bring to a boil. Reduce heat; cook and stir for 2 minutes or until thickened. Add to the soup with tomatoes; simmer for 10 minutes or until heated through.

FAST FIX

STUFFED BARBECUE BURGERS

These big burgers are almost a meal by themselves. With a delectable cheese and vegetable filling, they'll surely satisfy any hungry appetite.

—LORETTA MOE GRAFTON, ND

START TO FINISH: 30 MIN. • **MAKES:** 4 SERVINGS

- **2 pounds ground beef**
- **1 cup (4 ounces) shredded cheese of your choice**
- **⅓ cup finely chopped green pepper**
- **⅓ cup finely chopped tomato**
- **3 fresh mushrooms, finely chopped**
- **2 green onions, finely chopped**
- **½ cup barbecue sauce**
- **1 tablespoon sugar**
- **4 hamburger buns, split**

1. Shape beef into eight patties. In a large bowl, combine the cheese, green pepper, tomato, mushrooms and onions. Top half of the patties with vegetable mixture. Cover with remaining patties and firmly press edges to seal.
2. Grill, covered, over medium heat or broil 4 in. from the heat for 3 minutes on each side. Brush with barbecue sauce and sprinkle with sugar. Grill, covered, or broil 5-6 minutes longer on each side or until a thermometer reads 160° and juices run clear, basting occasionally. Serve on buns.

"Yum! We added a fried egg and bacon to these burgers. They were delicious!"

—JOANNRANDALL
FROM TASTEOFHOME.COM

POTATO MINESTRONE

Even the die-hard meat lovers in your family won't be able to get enough of this savory meatless soup. If you prefer a thicker consistency, mash half of the garbanzo beans before adding them to the slow cooker.

—PAULA ZSIRAY LOGAN, UT

PREP: 10 MIN. • **COOK:** 8½ HOURS
MAKES: 12 SERVINGS (ABOUT 3 QUARTS)

- **2 cans (14½ ounces each) chicken or vegetable broth**
- **1 can (28 ounces) crushed tomatoes**
- **1 can (16 ounces) kidney beans, rinsed and drained**
- **1 can (15 ounces) garbanzo beans or chickpeas, rinsed and drained**
- **1 can (14½ ounces) beef broth**
- **2 cups frozen cubed hash brown potatoes, thawed**
- **1 tablespoon dried minced onion**
- **1 tablespoon dried parsley flakes**
- **1 teaspoon salt**
- **1 teaspoon dried oregano**
- **½ teaspoon garlic powder**
- **½ teaspoon dried basil**
- **½ teaspoon dried marjoram**
- **1 package (10 ounces) frozen chopped spinach, thawed and drained**
- **2 cups frozen peas and carrots, thawed**

In a 5-qt. slow cooker, combine the first 13 ingredients. Cover and cook on low for 8 hours. Stir in the spinach and the peas and carrots; cook 30 minutes or until heated through.

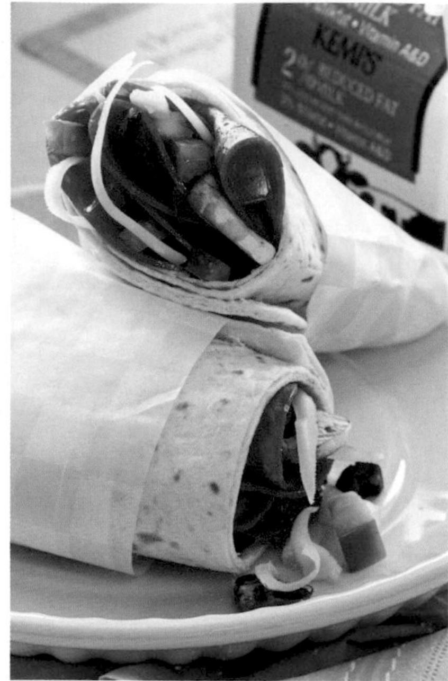

FAST FIX

PIZZA WRAPS

This recipe features the flavors of your favorite pie—and there's no cooking or baking required. It's the perfect quick-to-fix lunch on those harried mornings you're rushing to get kids off to school.
—ELIZABETH DUMONT BOULDER, CO

START TO FINISH: 15 MIN.
MAKES: 4 WRAPS

- **1 package (8 ounces) sliced pepperoni**
- **4 flour tortillas (8 inches), room temperature**
- **½ cup chopped tomatoes**
- **¼ cup each chopped sweet onion, chopped fresh mushrooms and chopped ripe olives**
- **¼ cup chopped green pepper, optional**
- **1 cup (4 ounces) shredded part-skim mozzarella cheese**

Arrange pepperoni off center on each tortilla. Top with the remaining ingredients. Fold sides and bottom edge over filling and roll up.

GRANDMA'S CHICKEN 'N' DUMPLING SOUP

The rich and comforting flavor of this soup can't be beat. But it holds a special place in my heart for another reason. My grandma passed the recipe to me over 40 years ago. Every time I make it, I think of her and what an amazing cook she was.
—PAULETTE BALDA PROPHETSTOWN, IL

PREP: 20 MIN. + COOLING • **COOK:** 2¾ HOURS
MAKES: 12 SERVINGS (3 QUARTS)

- **1 broiler/fryer chicken (3½-4 pounds), cut up**
- **2¼ quarts cold water**
- **5 chicken bouillon cubes**
- **6 whole peppercorns**
- **3 whole cloves**
- **1 can (10¾ ounces) condensed cream of chicken soup, undiluted**
- **1 can (10¾ ounces) condensed cream of mushroom soup, undiluted**
- **1½ cups chopped carrots**
- **1 cup fresh or frozen peas**
- **1 cup chopped celery**
- **1 cup chopped peeled potatoes**
- **¼ cup chopped onion**
- **1½ teaspoons seasoned salt**
- **¼ teaspoon pepper**
- **1 bay leaf**

DUMPLINGS

- **2 cups all-purpose flour**
- **4 teaspoons baking powder**
- **1 teaspoon salt**
- **¼ teaspoon pepper**
- **1 large egg, beaten**
- **2 tablespoons butter, melted**
- **¾ to 1 cup milk**
- **Snipped fresh parsley, optional**

1. Place the chicken, water, bouillon, peppercorns and cloves in a stockpot. Cover and bring to a boil; skim foam. Reduce heat; cover and simmer for 45-60 minutes or until chicken is tender. Strain broth; return to pot.
2. Remove chicken and set aside until cool. Remove meat from bones; discard bones and skin and cut chicken into chunks. Cool broth and skim off fat.
3. Return chicken to stockpot with soups, vegetables and seasonings; bring to a boil. Reduce heat; cover and simmer for 1 hour. Uncover; increase heat to a gentle boil. Discard bay leaf.
4. For dumplings, combine the dry ingredients. Stir in egg, butter and enough milk to make a moist stiff batter. Drop by teaspoonfuls into soup. Cover; cook covered for 18-20 minutes. Sprinkle with parsley if desired.

FAST FIX

STATE FAIR SUBS

My college roommate and I first tried these meaty sandwiches at the Iowa State Fair. After a little experimenting, we re-created the recipe. We ate the subs often because they were fast to fix between classes and didn't break our next-to-nothing grocery budget.
—CHRISTI ROSS MILL CREEK, OK

PREP: 20 MIN. • **BAKE:** 20 MIN.
MAKES: 6 SERVINGS

1 loaf (1 pound unsliced) French bread
2 large eggs
¼ cup milk
½ teaspoon pepper
¼ teaspoon salt
1 pound bulk Italian sausage
1½ cups chopped onion
2 cups (8 ounces) shredded part-skim mozzarella cheese

1. Cut bread in half lengthwise; carefully hollow out top and bottom of loaf, leaving a 1-in. shell. Cube removed bread. In a large bowl, beat the eggs, milk, pepper and salt. Add bread cubes and toss to coat; set aside.
2. In a skillet over medium heat, cook sausage and onion until the meat is no longer pink; drain. Add to the bread mixture. Spoon filling into bread shells; sprinkle with cheese. Wrap each in foil. Bake at 400° for 20-25 minutes or until cheese is melted. Cut into serving-size slices.

TOP TIP

Super Subs

When I make State Fair Subs, it's usually for a large, hungry group so I typically double the recipe. I mix mild Italian sausage with a hot variety for a little kick. Sometimes I saute fresh garlic, mushrooms and green peppers with the meat and onions. It's also fun to use flavored French breads that you can find at your local deli or bakery. When the sandwich is assembled, I brush the bread with melted garlic butter for the final touch.
—JEWELLMRS
FROM TASTEOFHOME.COM

RICH FRENCH ONION SOUP

When entertaining guests, I bring out this savory soup while we're waiting for the main course. I recommend sauting the onions early in the day and letting the soup simmer until it's time to eat.
—LINDA ADOLPH EDMONTON, AB

PREP: 10 MIN. • **COOK:** 5 HOURS • **MAKES:** 10 SERVINGS

- **6 large onions, chopped**
- **½ cup butter**
- **6 cans (10½ ounces each) condensed beef broth, undiluted**
- **1½ teaspoons Worcestershire sauce**
- **3 bay leaves**
- **10 slices French bread, toasted**
- **Shredded Parmesan and shredded part-skim mozzarella cheese**

1. In a large skillet, saute the onions in butter until crisp-tender. Transfer to a 5-qt. slow cooker. Add the beef broth, Worcestershire sauce and bay leaves.
2. Cover and cook on low for 5-7 hours or until the onions are tender. Discard bay leaves.
3. Ladle soup into ovenproof bowls. Top each with a slice of toast; sprinkle with desired amount of cheese. Place bowls on a baking sheet. Broil for 2-3 minutes or until the cheese is lightly golden.

"Delicious! We finished off the soup by adding macaroni—we liked it even better that way."
—DCCOOKIN FROM TASTEOFHOME.COM

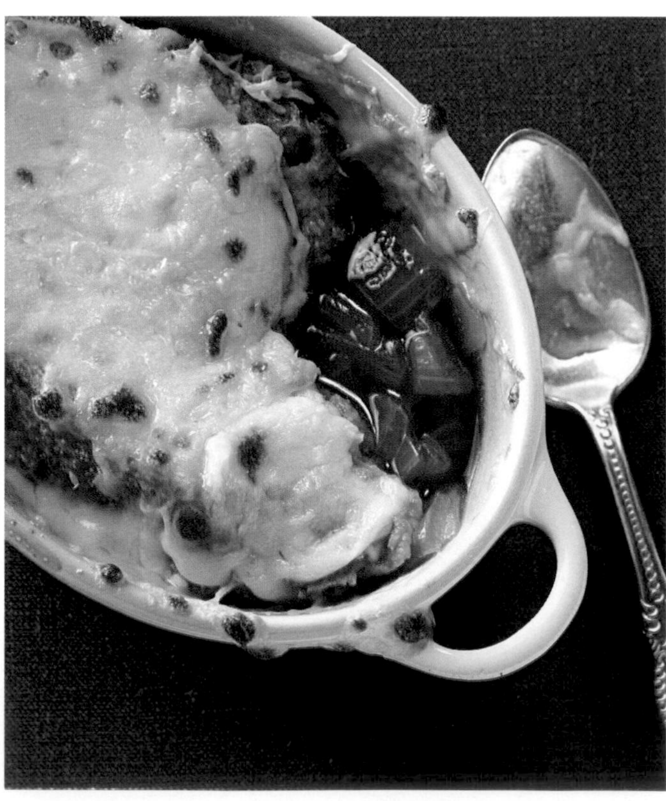

PASTA PIZZA SOUP

A steaming bowl of this soup hits the spot on a chilly day, which we have in abundance here in Alaska. Oregano adds fast flavor to the pleasant combination of tender vegetables, pasta spirals and ground beef.
—LINDA FOX SOLDOTNA, AK

PREP: 10 MIN. • **COOK:** 30 MIN.
MAKES: 8 SERVINGS (ABOUT 2 QUARTS)

- **1 pound ground beef**
- **1¾ cups sliced fresh mushrooms**
- **1 medium onion, chopped**
- **1 celery rib, thinly sliced**
- **1 garlic clove, minced**
- **4 cups water**
- **1 can (14½ ounces) Italian diced tomatoes, undrained**
- **2 medium carrots, sliced**
- **4 teaspoons beef bouillon granules**
- **1 bay leaf**
- **1½ teaspoons dried oregano**
- **1½ cups cooked tricolor spiral pasta**

1. In a large saucepan over medium heat, cook the beef, mushrooms, onion and celery until meat is no longer pink. Add garlic; cook 1 minute longer. Drain.
2. Stir in the water, tomatoes, carrots, bouillon, bay leaf and oregano. Bring to a boil. Reduce heat; cover and simmer for 20-25 minutes or until carrots are tender. Stir in pasta; heat through. Discard bay leaf.

FAST FIX

CHICKEN SALAD PARTY SANDWICHES

My famous chicken salad arrives at the party chilled in a plastic container. When it's time to set out the food, I stir in the pecans and assemble the sandwiches. They're ideal for buffet-style potlucks.

—TRISHA KRUSE EAGLE, ID

START TO FINISH: 25 MIN. • **MAKES:** 15 SERVINGS

- **4 cups cubed cooked chicken breast**
- **1½ cups dried cranberries**
- **2 celery ribs, finely chopped**
- **2 green onions, thinly sliced**
- **¼ cup chopped sweet pickles**
- **1 cup fat-free mayonnaise**
- **½ teaspoon curry powder**
- **¼ teaspoon coarsely ground pepper**
- **½ cup chopped pecans, toasted**
- **15 whole wheat dinner rolls**
- **Torn leaf lettuce**

1. In a large bowl, combine the first five ingredients. In a small bowl, combine the mayonnaise, curry and pepper. Add to chicken mixture; toss to coat. Chill until serving.
2. Stir pecans into chicken salad. Serve on rolls lined with leaf lettuce.

CAJUN CORN SOUP

I found this recipe years ago and substituted Cajun stewed tomatoes for a bolder taste. Now I prepare my soup often for out-of-state guests who want to try Cajun food. Adjust the ingredients and seasonings to your own taste.

—SUE FONTENOT KINDER, LA

PREP: 20 MIN. • **COOK:** 1 HOUR 20 MIN. • **MAKES:** 12-14 SERVINGS

- **1 cup chopped onion**
- **1 cup chopped green pepper**
- **6 green onions, sliced**
- **½ cup canola oil**
- **½ cup all-purpose flour**
- **3 cups water**
- **2 packages (16 ounces each) frozen corn**
- **1½ pounds smoked sausage, cut into ¼-inch pieces**
- **3 cups cubed fully cooked ham**
- **1 can (14½ ounces) stewed tomatoes**
- **2 cups chopped peeled tomatoes**
- **1 can (6 ounces) tomato paste**
- **⅛ teaspoon cayenne pepper or to taste**
- **Salt to taste**
- **Hot pepper sauce to taste**

1. In a Dutch oven, saute the onion, green pepper and green onions in oil for 5-6 minutes or until tender. Stir in flour and cook until bubbly. Gradually add water; bring to a boil. Add the corn, sausage, ham, tomatoes, tomato paste, cayenne, salt and pepper sauce.

2. Reduce heat; simmer, uncovered, for 1 hour, stirring occasionally.

ONION BEEF AU JUS

Garlic, sweet onions and soy sauce make a succulent juice for dipping these savory open-faced sandwiches. Any leftover beef makes delicious cold sandwiches, too.

—MARILYN BROWN WEST UNION, IA

PREP: 20 MIN. • **BAKE:** 2½ HOURS + STANDING
MAKES: 12 SERVINGS

- **1 beef rump roast or bottom round roast (4 pounds)**
- **2 tablespoons canola oil**
- **2 large sweet onions, cut into ¼-inch slices**
- **6 tablespoons butter, softened, divided**
- **5 cups water**
- **½ cup reduced-sodium soy sauce**
- **1 envelope onion soup mix**
- **1 garlic clove, minced**
- **1 teaspoon browning sauce, optional**
- **1 loaf (1 pound) French bread**
- **1 cup (4 ounces) shredded Swiss cheese**

1. In a Dutch oven over medium-high heat, brown roast on all sides in oil; drain. In a large skillet, saute onions in 2 tablespoons of butter until tender. Add the water, soy sauce, soup mix, garlic and, if desired, browning sauce. Pour juice over roast.

2. Cover and bake roast at 325° for 2½ hours or until the meat is tender.

3. Let meat stand for 10 minutes, then thinly slice. Return meat to pan juices. Split bread lengthwise; cut into 3-in. sections. Spread with remaining butter. Place bread on a baking sheet.

4. Broil bread 4-6 in. from the heat for 2-3 minutes or until golden brown. Top with beef and onions; sprinkle with cheese. Broil for 1-2 minutes or until cheese is melted. Serve with pan juices.

HEARTY HAMBURGER SOUP

My clan looks forward to this spirit-warming soup whenever I have them over for family get-togethers. I serve it with a fresh loaf of homemade bread and tall glasses of milk. The soup has robust flavor and plenty of fresh ingredients, and it's easy to make.
—BARBARA BROWN JANESVILLE, WI

PREP: 10 MIN. • **COOK:** 30 MIN. • **MAKES:** 8 SERVINGS (2 QUARTS)

- **1 pound ground beef**
- **4 cups water**
- **1 can (14½ ounces) diced tomatoes, undrained**
- **3 medium carrots, sliced**
- **2 medium potatoes, peeled and cubed**
- **1 medium onion, chopped**
- **½ cup chopped celery**
- **4 teaspoons beef bouillon granules**
- **1½ teaspoons salt**
- **¼ teaspoon pepper**
- **¼ teaspoon dried oregano**
- **1 cup cut fresh or frozen green beans**

1. In a large saucepan, brown beef; drain. Add the next 10 ingredients; bring to a boil.
2. Reduce heat; cover and simmer for 15 minutes or until potatoes and carrots are tender. Add green beans. Cover and simmer 15 minutes longer or until the beans are tender.

FAST FIX

GYRO-STYLE TURKEY PITAS

For a unique twist on traditional gyros, try these flavorful pitas stuffed with turkey, sauerkraut and a zesty cream sauce.
—WANDA ALLENDE ORLANDO, FL

START TO FINISH: 30 MIN. • **MAKES:** 4 SERVINGS

- **1 pound ground turkey**
- **1 small onion, chopped**
- **½ cup sauerkraut, rinsed and well drained**
- **2 tablespoons brown sugar**
- **½ teaspoon salt**
- **⅔ cup sour cream**
- **3 tablespoons mayonnaise**
- **2 tablespoons prepared ranch salad dressing**
- **1 small tomato, chopped**
- **⅓ cup chopped cucumber**
- **4 pita breads (6 inches), halved and warmed**
- **Shredded lettuce**

1. In a large skillet, cook the turkey, onion, sauerkraut, brown sugar and salt over medium heat until meat is no longer pink; drain.
2. In a small bowl, combine the sour cream, mayonnaise and salad dressing. Stir in tomato and cucumber. Fill pita halves with turkey mixture, lettuce and sauce.

VEGETABLE CARROT SOUP

This blended soup is so smooth and delicious that you'll forget it packs a powerhouse of nutrition from carrots and other veggies. Its lovely golden color adds a special touch to the table, too.
—BERTHA MCCLUNG SUMMERSVILLE, WV

PREP: 15 MIN. • **COOK:** 40 MIN. • **MAKES:** 4 SERVINGS

- **3 cups thinly sliced carrots**
- **1 cup chopped onion**
- **⅔ cup chopped celery**
- **1½ cups diced peeled potatoes**
- **1 garlic clove, minced**
- **½ teaspoon sugar**
- **2 teaspoons canola oil**
- **4 cups reduced-sodium chicken broth**
- **Dash ground nutmeg**
- **Pepper to taste**

1. In a Dutch oven or soup kettle over medium-low heat, saute carrots, onion, celery, potatoes, garlic and sugar in oil for 5 minutes. Add broth, nutmeg and pepper; bring to a boil. Reduce heat; cover and simmer for 30-40 minutes or until vegetables are tender.
2. Remove from the heat and cool to room temperature. Puree in batches in a blender or food processor. Return to the kettle and heat through.

SCORED POTATOES, 75

GERMAN POTATO SALAD, 72

CAJUN CABBAGE, 67

SPICY APPLESAUCE, 70

SIDE DISHES, SALADS & MORE

When it comes to sensational salads, side dishes and other mealtime accompaniments, this chapter has the pick of the crop! Enjoy mouthwatering medleys of fresh greens, veggies, fruits, pasta, rice, potatoes and more. You and your family will relish every bite when your favorite foods are topped with any of the country-style jams and condiments featured here. See for yourself how these superb sidekicks make the perfect dinner a reality!

(5) INGREDIENTS

EASY LEMON-BLUEBERRY JAM

This delightfully sweet and simple jam comes together quickly. It makes a great gift for family and friends.

—**JOYCE ROBBINS** OLD HICKORY, TN

PREP: 5 MIN. • **COOK:** 10 MIN. + CHILLING
MAKES: 4 HALF-PINTS

- **4 cups fresh blueberries**
- **2 cups sugar**
- **1 package (3 ounces) lemon gelatin**

In a large saucepan, slightly crush 2 cups of blueberries. Add remaining berries and sugar, mix well. Bring to a boil, stirring constantly. Remove from the heat; stir in gelatin until dissolved. Pour hot jam into jars or containers. Cover and cool. Refrigerate.

(5) INGREDIENTS

SLOW-COOKED GREEN BEANS

I presented a cooking demo to women from my church, and these easy green beans were my star attraction.

—**ALICE WHITE** WILLOW SPRING, NC

PREP: 10 MIN. • **COOK:** 2 HOURS
MAKES: 12 SERVINGS

- **3 packages (16 ounces each) frozen french-style green beans, thawed**
- **½ cup packed brown sugar**
- **½ cup butter, melted**
- **1½ teaspoons garlic salt**
- **¾ teaspoon reduced-sodium soy sauce**

Place green beans in a 5-qt. slow cooker. In a small bowl, mix remaining ingredients; pour over beans and toss to coat. Cook, covered, on low 2-3 hours or until heated through. Serve with a slotted spoon.

VEGGIE-TOPPED POLENTA SLICES

One night we didn't have too many ingredients in the kitchen. I got creative and tinkered with what we did have, and this amazing dish was the result!

—**JENNIFER TIDWELL** FAIR OAKS, CA

PREP: 20 MIN. • **COOK:** 20 MIN.
MAKES: 4 SERVINGS

- **1 tube (1 pound) polenta, cut into 12 slices**
- **2 tablespoons olive oil, divided**
- **1 medium zucchini, chopped**
- **2 shallots, minced**
- **2 garlic cloves, minced**
- **3 tablespoons reduced-sodium chicken broth**
- **½ teaspoon pepper**
- **⅛ teaspoon salt**
- **4 plum tomatoes, seeded and chopped**
- **2 tablespoons minced fresh basil or 2 teaspoons dried basil**
- **1 tablespoon minced fresh parsley**
- **½ cup shredded part-skim mozzarella cheese**

1. In a large nonstick skillet, cook polenta in 1 tablespoon oil over medium heat for 9-11 minutes on each side or until golden brown.
2. Meanwhile, in another large skillet, saute zucchini in remaining oil until tender. Add shallots and garlic; cook 1 minute longer. Add the broth, pepper and salt. Bring to a boil; cook until liquid is almost evaporated.
3. Stir in the tomatoes, basil and parsley; heat through. Serve with polenta; sprinkle with cheese.

"Our family loves this! So yummy, quick and healthy."

—CMABKB
FROM TASTEOFHOME.COM

CAJUN CABBAGE

Looking for a different way to enjoy cabbage? Try this spicy cheese-topped dish I adapted from a friend's recipe. Not only do my husband and kids like it, but it also gets rave reviews when I make it for company or church functions.

—BOBBIE SOILEAU OPELOUSAS, LA

PREP: 15 MIN. • **BAKE:** 65 MIN.
MAKES: 6-8 SERVINGS

1 pound ground beef
1 medium green pepper, chopped
1 medium onion, chopped
2 garlic cloves, minced
1 can (10 ounces) diced tomatoes and green chilies
1 can (8 ounces) tomato sauce
½ cup uncooked long grain rice
1 teaspoon salt
½ teaspoon dried basil
½ teaspoon dried oregano
¼ to ½ teaspoon each white, black and cayenne pepper
4 to 6 drops hot pepper sauce
1 small head cabbage, chopped
1 cup (4 ounces) shredded Colby cheese

1. In a skillet, cook the beef, green pepper, onion and garlic over medium heat until meat is no longer pink; drain. Stir in tomatoes, tomato sauce, rice and seasonings.
2. Spread into an ungreased 13x9-in. baking dish. Top with the cabbage and cheese. Cover and bake at 350° for 65-75 minutes or until rice is tender.

SWEET 'N' SOUR BEANS

This recipe is popular on both sides of the border. It came from a friend in Alaska, then traveled with me to Mexico, where I lived for 5 years, and is now a potluck favorite in my Arkansas community. It's easy to keep the beans warm and serve from a slow cooker.

—BARBARA SHORT MENA, AR

PREP: 20 MIN. • **COOK:** 3 HOURS
MAKES: 20 SERVINGS (½ CUP EACH)

8 bacon strips, diced
2 medium onions, halved and thinly sliced
1 cup packed brown sugar
½ cup cider vinegar
1 teaspoon salt
1 teaspoon ground mustard
½ teaspoon garlic powder
1 can (28 ounces) baked beans, undrained
1 can (16 ounces) kidney beans, rinsed and drained
1 can (15 ounces) pinto beans, rinsed and drained
1 can (15 ounces) lima beans, rinsed and drained
1 can (15½ ounces) black-eyed peas, rinsed and drained

1. In a large skillet, cook bacon over medium heat until crisp. Remove with slotted spoon to paper towels. Drain, reserving 2 tablespoons drippings. Saute onions in the drippings until tender. Add the brown sugar, vinegar, salt, mustard and garlic powder. Bring to a boil.
2. In a 5-qt. slow cooker, combine the beans and peas. Add onion mixture and bacon; mix well. Cover and cook on high for 3-4 hours or until heated through.

CORN BREAD PUDDING

This comforting side dish pairs perfectly with shrimp and other seafood. I adapted the dish from my mom's recipe. It never fails to please.

—BOB GEBHARDT WAUSAU, WI

PREP: 5 MIN. • **BAKE:** 40 MIN. • **MAKES:** 12 SERVINGS

- **2 large eggs**
- **1 cup (8 ounces) sour cream**
- **1 can (15¼ ounces) whole kernel corn, drained**
- **1 can (14¾ ounces) cream-style corn**
- **½ cup butter, melted**
- **1 package (8½ ounces) corn bread/muffin mix**
- **¼ teaspoon paprika**

1. In a large bowl, combine the first five ingredients. Stir in corn bread mix just until blended. Pour into a greased 3-qt. baking dish. Sprinkle with paprika.
2. Bake, uncovered, at 350° for 40-45 minutes or until a knife inserted near the center comes out clean. Serve warm.

CREAMY CRANBERRY SALAD

One of my piano students gave me the recipe for this luscious cranberry fluff. Studded with berries, pineapple, marshmallows and nuts, it's almost good enough to be dessert.

—ALEXANDRA LYPECKY DEARBORN, MI

PREP: 15 MIN. + CHILLING • **MAKES:** 16 SERVINGS (½ CUP EACH)

- **3 cups fresh or frozen cranberries (thawed), chopped**
- **1 can (20 ounces) unsweetened crushed pineapple, drained**
- **2 cups miniature marshmallows**
- **1 medium apple, chopped**
- **⅔ cup sugar**
- **⅛ teaspoon salt**
- **2 cups heavy whipping cream**
- **¼ cup chopped walnuts**

1. In a large bowl, mix the first six ingredients until blended. Refrigerate, covered, overnight.
2. In a large bowl, beat cream until stiff peaks form. Just before serving, fold cream and walnuts into cranberry mixture.

FAST FIX

SMOKED TURKEY AND APPLE SALAD

An eye-catching dish, this refreshing salad is a great main course for summer. Dijon dressing pairs nicely with the turkey, while apples and walnuts add crunch.

—CAROLYN JOHNS LACEY, WA

START TO FINISH: 20 MIN. • **MAKES:** 4 SERVINGS

DRESSING

- **5 tablespoons olive oil**
- **2 tablespoons cider vinegar**
- **1 tablespoon Dijon mustard**
- **1 teaspoon lemon-pepper seasoning**
- **½ teaspoon salt, optional**

SALAD

- **6 to 8 cups torn watercress or romaine**
- **1 medium carrot, julienned**
- **10 cherry tomatoes, halved**
- **8 ounces smoked turkey, julienned**
- **4 medium apples, sliced**
- **⅓ cup chopped walnuts, toasted**

1. Whisk together dressing ingredients; set aside.
2. Just before serving, arrange salad greens on a platter or individual plates. Top with carrot, tomatoes, turkey and apples. Drizzle dressing over salad; toss to coat. Sprinkle with walnuts.

LOADED MASHED POTATOES

Tired of the same old mashed potatoes, I whipped up this new family favorite. We can't get enough of them at our house. Often, I'll prepare this dish ahead and refrigerate it. Then I bake it just before serving.

—DAWN REUTER OXFORD, WI

PREP: 20 MIN. • **BAKE:** 30 MIN. • **MAKES:** 14 SERVINGS

- **5 pounds potatoes, peeled and cubed**
- **¾ cup sour cream**
- **½ cup milk**
- **3 tablespoons butter**
- **Salt and pepper to taste**
- **3 cups (12 ounces) shredded cheddar cheese blend, divided**
- **½ pound sliced bacon, cooked and crumbled**
- **3 green onions, sliced**

1. Place potatoes in a Dutch oven and cover with water. Bring to a boil. Reduce heat; cover and simmer 10-15 minutes or until tender. Drain and place in a large bowl. Add the sour cream, milk, butter, salt and pepper. Beat on medium-low speed until light and fluffy. Stir in 2 cups cheddar cheese, bacon and onions.
2. Transfer to a greased 3-qt. baking dish. Top with the remaining cheese. Bake, uncovered, at 350° for 30 minutes or until heated through and cheese is melted.

FAST FIX

CREAMY COLESLAW

Packaged coleslaw mix cuts down on prep time. My recipe is great for potlucks or to serve your family on a busy weeknight.

—RENEE ENDRESS GALVA, IL

START TO FINISH: 10 MIN. • **MAKES:** 6 SERVINGS

- **1 package (14 ounces) coleslaw mix**
- **¾ cup mayonnaise**
- **⅓ cup sour cream**
- **¼ cup sugar**
- **¾ teaspoon seasoned salt**
- **½ teaspoon ground mustard**
- **¼ teaspoon celery salt**

Place coleslaw mix in a large bowl. In a small bowl, combine the remaining ingredients; stir until blended. Pour over coleslaw mix and toss to coat. Refrigerate until serving.

5 INGREDIENTS

SPICY APPLESAUCE

Every year, we have an apple-picking party and end up with loads of apples. This is one of the recipes I always look forward to making with our harvest.
—MARIAN PLATT SEQUIM, WA

PREP: 25 MIN. • **COOK:** 30 MIN.
MAKES: 8 CUPS

- **5 pounds tart apples (about 16 medium), peeled and sliced**
- **1 cup apple juice**
- **1 teaspoon ground cinnamon**
- **½ teaspoon ground allspice**
- **½ teaspoon ground cloves**

In a Dutch oven, combine all ingredients; bring to a boil. Reduce heat; simmer, covered, 25-35 minutes or until apples are tender, stirring occasionally. Remove from heat; mash apples to desired consistency. Serve warm or cold.

FREEZE OPTION *Freeze cooled applesauce in freezer containers. To use, thaw in refrigerator overnight. Serve cold or heat through in a saucepan, stirring occasionally.*

FAST FIX

PICNIC PASTA SALAD

My family's not big on traditional pasta salads made with mayonnaise. So when I served this colorful version that uses Italian dressing, it was a big hit.
—FELICIA FIOCCHI VINELAND, NJ

START TO FINISH: 25 MIN.
MAKES: 14-16 SERVINGS

- **1 package (12 ounces) tricolor spiral pasta**
- **1 package (10 ounces) refrigerated tricolor tortellini**
- **1 jar (7½ ounces) marinated artichoke hearts, undrained**
- **½ pound fresh broccoli florets (about 1¾ cups)**
- **12 ounces provolone cheese, cubed**
- **12 ounces hard salami, cubed**
- **1 medium sweet red pepper, chopped**
- **1 medium green pepper, chopped**
- **1 can (15 ounces) garbanzo beans or chickpeas, rinsed and drained**
- **2 cans (2¼ ounces each) sliced ripe olives, drained**
- **1 medium red onion, chopped**
- **4 garlic cloves, minced**
- **2 envelopes Italian salad dressing mix**

1. Cook spiral pasta and tortellini according to package directions. Drain and rinse in cold water. Place in a large bowl; add the artichokes, broccoli, provolone cheese, salami, peppers, beans, olives, onion and garlic.
2. Prepare salad dressing according to package directions; pour over salad and toss to coat. Serve immediately or cover and refrigerate.

5 INGREDIENTS

OVEN-FRIED POTATOES

These spuds are a family favorite. They're easy to make, and they travel well to potlucks. We enjoy them for breakfast or alongside poultry, beef or pork for supper.
—DELORES BILLINGS KOKSILAH, BC

PREP: 10 MIN. • **BAKE:** 40 MIN.
MAKES: 12-14 SERVINGS

- **12 medium potatoes, peeled and cubed**
- **¼ cup grated Parmesan cheese**
- **2 teaspoons salt**
- **1 teaspoon garlic powder**
- **1 teaspoon paprika**
- **½ teaspoon pepper**
- **⅓ cup vegetable oil**

1. Place potatoes in two large resealable plastic bags. Combine the Parmesan cheese and seasonings; add to potatoes. Seal bag and shake to coat.
2. Pour oil into two 15x10x1-in. baking pans; pour potatoes into pans. Bake, uncovered, at 375° for 40-50 minutes or until tender.

FAST FIX

TORTELLINI & CHICKEN CAESAR SALAD

My family loves classic Caesar salad, and the addition of the tortellini makes it extra hearty. It's one I serve often.
—LEE REESE ROLLA, MO

START TO FINISH: 25 MIN.
MAKES: 6 SERVINGS

- **1 package (20 ounces) refrigerated cheese tortellini**
- **1 pound boneless skinless chicken breasts, cut into 1½-inch pieces**
- **⅓ cup finely chopped onion**
- **1 tablespoon olive oil**
- **2 garlic cloves, minced**
- **¾ teaspoon salt**
- **¼ teaspoon pepper**
- **1 package (10 ounces) hearts of romaine salad mix**
- **1½ cups grape tomatoes**
- **1 can (6½ ounces) sliced ripe olives, drained**
- **¾ cup creamy Caesar salad dressing**
- **¾ cup shredded Parmesan cheese**
- **6 bacon strips, cooked and crumbled**

1. Cook tortellini according to package directions. Drain; rinse with cold water.
2. Meanwhile, in a small bowl, combine chicken, onion, oil, garlic, salt and pepper; toss to coat. Heat a large skillet over medium-high heat. Add chicken mixture; cook and stir 4-6 minutes or until chicken is no longer pink. Remove from heat.
3. In a large bowl, combine salad mix, tomatoes, olives, tortellini and chicken mixture. Drizzle with dressing; toss to coat. Sprinkle with cheese and bacon. Serve immediately.

TOP TIP

Speedy Salad

A visit to the supermarket salad bar can save a great deal of time (and mess) after a busy day. For a tossed salad, buy a bag of lettuce and pick up as many of the other chopped and ready-to-go salad fixings that are available at the salad bar. This is also great when a recipe doesn't call for an entire vegetable.
—TERRYANN M. OAKLYN, NJ

STRAWBERRY-KIWI JAM

In my family, we love to give jams and jellies as gifts. Strawberries and kiwi make a wonderful combination in this tasty spread.
—KATHY KITTELL LENEXA, KS

PREP: 20 MIN. • **COOK:** 15 MIN. + STANDING • **MAKES:** 5¾ CUPS

- **6 cups fresh strawberries**
- **3 medium kiwifruit, peeled and finely chopped**
- **1 tablespoon lemon juice**
- **1 tablespoon chopped crystallized ginger**
- **1 package (1¾ ounces) powdered fruit pectin**
- **5 cups sugar**

1. Rinse six 1-cup plastic containers and lids with boiling water. Dry thoroughly. In a large bowl, mash berries; transfer to a Dutch oven. Add kiwi, lemon juice and crystallized ginger. Stir in pectin. Bring to a full rolling boil over high heat, stirring constantly.
2. Stir in sugar; return to a full rolling boil. Boil 1 minute, stirring constantly.
3. Remove from heat; skim off foam. Immediately fill all containers to within ½ in. of tops. Wipe off top edges of containers and cool to room temperature, about 1 hour. Cover and let stand at room temperature 24 hours.
4. Jam is now ready to use. Refrigerate up to 3 weeks or freeze extra containers up to 12 months. Thaw frozen jam in refrigerator before serving.

FAST FIX

APPLE SALAD WITH MAPLE-MUSTARD VINAIGRETTE

This seasonal salad will be a hit at any gathering. It's also easy for weeknights; simply halve the recipe whenever you're serving a smaller crowd.
—BETH DAUENHAUER PUEBLO, CO

START TO FINISH: 15 MIN. • **MAKES:** 12 SERVINGS (1 CUP EACH)

- **¼ cup thawed frozen apple juice concentrate**
- **2 tablespoons cider vinegar**
- **2 tablespoons canola oil**
- **2 tablespoons spicy brown mustard**
- **2 tablespoons maple syrup**
- **¼ teaspoon salt**
- **⅛ teaspoon pepper**

SALAD

- **9 cups torn mixed salad greens**
- **2 large tart apples, chopped**
- **1 small red onion, thinly sliced**
- **⅓ cup chopped walnuts, toasted**

In a small bowl, whisk the first seven ingredients. In a large bowl, combine salad greens, apples, onion and walnuts. Drizzle with vinaigrette; toss to coat.

NOTE *To toast nuts, bake in a shallow pan in a 350° oven for 5-10 minutes or cook in a skillet over low heat until lightly browned, stirring occasionally.*

FAST FIX

GERMAN POTATO SALAD

I'd always loved my German grandmother's potato salad. So when I married a potato farmer—and had spuds in abundance—I played with several recipes that sounded similar and came up with this salad that reminds me of hers.
—SUE HARTMAN PARMA, ID

START TO FINISH: 25 MIN. • **MAKES:** 6-8 SERVINGS

- **5 bacon strips**
- **¾ cup chopped onion**
- **2 tablespoons all-purpose flour**
- **1 teaspoon salt**
- **⅛ teaspoon pepper**
- **1⅓ cups water**
- **⅔ cup cider vinegar**
- **¼ cup sugar**
- **6 cups sliced cooked peeled potatoes**

1. In a large skillet, fry bacon until crisp; remove and set aside. Drain all but 2-3 tablespoons of drippings; cook onion until tender. Stir in the flour, salt and pepper until blended. Add water and vinegar; cook and stir for 1 minute or until slightly thickened.
2. Stir in sugar until dissolved. Crumble bacon; gently stir in bacon and potatoes. Heat through, stirring lightly to coat potatoes. Serve warm.

RICH
BLACK CHERRY
TASTE

"I took this to a luncheon and the ladies loved it! The dressing is light and refreshing. Definitely a crowd pleaser!"
—**JVROLLINS** FROM TASTEOFHOME.COM

STRAWBERRY-ORANGE SPINACH SALAD

Here's a colorful medley packed full of flavor and nutrition. Toasted walnuts add texture and crunch.
—**MARY BUFORD SHAW** MT. PLEASANT, SC

PREP: 25 MIN. • **COOK:** 10 MIN. • **MAKES:** 8 SERVINGS

- **3 bacon strips, chopped**
- **3 tablespoons rice vinegar**
- **2 tablespoons honey**
- **5 teaspoons olive oil**
- **1 teaspoon Dijon mustard**
- **½ teaspoon pepper**
- **¼ teaspoon salt**
- **1 package (6 ounces) fresh baby spinach**
- **2 medium navel oranges, peeled and chopped**
- **12 fresh strawberries, quartered**
- **1 cup thinly sliced cucumber**
- **½ cup thinly sliced red onion**
- **1 medium carrot, shredded**
- **½ cup chopped walnuts, toasted**

1. In a small skillet, cook bacon over medium heat until crisp. Remove to paper towels with a slotted spoon; drain.
2. In a small bowl, whisk the vinegar, honey, oil, mustard, pepper and salt. In a large bowl, combine the spinach, oranges, strawberries, cucumber, onion and carrot. Pour dressing over salad; toss to coat. Sprinkle with walnuts and bacon. Serve immediately.

GRILLED GREEK POTATO SALAD

The Greek vinaigrette and fresh oregano add just the right flavor to this savory potato salad. It's my most requested summer recipe and tastes delicious warm, cold or at room temperature.
—**KATHY RUNDLE** FOND DU LAC, WI

PREP: 30 MIN. • **GRILL:** 20 MIN. • **MAKES:** 16 SERVINGS (¾ CUP EACH)

- **3 pounds small red potatoes, halved**
- **2 tablespoons olive oil**
- **½ teaspoon salt**
- **¼ teaspoon pepper**
- **1 large sweet yellow pepper, chopped**
- **1 large sweet red pepper, chopped**
- **1 medium red onion, halved and sliced**
- **1 medium cucumber, chopped**
- **1¼ cups grape tomatoes, halved**
- **½ pound fresh mozzarella cheese, cubed**
- **¾ cup Greek vinaigrette**
- **½ cup halved Greek olives**
- **1 can (2¼ ounces) sliced ripe olives, drained**
- **2 tablespoons minced fresh oregano or 1 teaspoon dried oregano**

1. Drizzle potatoes with oil and sprinkle with salt and pepper; toss to coat. Grill potatoes, covered, over medium heat or broil 4 in. from the heat for 20-25 minutes or until tender.
2. Place in a large bowl. Add the remaining ingredients; toss to coat. Serve salad warm or cold.

5 INGREDIENTS FAST FIX

PARMESAN ASPARAGUS

Nothing could be more simple than this tasty side dish. With just four ingredients, it goes together in no time. We're Parmesan fans, but you could also try blue cheese or feta.

—**MARY ANN MARINO** WEST PITTSBURGH, PA

START TO FINISH: 20 MIN. • **MAKES:** 10-12 SERVINGS

4 pounds fresh asparagus, trimmed
¼ pound butter, melted
2 cups shredded Parmesan cheese
½ teaspoon pepper

1. In a large saucepan, bring 1/2 in. of water to a boil. Add the asparagus; cover and boil for 3 minutes or until crisp-tender. Drain.
2. Arrange asparagus in a greased 13x9-in. baking dish. Drizzle with butter; sprinkle with Parmesan cheese and pepper. Bake, uncovered, at 350° for 10-15 minutes or until cheese is melted.

FAST FIX

BLT MACARONI SALAD

A friend served this salad, and I had to have the recipe. My husband loves BLT sandwiches, so this has become a favorite of his. It's nice to serve on hot and humid days, which we frequently get during summer here in Virginia.

—**MRS. HAMILTON MYERS JR.** CHARLOTTESVILLE, VA

START TO FINISH: 30 MIN. • **MAKES:** 6 SERVINGS

½ cup mayonnaise
3 tablespoons chili sauce
2 tablespoons lemon juice
1 teaspoon sugar
3 cups cooked elbow macaroni
½ cup chopped seeded tomato
2 tablespoons chopped green onions
3 cups shredded lettuce
4 bacon strips, cooked and crumbled

In a large bowl, combine the first four ingredients. Add the macaroni, tomatoes and onions; toss to coat. Cover and refrigerate. Just before serving, add the lettuce and bacon; toss to coat.

5 INGREDIENTS

SCORED POTATOES

These well-seasoned baked potatoes are a fun alternative to plain baked potatoes. It's easy to help yourself to just the amount you want, too, since the potato halves are scored into sections. They're great alongside your favorite entree.

—**BARBARA WHEELER** SPARKS GLENCOE, MD

PREP: 10 MIN. • **BAKE:** 50 MIN. • **MAKES:** 4 SERVINGS

4 large baking potatoes
2 tablespoons butter, melted, divided
⅛ teaspoon paprika
1 tablespoon minced fresh parsley
Salt and pepper to taste

1. With a sharp knife, cut potatoes in half lengthwise. Slice each half widthwise six times, but not all the way through; fan potatoes slightly.
2. Place in a shallow baking dish. Brush potatoes with 1 tablespoon butter. Sprinkle with paprika, parsley, salt and pepper. Bake, uncovered, at 350° for 50 minutes or until tender. Drizzle with remaining butter.

FRESH TOMATO RELISH

This relish packs a flavor punch. I enjoy a small sampling as a condiment to my favorite dishes, but my two grown sons love it so much they eat it on its own as a salad. The recipe is from my late husband's mother. I usually make a batch as soon as the first tomatoes of the season are ripe for the picking.

—LELA BASKINS WINDSOR, MO

PREP: 30 MIN. + CHILLING
MAKES: ABOUT 6 PINTS

- **2 cups white vinegar**
- **½ cup sugar**
- **8 cups chopped tomatoes (about 11 large)**
- **½ cup chopped onion**
- **1 medium green pepper, diced**
- **1 celery rib, diced**
- **¼ cup prepared horseradish**
- **2 tablespoons salt**
- **1 tablespoon mustard seed**
- **1½ teaspoons pepper**
- **½ teaspoon ground cinnamon**
- **½ teaspoon ground cloves**

1. In a large saucepan, bring vinegar and sugar to a boil. Remove from the heat; cool completely.
2. In a large bowl, combine the remaining ingredients; add vinegar mixture and mix well. Spoon into storage containers, allowing ½-in. headspace. Refrigerate up to 2 weeks or freeze up to 12 months. Serve relish with a slotted spoon.

FAST FIX

CHICKEN FIESTA SALAD

This hearty, slightly spicy medley is always a winner at our house. It's colorful, crunchy and easy to assemble. The best part is I can get it on the table in about 15 minutes, thanks to the quick convenience of my broiler.

—KATIE RANKIN COLUMBUS, OH

START TO FINISH: 30 MIN.
MAKES: 2 SERVINGS

- **1½ teaspoons lemon-pepper seasoning**
- **1½ teaspoons chili powder**
- **1½ teaspoons dried basil**
- **¾ pound boneless skinless chicken breasts, cut into 1-inch pieces**
- **4 cups torn mixed salad greens**
- **⅔ cup canned black beans, rinsed and drained**
- **¼ cup thinly sliced red onion**
- **1 small tomato, sliced**
- **½ cup shredded cheddar cheese**
- **Tortilla chips, salsa and ranch salad dressing**

1. In a large resealable plastic bag, combine the seasonings. Add chicken, a few pieces at a time, and shake to coat.
2. Place chicken on a greased broiler pan. Broil 3-4 in. from heat 3-4 minutes on each side or until no longer pink.
3. On two plates, arrange the salad greens, black beans, onion and tomato. Top with chicken and cheddar cheese. Serve with tortilla chips, salsa and ranch dressing.

(5) INGREDIENTS FAST FIX

ROASTED CARROTS WITH THYME

Cutting the carrots lengthwise makes this dish extra pretty.

—DEIRDRE COX KANSAS CITY, MO

START TO FINISH: 30 MIN.
MAKES: 4 SERVINGS

- **1 pound medium carrots, halved lengthwise**
- **2 teaspoons minced fresh thyme or ½ teaspoon dried thyme**
- **2 teaspoons canola oil**
- **1 teaspoon honey**
- **¼ teaspoon salt**

Preheat oven to 400°. Place carrots in a greased 15x10x1-in. baking pan. In a small bowl, mix the thyme, oil, honey and salt; brush over carrots. Roast 20-25 minutes or until tender.

GOLDEN MASHED POTATOES

This is a tasty alternative to regular mashed potatoes and gravy. I make it often to take to picnics and church socials. My husband even made it for his family's reunion one year, and they loved it!
—CINDY STITH WICKLIFFE, KY

PREP: 40 MIN. • **BAKE:** 30 MIN.
MAKES: 10-12 SERVINGS

- **9 large potatoes (about 4 pounds), peeled and cubed**
- **1 pound carrots, cut into ½-inch chunks**
- **8 green onions, thinly sliced**
- **½ cup butter**
- **1 cup (8 ounces) sour cream**
- **1½ teaspoons salt**
- **⅛ teaspoon pepper**
- **¾ cup shredded cheddar cheese**

1. In a soup kettle or Dutch oven, cook the potatoes and carrots in boiling salted water until tender; drain. Place in a bowl; mash and set aside.
2. In a skillet, saute onions in butter until tender. Add to potato mixture. Add sour cream, salt and pepper; mix until blended.
3. Transfer to a greased 13x9-in. baking dish. Sprinkle with the cheddar cheese. Bake, uncovered, at 350° for 30-40 minutes or until heated through.

FREEZE OPTION *Cool unbaked casserole; cover and freeze. To use, partially thaw in refrigerator overnight. Remove from refrigerator 30 minutes before baking. Preheat oven to 350°. Bake casserole as directed, increasing time as necessary to heat through and for a thermometer inserted in center to read 165°.*

TOP TIP

Freeze Extra Mashed Potatoes

When I have leftover mashed potatoes, I freeze individual servings in muffin cups. Once they're frozen, I pop them out and store in resealable plastic freezer bags. During the week, I pull out as many servings as I need and heat them in the microwave.
—GRETCHEN B. SURPRISE, AZ

FAST FIX

CREAMED CORN WITH BACON

Creamed corn is delicious on its own, but add bacon and it's out of this world! It's particularly good with fresh corn from our local farmers market.

—**TINA MIRILOVICH** JOHNSTOWN, PA

START TO FINISH: 25 MIN. • **MAKES:** 6 SERVINGS

- **1 small onion, finely chopped**
- **1 tablespoon butter**
- **4 cups fresh or frozen corn, thawed**
- **1 cup heavy whipping cream**
- **¼ cup chicken broth**
- **4 bacon strips, cooked and crumbled**
- **¼ teaspoon pepper**
- **¼ cup grated Parmesan cheese**
- **2 tablespoons minced fresh parsley**

1. In a large skillet, saute onion in butter for 3 minutes. Add corn; saute 1-2 minutes longer or until tender.
2. Stir in the cream, broth, bacon and pepper. Cook and stir for 5-7 minutes or until slightly thickened. Stir in the cheese and parsley.

(5)INGREDIENTS FAST FIX

WATERMELON GRAPE SALAD

Enjoy this easy fruit salad on a warm summer day when watermelon is at its best, or serve it with a scoop of lemon sherbet for a refreshing dessert.

—**SUE GRONHOLZ** BEAVER DAM, WI

START TO FINISH: 10 MIN. • **MAKES:** 2 SERVINGS

- **1 cup cubed seeded watermelon**
- **1 cup seedless red grapes**
- **2 tablespoons white grape juice**
- **½ teaspoon finely chopped fresh tarragon**
- **½ teaspoon honey**

In a small bowl, combine watermelon and grapes. In another bowl, whisk the grape juice, tarragon and honey. Pour over fruit and toss to coat. Serve immediately.

(5)INGREDIENTS FAST FIX

FRESH GREEN BEANS & GARLIC

When it comes to food, I believe fresh is best. I developed this recipe to take advantage of our garden's bounty. It shows off the full flavor of the green beans.

—**CAROL MAYER** SPARTA, IL

START TO FINISH: 25 MIN. • **MAKES:** 8 SERVINGS

- **2 tablespoons canola oil**
- **2 tablespoons butter**
- **4 garlic cloves, sliced**
- **2 pounds fresh green beans**
- **1 cup reduced-sodium chicken broth**
- **½ teaspoon salt**
- **¼ teaspoon pepper**

1. In a Dutch oven, heat oil and butter over medium-high heat. Add garlic; cook and stir 45-60 seconds or until golden. Using a slotted spoon, remove garlic from pan; reserve. Add green beans to pan; cook and stir 4-5 minutes or until crisp-tender.
2. Stir in broth, salt and pepper. Bring to a boil. Reduce heat; simmer, uncovered, 8-10 minutes or just until beans are tender and broth is almost evaporated, stirring occasionally. Stir in reserved garlic.

FAST FIX

MOM'S SPANISH RICE

My mom is famous for her Spanish rice, the ultimate comfort food. When I want a taste of home, I pull out this recipe.
—**JOAN HALLFORD**
NORTH RICHLAND HILLS, TX

START TO FINISH: 20 MIN.
MAKES: 4 SERVINGS

- **1 pound lean ground beef (90% lean)**
- **1 large onion, chopped**
- **1 medium green pepper, chopped**
- **1 can (15 ounces) tomato sauce**
- **1 can (14½ ounces) no-salt-added diced tomatoes, drained**
- **1 teaspoon ground cumin**
- **1 teaspoon chili powder**
- **½ teaspoon garlic powder**
- **¼ teaspoon salt**
- **2⅔ cups cooked brown rice**

1. In a large skillet, cook the beef, onion and pepper over medium heat 6-8 minutes or until beef is no longer pink and onion is tender, breaking up beef into crumbles; drain.
2. Stir in tomato sauce, tomatoes and seasonings; bring to a boil. Add rice; heat through, stirring occasionally.

(5) INGREDIENTS FAST FIX

TANGY BUTTERMILK SALAD DRESSING

Buttermilk gives a tangy twist to this mild and creamy salad dressing. You'll love drizzling it on your favorite fresh greens and vegetables.
—***TASTE OF HOME* TEST KITCHEN**

START TO FINISH: 5 MIN. • **MAKES:** 2 CUPS

- **1 cup mayonnaise**
- **1 cup buttermilk**
- **½ teaspoon onion salt**
- **¼ teaspoon paprika**
- **⅛ teaspoon pepper**
- **Mixed salad greens**

In a small bowl, whisk the mayonnaise, buttermilk, onion salt, paprika and pepper. Serve with salad greens. Refrigerate leftovers.

HOMEMADE ANTIPASTO SALAD

This colorful salad is a tasty favorite. Guests love the homemade salad dressing, which is a nice change from bottled Italian.
—**LINDA HARRINGTON** WINDHAM, NH

PREP: 1 HOUR + CHILLING
MAKES: 50 (¾-CUP) SERVINGS

- **2 packages (1 pound each) spiral pasta**
- **4 cups chopped green peppers**
- **4 cups chopped seeded tomatoes**
- **3 cups chopped onions**
- **2 cans (15 ounces each) garbanzo beans or chickpeas, rinsed and drained**
- **1 pound thinly sliced Genoa salami, julienned**
- **1 pound sliced pepperoni, julienned**
- **½ pound provolone cheese, cubed**
- **1 cup pitted ripe olives, halved**

DRESSING

- **1 cup red wine vinegar**
- **½ cup sugar**
- **2 tablespoons dried oregano**
- **2 teaspoons salt**
- **1 teaspoon pepper**
- **1½ cups olive oil**

1. Cook pasta according to package directions. Drain; rinse with cold water. In several large bowls, combine pasta, green peppers, tomatoes, onions, beans, salami, pepperoni, cheese and olives.
2. Place vinegar, sugar, oregano, salt and pepper in a blender. While processing, gradually add oil in a steady stream. Pour over pasta salad; toss to coat. Refrigerate, covered, 4 hours or overnight.

FAST FIX

SKILLET SAUSAGE STUFFING

I gave regular boxed stuffing mix a flavorful upgrade by adding pork sausage, mushrooms, celery and onion. It impressed my in-laws, so I knew it was a keeper! My husband and children love it, too.

—JENNIFER LYNN CULLEN TAYLOR, MI

START TO FINISH: 25 MIN.
MAKES: 8 SERVINGS

1 pound bulk pork sausage
1¼ cups chopped celery
½ cup chopped onion
½ cup sliced fresh mushrooms
1 large garlic clove, minced
1½ cups reduced-sodium chicken broth
1 teaspoon rubbed sage
1 package (6 ounces) stuffing mix

1. In a large skillet, cook the sausage, celery, onion and mushrooms over medium heat until meat is no longer pink. Add garlic; cook 1 minute longer; drain. Stir in broth and sage.
2. Bring to a boil. Stir in stuffing mix. Cover and remove from the heat; let stand for 5 minutes. Fluff with a fork.

(5) INGREDIENTS

ROSEMARY SWEET POTATO FRIES

I'm hooked on the sweet potato fries at one of my favorite local restaurants. One day I decided to make them on my own. Mine boast the same great flavor but are baked instead of deep fried.

—JACKIE GREGSTON HALLSVILLE, TX

PREP: 15 MIN. • **BAKE:** 30 MIN.
MAKES: 4 SERVINGS

3 tablespoons olive oil
1 tablespoon minced fresh rosemary
1 garlic clove, minced
1 teaspoon cornstarch
¾ teaspoon salt
⅛ teaspoon pepper
3 large sweet potatoes, peeled and cut into ¼-inch julienned strips (about 2¼ pounds)

1. Preheat oven to 425°. In a large resealable plastic bag, combine the first six ingredients. Add sweet potatoes; shake to coat.
2. Arrange in a single layer on two 15x10x1-in. baking pans coated with cooking spray. Bake, uncovered, for 30-35 minutes or until tender and lightly browned, turning occasionally.

(5) INGREDIENTS FAST FIX

SWEET HONEY ALMOND BUTTER

This homemade butter makes a nice gift when paired with a fresh loaf of bread. It's a great topper for muffins, biscuits, rolls and even slices of pound cake.

—EVELYN HARRIS WAYNESBORO, VA

START TO FINISH: 10 MIN.
MAKES: 2 CUPS

1 cup butter, softened
¾ cup honey
¾ cup confectioners' sugar
¾ cup finely ground almonds
¼ to ½ teaspoon almond extract

In a bowl, combine all ingredients; mix well. Refrigerate up to 1 week or freeze up to 3 months.

MEDITERRANEAN COBB SALAD

I'm a huge fan of taking classic dishes and adding flair to them. I also like to change up heavier dishes, like the classic Cobb salad. I've traded out typical chicken for crunchy falafel that's just as satisfying.
—JENNIFER TIDWELL FAIR OAKS, CA

PREP: 1 HOUR • **COOK:** 5 MIN./BATCH
MAKES: 10 SERVINGS

- **1 package (6 ounces) falafel mix**
- **½ cup sour cream or plain yogurt**
- **¼ cup chopped seeded peeled cucumber**
- **¼ cup 2% milk**
- **1 teaspoon minced fresh parsley**
- **¼ teaspoon salt**
- **4 cups torn romaine**
- **4 cups fresh baby spinach**
- **3 hard-cooked large eggs, chopped**
- **2 medium tomatoes, seeded and finely chopped**
- **1 medium ripe avocado, peeled and finely chopped**
- **¾ cup crumbled feta cheese**
- **8 bacon strips, cooked and crumbled**
- **½ cup pitted Greek olives, finely chopped**

1. Prepare and cook falafel according to package directions. When cool enough to handle, crumble or coarsely chop falafel.
2. In a small bowl, mix sour cream, cucumber, milk, parsley and salt. In a large bowl, combine romaine and spinach; transfer to a platter. Arrange crumbled falafel and remaining ingredients over greens. Drizzle with dressing.

SHARP CHEDDAR SCALLOPED POTATOES

I like to mix things up in the kitchen, so I rarely follow a recipe exactly as written. Here's what I came up with when I experimented with a friend's recipe for cheesy scalloped potatoes. They're so good, you'll keep going back for more.
—**SUSAN SIMONS** EATONVILLE, WA

PREP: 30 MIN. • **BAKE:** 70 MIN.
MAKES: 8 SERVINGS

- **¼ cup butter, cubed**
- **⅓ cup all-purpose flour**
- **¾ teaspoon salt**
- **½ teaspoon ground mustard**
- **½ teaspoon white pepper**
- **2 cups half-and-half cream**
- **1½ cups (6 ounces) shredded sharp white cheddar cheese**
- **1½ cups (6 ounces) shredded sharp cheddar cheese**
- **6 cups thinly sliced peeled Yukon Gold potatoes (about 2 pounds)**
- **2 small onions, finely chopped**

1. Preheat oven to 350°. In a large saucepan, heat butter over medium heat. Stir in the flour, salt, mustard and pepper until blended; cook and stir 2-3 minutes or until lightly browned. Gradually whisk in cream. Bring to a boil, stirring constantly; cook and stir 1-2 minutes or until thickened. Remove from heat.
2. In a small bowl, combine cheeses. Layer a third of the potatoes, a third of the onions and ¾ cup cheese mixture in a greased 3-qt. baking dish. Repeat layers twice. Pour sauce over top; sprinkle with remaining cheese.
3. Bake, covered, for 45 minutes. Uncover; bake 25-30 minutes longer or until potatoes are tender and top is lightly browned.

COLORFUL QUINOA SALAD

My youngest daughter recently learned she has to avoid gluten, dairy and eggs, which gave me a new challenge in the kitchen. I put this dish together as a side we could all share. We love it for leftovers, too.
—CATHERINE TURNBULL BURLINGTON, ON

PREP: 30 MIN. + COOLING • **MAKES:** 8 SERVINGS

- **2 cups water**
- **1 cup quinoa, rinsed**
- **2 cups fresh baby spinach, thinly sliced**
- **1 cup grape tomatoes, halved**
- **1 medium cucumber, seeded and chopped**
- **1 medium sweet orange pepper, chopped**
- **1 medium sweet yellow pepper, chopped**
- **2 green onions, chopped**

DRESSING

- **3 tablespoons lime juice**
- **2 tablespoons olive oil**
- **4 teaspoons honey**
- **1 tablespoon grated lime peel**
- **2 teaspoons minced fresh gingerroot**
- **¼ teaspoon salt**

1. In a large saucepan, bring water to a boil. Add quinoa. Reduce heat; simmer, covered, 12-15 minutes or until liquid is absorbed. Remove from heat; fluff with a fork. Transfer to a large bowl; cool completely.
2. Stir spinach, tomatoes, cucumber, peppers and green onions into quinoa. In a small bowl, whisk dressing ingredients until blended. Drizzle over quinoa mixture; toss to coat. Refrigerate until serving.

CRISPY POTATO PUFFS

Crunchy cornflakes and sesame seeds surround a velvety potato filling in these adorable puffs. They are the perfect side dish.
—EVA TOMLINSON BRYAN, OH

PREP: 35 MIN. • **BAKE:** 15 MIN. • **MAKES:** 12 SERVINGS (2 PUFFS EACH)

- **4 pounds cubed peeled potatoes (about 11 cups)**
- **½ cup 2% milk**
- **¼ cup butter, cubed**
- **1½ teaspoons salt**
- **½ cup shredded cheddar cheese**
- **1½ cups crushed cornflakes**
- **6 tablespoons sesame seeds, toasted**

1. Place potatoes in a large saucepan; add water to cover. Bring to a boil. Reduce heat; cook, uncovered, 10-15 minutes or until tender. Drain; return to pan.
2. Mash potatoes, gradually adding milk, butter and salt; stir in cheese. Transfer to a large bowl; refrigerate, covered, 2 hours or until firm enough to shape.
3. In a shallow dish, combine the cornflakes and sesame seeds. Shape potato mixture into 1½-in. balls; roll in the cornflake mixture.
4. Place on greased baking sheets; bake 7-9 minutes or until golden brown.

FREEZE OPTION *Place unbaked puffs on baking sheets; cover and freeze until firm. Transfer to resealable plastic freezer bags. Freeze up to 3 months. To use, preheat oven to 400°. Place frozen potato puffs on greased baking sheets. Bake 15-20 minutes or until golden brown and heated through.*

“My family really likes these. I added some cream cheese to boost the flavor.”

—**ELLENGREGORY** FROM TASTEOFHOME.COM

ZUCCHINI BOATS, 89

CRISPY FRIED CHICKEN, 97

PORK LOIN WITH RASPBERRY SAUCE, 94

EASY CHICKEN ENCHILADAS, 87

HEARTY MAIN DISHES

There's nothing like coming home after a long day to enjoy the piping hot goodness of a home-cooked meal. And the star of any meal is always the main course. Whether your family is partial to succulent cuts of beef or pork, juicy chicken or turkey, big bowls of pasta, barbecued chops, easy-as-pie pizzas, fresh fish, or ethnic cuisine, you're sure to find the perfect offering in this collection of flavorful entrees. From timeless classics to new taste twists, each of these sensational mainstays is guaranteed to bring everyone running to the table!

FAST FIX

THAI CHICKEN PEANUT NOODLES

My husband loves the spicy Thai flavors in this speedy dish. We break out the chopsticks for a more authentic experience.

—JENNIFER FISHER AUSTIN, TX

START TO FINISH: 30 MIN.
MAKES: 6 SERVINGS

- **¼ cup creamy peanut butter**
- **½ cup reduced-sodium chicken broth**
- **¼ cup lemon juice**
- **¼ cup reduced-sodium soy sauce**
- **4 teaspoons Sriracha Asian hot chili sauce**
- **¼ teaspoon crushed red pepper flakes**
- **12 ounces uncooked multigrain spaghetti**
- **1 pound lean ground chicken**
- **1½ cups julienned carrots**
- **1 medium sweet red pepper, chopped**
- **1 garlic clove, minced**
- **½ cup finely chopped unsalted peanuts**
- **4 green onions, chopped**

1. In a small bowl, whisk the first six ingredients until blended. Cook the spaghetti according to the package directions; drain.

2. Meanwhile, in a large skillet, cook chicken, carrots, pepper and garlic over medium heat for 5-6 minutes or until chicken is no longer pink, breaking up chicken into crumbles; drain.

3. Stir in the peanut butter mixture; bring to a boil. Reduce heat; simmer, uncovered, 3-5 minutes or until the sauce is slightly thickened. Serve with spaghetti. Top with the peanuts and green onions.

FAST FIX

APRICOT PORK MEDALLIONS

There's nothing we love more than a great pork dish for supper, and this recipe ranks up there with the best of them. Apricot preserves give the pork just the right amount of sweetness without being overwhelming.

—CRYSTAL JO BRUNS ILIFF, CO

START TO FINISH: 20 MIN.
MAKES: 4 SERVINGS

- **1 pork tenderloin (1 pound), cut into eight slices**
- **1 tablespoon plus 1 teaspoon butter, divided**
- **½ cup apricot preserves**
- **2 green onions, sliced**
- **1 tablespoon cider vinegar**
- **¼ teaspoon ground mustard**

1. Pound pork slices with a meat mallet to ½-in. thickness. In a large skillet, heat 1 tablespoon butter over medium heat. Brown the pork on each side. Remove pork from pan, reserving drippings.

2. Add preserves, green onions, vinegar, mustard and remaining butter to pan; bring just to a boil, stirring to loosen browned bits from pan. Reduce heat; simmer, covered, 3-4 minutes to allow flavors to blend.

3. Return the pork to pan; cook until pork is tender. Let stand for 5 minutes before serving.

EASY CHICKEN ENCHILADAS

This family favorite is a must for any Mexican meal at my house. Try it as a main dish or include the enchiladas as part of a buffet.

—CHERYL POMRENKE COFFEYVILLE, KS

PREP: 15 MIN. • **BAKE:** 25 MIN. + STANDING
MAKES: 10 SERVINGS

- **3 cups (12 ounces) shredded cheddar cheese, divided**
- **2 cups (8 ounces) shredded Monterey Jack cheese**
- **2 cups chopped cooked chicken**
- **2 cups (16 ounces) sour cream**
- **1 can (10¾ ounces) condensed cream of chicken soup, undiluted**
- **1 can (4 ounces) chopped green chilies**
- **2 tablespoons finely chopped onion**
- **¼ teaspoon pepper**
- **⅛ teaspoon salt**
- **10 flour tortillas (8 inches), warmed**
- **Pico de gallo, optional**

1. In a large bowl, combine 2 cups cheddar cheese, Monterey Jack cheese, chicken, sour cream, soup, chilies, onion, pepper and salt. Spoon about 1/2 cup off center on each tortilla; roll up. Place seam side down in a greased 13x9-in. baking dish.

2. Cover dish and bake at 350° for 20 minutes. Uncover; sprinkle with the remaining cheddar cheese. Bake 5 minutes longer or until cheese is melted. Let stand for 10 minutes before serving. If desired, serve with pico de gallo.

TOP TIP

Time-Saver Chicken

To make chopped cooked chicken for recipes, simmer some boneless chicken breasts in water seasoned with salt, pepper and your favorite herbs. Cool and dice; keep them in the freezer for later.

GRILLED HULI HULI CHICKEN

When I lived in Hawaii, a friend gave me this recipe for chicken marinated in a succulent ginger-soy sauce. *Huli* means "turn" in Hawaiian and refers to turning the meat on the grill.
—SHARON BOLING CORONADO, CA

PREP: 15 MIN. + MARINATING
GRILL: 15 MIN.
MAKES: 12 SERVINGS

- **1 cup packed brown sugar**
- **¾ cup ketchup**
- **¾ cup reduced-sodium soy sauce**
- **⅓ cup sherry or chicken broth**
- **2½ teaspoons minced fresh gingerroot**
- **1½ teaspoons minced garlic**
- **24 boneless skinless chicken thighs (about 5 pounds)**

1. In a small bowl, mix the first six ingredients. Reserve 1⅓ cups for basting; cover and refrigerate. Divide remaining marinade between two large resealable plastic bags. Add 12 chicken thighs to each; seal the bags and turn to coat. Refrigerate for 8 hours or overnight.
2. Drain and discard marinade from chicken. Moisten a paper towel with cooking oil; using long-handled tongs, lightly coat the grill rack.
3. Grill the chicken, covered, over medium heat for 6-8 minutes on each side or until no longer pink; baste occasionally with reserved marinade during the last 5 minutes.

"Hands down, the best grilled chicken I've ever eaten. I didn't change a thing, other than scaling back all quantities for less chicken. The full recipe will be fantastic for summer get-togethers with more of a crowd."
—SHANNONDOBOS
FROM TASTEOFHOME.COM

GRILLED SIRLOIN WITH CHILI-BEER BARBECUE SAUCE

We came up with this recipe as a tasty way to cook with beer, but the combination of seasonings in the sauce is what makes this recipe a standout.
—*TASTE OF HOME* TEST KITCHEN

PREP: 40 MIN. • **GRILL:** 20 MIN.
MAKES: 8 SERVINGS

- **1½ cups beer or nonalcoholic beer**
- **1 small onion, chopped**
- **¾ cup chili sauce**
- **2 tablespoons soy sauce**
- **1 tablespoon brown sugar**
- **2 teaspoons chili powder**
- **2 garlic cloves, minced**
- **¼ teaspoon cayenne pepper**
- **¼ teaspoon ground mustard**
- **⅛ teaspoon ground cumin**
- **2 beef top sirloin steaks (1½ pounds each)**
- **½ teaspoon salt**
- **½ teaspoon pepper**

1. In a small saucepan, combine the first 10 ingredients. Bring to a boil. Reduce heat; simmer, uncovered, for 25-30 minutes or until thickened. Set aside ¾ cup and keep warm.

2. Sprinkle steaks with salt and pepper. Grill the steaks, covered, over medium heat or broil 4 in. from the heat for 9-13 minutes on each side or until meat reaches desired doneness (for medium-rare, a thermometer should read 145°; medium 160°; well-done 170°), basting occasionally with remaining sauce. Slice the meat and serve with the reserved sauce.

STRING CHEESE MEAT LOAF

My daughter likes the cheese stuffed into this flavorful meat loaf made with a blend of ground beef and Italian sausage. Served with a salad and sourdough bread, the meal is special enough for company.
—LAURA LAWRENCE SALINAS, CA

PREP: 15 MIN.
BAKE: 1 HOUR 25 MIN. + STANDING
MAKES: 6 SERVINGS

- **1 cup meatless spaghetti sauce, divided**
- **1 large egg, lightly beaten**
- **1 cup seasoned bread crumbs**
- **2 garlic cloves, minced**
- **1½ teaspoons dried rosemary, crushed**
- **1 pound lean ground beef**
- **8 ounces bulk Italian sausage**
- **3 pieces string cheese**

1. In a large bowl, combine ½ cup spaghetti sauce, egg, bread crumbs, garlic and rosemary. Crumble meat over mixture and mix well.

2. Press half into a greased 8x4-in. loaf pan. Place two pieces of cheese, side by side, near one end of loaf. Cut the remaining piece of cheese in half; place side by side on opposite end of loaf. Top with remaining meat mixture; press down firmly to seal.

3. Bake meat loaf, uncovered, at 350° for 1¼-1½ hours or until meat is no longer pink and a thermometer reads 160°; drain. Drizzle with the remaining spaghetti sauce; bake 10 minutes longer. Let stand for 10 minutes before slicing.

NOTE *Three ounces of mozzarella cheese cut into four ½-inch sticks may be substituted for the string cheese.*

5 INGREDIENTS

GARLIC ROSEMARY TURKEY

Garlic, herbs and lemon may seem like simple flavor accents, but they are all you need to make this turkey shine. Our house smells incredible while the bird is roasting, and my family can hardly wait to sit down at the table to eat.

—CATHY DOBBINS RIO RANCHO, NM

PREP: 10 MIN. • **BAKE:** 3 HOURS + STANDING • **MAKES:** 10 SERVINGS

- **1 turkey (10 to 12 pounds)**
- **6 to 8 garlic cloves, peeled**
- **2 large lemons, halved**
- **2 tablespoons olive oil**
- **2 teaspoons dried rosemary, crushed**
- **1 teaspoon rubbed sage**

1. Preheat oven to 325°. Cut six to eight small slits in turkey skin; insert garlic under the skin. Squeeze two lemon halves inside the turkey; squeeze remaining halves over outside of turkey. Place lemons in the cavity.

2. Tuck wings under turkey; tie drumsticks together. Place on a rack in a shallow roasting pan, breast side up. Brush with oil; sprinkle with rosemary and sage. Roast 1 hour.

3. Cover turkey with foil; roast 2-2½ hours longer or until a thermometer inserted in thickest part of thigh reads 170°-175°. Baste occasionally with pan drippings.

4. Remove turkey from oven. Let stand 20 minutes before carving. If desired, skim fat and thicken pan drippings for gravy. Serve with turkey.

5 INGREDIENTS FAST FIX

PAN-FRIED VENISON STEAK

This recipe was a family favorite when we had deer meat while I was growing up. I loved it, and now my children do, too!

—GAYLEEN GROTE BATTLEVIEW, ND

START TO FINISH: 25 MIN. • **MAKES:** 4 SERVINGS

- **1 pound venison or beef tenderloin, cut into ½-inch slices**
- **2 cups crushed saltines**
- **2 large eggs**
- **¾ cup milk**
- **1 teaspoon salt**
- **½ teaspoon pepper**
- **5 tablespoons canola oil**

1. Flatten venison to ¼-in. thickness. Place saltines in a shallow bowl. In another shallow bowl, whisk the eggs, milk, salt and pepper. Coat venison with saltines, then dip in egg mixture and coat a second time with saltines.

2. In a large skillet over medium heat, cook venison in oil in batches for 2-3 minutes on each side or until meat reaches desired doneness (for medium-rare, a thermometer should read 145°; medium, 160°; well-done, 170°).

5 INGREDIENTS FAST FIX

HADDOCK WITH LIME-CILANTRO BUTTER

In Louisiana, the good times roll when we broil fish and serve it with lots of lime juice, cilantro and butter.

—DARLENE MORRIS FRANKLINTON, LA

START TO FINISH: 15 MIN. • **MAKES:** 4 SERVINGS

- **4 haddock fillets (6 ounces each)**
- **½ teaspoon salt**
- **¼ teaspoon pepper**
- **3 tablespoons butter, melted**
- **2 tablespoons minced fresh cilantro**
- **1 tablespoon lime juice**
- **1 teaspoon grated lime peel**

1. Preheat broiler. Sprinkle fillets with salt and pepper. Place on a greased broiler pan. Broil 4-5 in. from heat 5-6 minutes or until fish flakes easily with a fork.

2. In a small bowl, mix remaining ingredients. Serve over fish.

TERIYAKI STEAK SKEWERS

When these flavorful skewered steaks are sizzling on the grill, the aroma makes everyone around stop what they're doing and come to see what's cooking. The tasty marinade is easy to make, and these little steaks are quick to cook and fun to eat.

—JERI DOBROWSKI BEACH, ND

PREP: 15 MIN. + MARINATING • **GRILL:** 10 MIN. • **MAKES:** 6 SERVINGS

- **½ cup reduced-sodium soy sauce**
- **¼ cup cider vinegar**
- **2 tablespoons brown sugar**
- **2 tablespoons finely chopped onion**
- **1 tablespoon canola oil**
- **1 garlic clove, minced**
- **½ teaspoon ground ginger**
- **⅛ teaspoon pepper**
- **2 pounds beef top sirloin steak**

1. In a large resealable plastic bag, combine the first eight ingredients. Trim fat from steak and slice across the grain into 1/2-in. strips. Add the beef to bag; seal bag and turn to coat. Refrigerate for 2-3 hours.

2. Drain and discard marinade. Loosely thread meat strips onto six metal or soaked wooden skewers. Grill, uncovered, over medium-hot heat for 7-10 minutes or until meat reaches desired doneness, turning often.

JAMBALAYA

This Southern dish is my family's favorite. They love the hearty combination of sausage, shrimp and rice. I appreciate the fact that it cooks in one pot for a marvelous meal.

—GLORIA KIRCHMAN EDEN PRAIRIE, MN

PREP: 20 MIN. • **COOK:** 30 MIN. • **MAKES:** 6-8 SERVINGS

- **¾ pound bulk hot or mild Italian sausage**
- **½ cup chopped onion**
- **½ cup chopped green pepper**
- **1 garlic clove, minced**
- **1 can (14½ ounces) diced tomatoes, undrained**
- **1 can (14½ ounces) chicken broth**
- **2 cups diced fully cooked ham**
- **¾ cup uncooked long grain rice**
- **1 bay leaf**
- **¼ teaspoon dried thyme**
- **1 pound fresh medium shrimp, peeled and deveined**

1. In a large skillet, cook sausage until browned; drain. Stir in onion and green pepper until vegetables are tender. Add garlic; cook 1 minute longer. Add the tomatoes, broth, ham, rice, bay leaf and thyme; cover skillet and simmer for 20-25 minutes or until tender.

2. Stir in shrimp; cover and cook for 3-4 minutes or until shrimp turn pink. Remove bay leaf.

(5) INGREDIENTS FAST FIX

BIG KAHUNA PIZZA

A prebaked crust and refrigerated barbecued pork make this pizza super fast and super easy. You'll agree it's super delicious! This can also double as a great last-minute appetizer when cut into bite-sized pieces.

—JONI HILTON ROCKLIN, CA

START TO FINISH: 30 MIN. • **MAKES:** 6 SERVINGS

- **1 prebaked 12-inch pizza crust**
- **1 carton (16 ounces) refrigerated fully cooked barbecued shredded pork**
- **1 can (20 ounces) pineapple chunks, drained**
- **⅓ cup chopped red onion**
- **2 cups (8 ounces) shredded part-skim mozzarella cheese**

1. Place pizza crust on an ungreased 12-in. pizza pan. Spread shredded pork over crust; top with pineapple and onion. Sprinkle with cheese.

2. Bake at 350° for 20-25 minutes or until cheese is melted.

PINEAPPLE-STUFFED CORNISH HENS

My mother brought this recipe back with her from Hawaii about 25 years ago. The tender meat, tropical stuffing and sweet-sour sauce made it a favorite with family and friends. I always keep copies of the recipe on hand to share.

—VICKI CORNERS ROCK ISLAND, IL

PREP: 20 MIN. • **BAKE:** 1 HOUR 25 MIN. • **MAKES:** 2 SERVINGS

- **½ teaspoon salt, divided**
- **2 Cornish game hens (20 to 24 ounces each)**
- **1 can (8 ounces) crushed pineapple**
- **3 cups cubed day-old bread (½-inch cubes), crusts removed**
- **1 celery rib, chopped**
- **½ cup flaked coconut**
- **⅔ cup butter, melted, divided**
- **¼ teaspoon poultry seasoning**
- **2 tablespoons steak sauce**
- **2 tablespoons cornstarch**
- **2 tablespoons brown sugar**
- **1 cup cold water**
- **1 tablespoon lemon juice**

1. Sprinkle 1/4 teaspoon salt inside hens; set aside. Drain pineapple, reserving juice. In a large bowl, combine the pineapple, bread cubes, celery and coconut. Add 1/3 cup butter; toss to coat. Loosely stuff hens with pineapple mixture.
2. Tuck wings under hens; tie legs together. Place on a rack in a greased shallow roasting pan. Place remaining stuffing in a greased 1½-cup baking dish; cover and set aside. Add poultry seasoning and remaining salt to remaining butter.
3. Spoon some butter mixture over hens. Bake, uncovered, at 350° for 40 minutes, basting twice with butter mixture.
4. Add steak sauce and reserved pineapple juice to any remaining butter mixture; baste hens. Bake reserved stuffing with hens for 30 minutes, basting the hens occasionally with remaining butter.
5. Uncover stuffing; bake 15-20 minutes longer or until a thermometer reads 185° for hens and 165° for stuffing in hens. Remove hens from pan; keep warm.
6. Pour drippings into a saucepan; skim fat. Combine cornstarch, brown sugar, water and lemon juice; add to the drippings. Bring to a boil; cook and stir 1-2 minutes or until thickened. Serve with hens and stuffing.

PORK LOIN WITH RASPBERRY SAUCE

Raspberries add lovely color and sweetness to this sauce, which enhances the savory pork roast. It's an easy way to transform ordinary pork into a special main dish.

—FLORENCE NURCZYK TORONTO, OH

PREP: 5 MIN. • **BAKE:** 1½ HOURS + STANDING • **MAKES:** 8 SERVINGS

- **1 boneless whole pork loin roast (3 pounds)**
- **1 teaspoon salt, divided**
- **1 teaspoon rubbed sage**
- **½ teaspoon pepper**
- **1 package (12 ounces) frozen unsweetened raspberries, thawed, divided**
- **¾ cup sugar**
- **1 tablespoon cornstarch**
- **¼ teaspoon each ground ginger, nutmeg and cloves**
- **¼ cup white vinegar**
- **1 tablespoon lemon juice**
- **1 tablespoon butter**

1. Place roast on a greased rack in a shallow roasting pan. Rub with 3/4 teaspoon salt, sage and pepper. Bake, uncovered, at 350° for 1½ hours or until a thermometer reads 160°.
2. Meanwhile, drain raspberries, reserving juice. Set aside 1/3 cup berries. In a sieve, mash remaining berries with the back of a spoon; reserve pulp and discard seeds.
3. In a large saucepan, combine the sugar, cornstarch, ginger, nutmeg, cloves and remaining salt. Stir in the vinegar, reserved raspberry juice and reserved pulp until blended. Add remaining raspberries. Bring to a boil; cook and stir for 2 minutes or until thickened. Remove from the heat; add lemon juice and butter. Stir until butter is melted. Let stand for 10 minutes before slicing. Serve with the raspberry sauce.
FREEZE OPTION *Prepare raspberry sauce; transfer to a freezer container. Place sliced pork in freezer containers. Cool and freeze. To use, partially thaw pork and sauce in refrigerator overnight. Heat sauce in a saucepan over medium heat until mixture comes to a boil. Remove from the heat. Microwave pork, covered, on high in a microwave-safe dish until heated through. Serve with sauce.*

FAST FIX

BEEF & SPINACH LO MEIN

If you like good Chinese food, you'll want to try my speedy lo mein. It combines hearty steak strips and colorful veggies with a tangy sauce. Quick-cooking spaghetti makes it a cinch to throw together when time is short.

—**DENISE PATTERSON** BAINBRIDGE, OH

START TO FINISH: 30 MIN.
MAKES: 5 SERVINGS

- **¼ cup hoisin sauce**
- **2 tablespoons soy sauce**
- **1 tablespoon water**
- **2 teaspoons sesame oil**
- **2 garlic cloves, minced**
- **¼ teaspoon crushed red pepper flakes**
- **1 pound beef top round steak, thinly sliced**
- **6 ounces uncooked spaghetti**
- **4 teaspoons canola oil, divided**
- **1 can (8 ounces) sliced water chestnuts, drained**
- **2 green onions, sliced**
- **1 package (10 ounces) fresh spinach, coarsely chopped**
- **1 red chili pepper, seeded and thinly sliced**

1. In a small bowl, mix the first six ingredients. Remove 1/4 cup mixture to a large bowl; add beef and toss to coat. Marinate at room temperature 10 minutes.

2. Cook spaghetti according to package directions. Meanwhile, in a large skillet, heat 1 1/2 teaspoons canola oil. Add half of the beef mixture; stir-fry 1-2 minutes or until meat is no longer pink. Remove from the pan. Repeat with an additional 1 1/2 teaspoons oil and remaining beef mixture.

3. Stir-fry the water chestnuts and green onions in remaining canola oil 30 seconds. Stir in the spinach and remaining hoisin mixture; cook until spinach is wilted. Return beef to pan; heat through.

4. Drain the spaghetti; add to the beef mixture and toss to combine. Sprinkle with chili pepper.

NOTE *Wear disposable gloves when cutting hot peppers; the oils can burn skin. Avoid touching your face.*

CRISPY FRIED CHICKEN

Always a picnic favorite, this chicken is delicious hot or cold.

—JEANNE SCHNITZLER LIMA, MT

PREP: 10 MIN. • **COOK:** 10 MIN./BATCH
MAKES: 8 SERVINGS

- **4 cups all-purpose flour, divided**
- **2 tablespoons garlic salt**
- **1 tablespoon paprika**
- **3 teaspoons pepper, divided**
- **2½ teaspoons poultry seasoning**
- **2 large eggs**
- **1½ cups water**
- **1 teaspoon salt**
- **2 broiler/fryer chickens (3½-4 pounds each), cut up**
- **Oil for deep-fat frying**

1. In a large resealable plastic bag, combine 2⅔ cups flour, garlic salt, paprika, 2½ teaspoons pepper and poultry seasoning. In a shallow bowl, beat eggs and water; add salt and the remaining flour and pepper. Dip the chicken in egg mixture, then place in the bag, a few pieces at a time. Seal bag and shake to coat.

2. In a deep-fat fryer, heat oil to 375°. Fry chicken, several pieces at a time, for 5-6 minutes on each side or until golden brown and juices run clear. Drain on paper towels.

"Excellent recipe! I used this with boneless chicken breasts and made sandwiches. My only regret is that I didn't make extra!"

—DSCHULTZ01
FROM TASTEOFHOME.COM

(5) INGREDIENTS FAST FIX

GRILLED TERIYAKI SALMON

For this sweet-and-sour glaze, I blend maple syrup from our neck of the woods with teriyaki sauce from the other side of the world. It helps the salmon stay moist. It's fantastic!

—LENITA SCHAFER ORMOND BEACH, FL

START TO FINISH: 30 MIN.
MAKES: 4 SERVINGS

- **¾ cup reduced-sodium teriyaki sauce**
- **½ cup maple syrup**
- **4 salmon fillets (6 ounces each)**
- **Mixed salad greens, optional**

1. In a small bowl, whisk teriyaki sauce and syrup. Pour 1 cup marinade into a large resealable plastic bag. Add salmon; seal bag and turn to coat. Refrigerate 15 minutes. Cover and refrigerate remaining marinade.

2. Drain the salmon, discarding marinade in bag. Moisten a paper towel with cooking oil; using long-handled tongs, rub on grill rack to coat lightly.

3. Place the salmon on grill rack, skin side down. Grill, covered, over medium heat or broil 4 in. from heat 8-12 minutes or until fish just begins to flake easily with a fork, basting frequently with reserved marinade. If desired, serve over lettuce salad.

POPCORN & PRETZEL CHICKEN TENDERS

My daughter, Alivia, thought it would be fun to coat chicken with two of our favorite movie-watching snacks—popcorn and pretzels. Crunchy and crispy, they bring a lot of smiles, especially when served with this sweet and creamy mustard sauce.
—SUZANNE CLARK PHOENIX, AZ

PREP: 25 MIN. + MARINATING • **BAKE:** 20 MIN.
MAKES: 6 SERVINGS (1 CUP SAUCE)

1½ pounds chicken tenderloins
1 cup buttermilk
2 teaspoons garlic powder
1 teaspoon salt
1 teaspoon onion powder
½ teaspoon pepper
¾ cup fat-free plain Greek yogurt
¼ cup peach preserves
1 tablespoon prepared mustard
4 cups miniature pretzels, crushed
2 cups air-popped popcorn, crushed
Cooking spray

1. In a large bowl, combine the first six ingredients; toss to coat. Refrigerate, covered, at least 30 minutes. In a small bowl, mix the yogurt, preserves and mustard; refrigerate until serving.
2. Preheat oven to 400°. In a large shallow dish, combine crushed pretzels and popcorn. Remove the chicken from marinade, discarding marinade. Dip both sides of chicken in pretzel mixture, patting to help coating adhere. Place tenders on a parchment paper-lined baking sheet; spritz with cooking spray.
3. Bake 20-25 minutes or until coating is golden brown and chicken is no longer pink. Serve with sauce.

MONTEREY CHICKEN WITH ROASTED VEGGIES

My clan often requests this baked chicken. Roasting the veggies brings out their sweetness. They're delicious with pasta or rice.
—GLORIA BRADLEY NAPERVILLE, IL

PREP: 15 MIN. • **BAKE:** 25 MIN. • **MAKES:** 6 SERVINGS

1 pound fresh asparagus, trimmed and cut into 2-inch pieces
2 large sweet red peppers, cut into strips
1 tablespoon olive oil
1½ teaspoons salt, divided
¾ teaspoon coarsely ground pepper, divided
6 boneless skinless chicken breast halves (6 ounces each)
5 tablespoons butter, divided
¼ cup all-purpose flour
1 cup chicken broth
1 cup heavy whipping cream
¼ cup white wine or additional chicken broth
1½ cups (6 ounces) shredded Monterey Jack cheese, divided

1. Preheat oven to 400°. Place asparagus and red peppers in a greased 13x9-in. baking dish; toss with oil, 1/2 teaspoon salt and 1/4 teaspoon pepper. Roast 5-8 minutes or just until crisp-tender. Remove vegetables from dish.
2. Season chicken with the remaining salt and pepper. In a large skillet, heat 1 tablespoon butter; brown 3 chicken breasts on both sides. Transfer to the same baking dish. Repeat with an additional 1 tablespoon butter and remaining chicken. Top chicken with roasted vegetables.
3. In same skillet, melt remaining butter over medium heat. Stir in flour until smooth; gradually whisk in broth, cream and wine. Bring to a boil, stirring constantly; cook and stir 2-3 minutes or until thickened. Stir in 1 cup cheese until melted. Pour over chicken.
4. Bake, uncovered, 25-30 minutes or until a thermometer inserted in chicken reads 165°. Sprinkle with remaining cheese.

HONEY CHIPOTLE RIBS

Nothing's better than having a finger-lickin' good barbecue sauce to smother your baby back ribs. This one calls for Guinness and honey so it's sure to be a winner. You can make the sauce up to a week in advance to keep prep easy on the day you plan to grill.
—CAITLIN HAWES WESTWOOD, MA

PREP: 5 MIN. • **COOK:** 1½ HOURS • **MAKES:** 12 SERVINGS

- **6 pounds pork baby back ribs**

BARBECUE SAUCE

- **3 cups ketchup**
- **2 bottles (11.2 ounces each) Guinness beer**
- **2 cups barbecue sauce**
- **⅔ cup honey**
- **1 small onion, chopped**
- **¼ cup Worcestershire sauce**
- **2 tablespoons Dijon mustard**
- **2 tablespoons chopped chipotle peppers in adobo sauce**
- **4 teaspoons ground chipotle pepper**
- **1 teaspoon salt**
- **1 teaspoon garlic powder**
- **½ teaspoon pepper**

1. Wrap ribs in large pieces of heavy-duty foil; seal edges of foil. Grill, covered, over indirect medium heat for 1-1½ hours or until tender.
2. In a large saucepan, combine sauce ingredients; bring to a boil. Reduce heat; simmer, uncovered, for about 45 minutes or until thickened, stirring occasionally.
3. Carefully remove ribs from foil. Place over direct heat; baste with some of the sauce. Grill, covered, over medium heat for about 30 minutes or until browned, turning once and basting occasionally with additional sauce. Serve with remaining sauce.

TOP TIP

Measuring Honey

When I need to measure honey for baking, I first oil the measuring cup. The honey comes out easily, and I get the full measure without the messy process of scraping the cup.
—BARBARA R. PORTLAND, OR

FAST FIX

CHICKEN NOODLE STIR-FRY

I rely on budget-friendly ramen noodles to stretch this appealing stir-fry. I usually toss in whichever veggies I happen to have on hand, so it's a unique flavor experience every time I make it.
—**DARLENE BRENDEN** SALEM, OR

START TO FINISH: 25 MIN. • **MAKES:** 4 SERVINGS

- **1 package (3 ounces) chicken-flavored ramen noodles**
- **1 pound boneless skinless chicken breasts, cut into strips**
- **1 tablespoon canola oil**
- **1 cup fresh broccoli florets**
- **1 cup fresh cauliflowerets**
- **1 cup sliced celery**
- **1 cup coarsely chopped cabbage**
- **2 medium carrots, thinly sliced**
- **1 medium onion, thinly sliced**
- **½ cup canned bean sprouts**
- **½ cup teriyaki or soy sauce**

1. Set aside seasoning packet from noodles. Cook noodles according to package directions. Meanwhile, in a large skillet or wok, stir-fry chicken in oil for 5-6 minutes or until no longer pink. Add vegetables; stir-fry for 3-4 minutes or until crisp-tender.
2. Drain noodles. Stir the noodles, contents of seasoning packet and teriyaki sauce into the chicken mixture until well combined.

FAST FIX

CORNED BEEF STIR-FRY

The celery seed really comes through in this colorful medley of carrots, cabbage and corned beef. A woman at church shared the recipe with me. My husband and son love its subtle sweetness.
—**ALESAH PADGETT** FRANKLIN, GA

START TO FINISH: 30 MIN. • **MAKES:** 4-6 SERVINGS

- **7 tablespoons canola oil, divided**
- **3 tablespoons white vinegar**
- **2 tablespoons sugar**
- **1 teaspoon celery seed**
- **¼ teaspoon salt**
- **6 cups coarsely chopped cabbage**
- **1 cup shredded carrots**
- **¼ cup chopped green onions**
- **½ pound thinly sliced deli corned beef**
- **Hot cooked rice, optional**

1. In a small bowl, whisk 4 tablespoons oil, vinegar, sugar, celery seed and salt until sugar is dissolved; set aside.
2. In a large skillet, saute the cabbage, carrots and onions in remaining oil for 15-16 minutes or until crisp-tender. Stir in vinegar-oil mixture and corned beef. Cover and simmer for 10 minutes or until heated through. If desired, serve with rice.

5 INGREDIENTS FAST FIX

SWEET POTATO & BEAN QUESADILLAS

Sweet potatoes and black beans pair up for a quesadilla that's easy, fast, fun and delicious.
BRITTANY HUBBARD GERING, NE

START TO FINISH: 30 MIN. • **MAKES:** 4 SERVINGS

- **2 medium sweet potatoes**
- **4 whole wheat tortillas (8 inches)**
- **¾ cup canned black beans, rinsed and drained**
- **½ cup shredded pepper jack cheese**
- **¾ cup salsa**

1. Scrub sweet potatoes; pierce several times with a fork. Place on a microwave-safe plate. Microwave, uncovered, on high 7-9 minutes or until very tender, turning once.
2. When cool enough to handle, cut each potato lengthwise in half. Scoop out pulp. Spread onto one half of each tortilla; top with beans and cheese. Fold other half of tortilla over filling.
3. Heat a griddle or skillet over medium heat. Cook quesadillas 2-3 minutes on each side or until golden brown and cheese is melted. Serve with salsa. .

FAST FIX

FAMILY-FAVORITE CHEESEBURGER PASTA

I created this recipe to satisfy a cheeseburger craving that hit me one day. The result was a home-style pasta that tastes just like a classic cheeseburger, but makes use of better-for-you ingredients.

—RAQUEL HAGGARD EDMOND, OK

START TO FINISH: 30 MIN. • **MAKES:** 4 SERVINGS

- **1½ cups uncooked whole wheat penne pasta**
- **¾ pound lean ground beef (90% lean)**
- **2 tablespoons finely chopped onion**
- **1 can (14½ ounces) no-salt-added diced tomatoes**
- **2 tablespoons dill pickle relish**
- **2 tablespoons prepared mustard**
- **2 tablespoons ketchup**
- **1 teaspoon steak seasoning**
- **¼ teaspoon seasoned salt**
- **¾ cup shredded reduced-fat cheddar cheese**
- **Chopped green onions, optional**

1. Cook pasta according to package directions. Meanwhile, in a large skillet, cook beef and onion over medium heat until meat is no longer pink; drain. Drain pasta; add to meat mixture.

2. Stir in the tomatoes, relish, mustard, ketchup, steak seasoning and seasoned salt. Bring to a boil. Reduce heat; simmer, uncovered, for 5 minutes.

3. Sprinkle with cheese. Remove from the heat; cover and

4. let stand until cheese is melted. Garnish pasta with green onions if desired.

NOTE *This recipe was tested with McCormick's Montreal Steak Seasoning. Look for it in the spice aisle.*

RICH CHICKEN ALFREDO PIZZA

Try this tasty twist on pizza night. Spinach and tender chunks of chicken combine with a smooth and buttery homemade Alfredo sauce for a pie that definitely lives up to its name.

—TAMMY HANKS GAINSVILLE, FL

PREP: 30 MIN. • **BAKE:** 15 MIN.
MAKES: 1 PIZZA (8 MAIN DISH OR 12 APPETIZER SLICES)

- **2½ teaspoons butter**
- **1 garlic clove, minced**
- **1½ cups heavy whipping cream**
- **3 tablespoons grated Parmesan cheese**
- **½ teaspoon salt**
- **¼ teaspoon pepper**
- **1 tablespoon minced fresh parsley**
- **1 prebaked 12-inch thin pizza crust**
- **1 cup cubed cooked chicken breast**
- **1 cup thinly sliced baby portobello mushrooms**
- **1 cup fresh baby spinach**
- **2 cups (8 ounces) shredded part-skim mozzarella cheese**

1. In a small saucepan over medium heat, melt butter. Add garlic; cook and stir for 1 minute. Add cream; cook until liquid is reduced by half, about 15-20 minutes. Add the Parmesan cheese, salt and pepper; cook and stir until thickened. Remove from heat; stir in parsley. Cool slightly.

2. Place crust on an ungreased baking sheet; spread with cream mixture. Top with chicken, mushrooms, spinach and mozzarella cheese. Bake at 450° for 15-20 minutes or until cheese is melted and crust is golden brown.

FAST FIX

MIXED PAELLA

Packed with chicken, shrimp, rice, tomatoes, peas and stuffed olives, this vibrant meal is quick and filling. It will take the chill off any cool evenings.

—LIBBY WALP CHICAGO, IL

START TO FINISH: 30 MIN.
MAKES: 6 SERVINGS

- **1¼ pounds boneless skinless chicken breasts, thinly sliced**
- **2 tablespoons olive oil**
- **1 medium onion, chopped**
- **2 garlic cloves, minced**
- **2¼ cups chicken broth**
- **1 cup uncooked long grain rice**
- **1 teaspoon dried oregano**
- **½ teaspoon ground turmeric**
- **½ teaspoon paprika**
- **¼ teaspoon salt**
- **¼ to ½ teaspoon pepper**
- **1 pound cooked medium shrimp, peeled and deveined**
- **1 can (14½ ounces) diced tomatoes, undrained**
- **¾ cup frozen peas, thawed**
- **½ cup sliced pimiento-stuffed olives**

1. In a large skillet, saute chicken in oil until no longer pink. Remove and keep warm. In the same skillet, saute onion until tender. Add garlic; cook 1 minute longer. Stir in the broth, rice and seasonings. Bring to a boil. Reduce heat; cover and simmer for 15-18 minutes or until rice is tender.
2. Stir in the shrimp, tomatoes, peas, olives and chicken; cover and cook for 3-4 minutes or until heated through.

FAST FIX

BLT SKILLET

With chunks of bacon and tomato, this skillet is reminiscent of a BLT. It's fast, too, so it makes a great weeknight meal. The whole wheat linguine gives the dish extra flavor and texture.

—EDRIE O'BRIEN DENVER, CO

START TO FINISH: 25 MIN.
MAKES: 2 SERVINGS

- **4 ounces uncooked whole wheat linguine**
- **4 bacon strips, cut into 1½-inch pieces**
- **1 plum tomato, cut into 1-inch pieces**
- **1 garlic clove, minced**
- **1½ teaspoons lemon juice**
- **¼ teaspoon salt**
- **¼ teaspoon pepper**
- **2 tablespoons grated Parmesan cheese**
- **1 tablespoon minced fresh parsley**

1. Cook linguine according to package directions. Meanwhile, in a large skillet, cook bacon over medium heat until crisp. Remove to paper towels; drain, reserving 1 teaspoon drippings.
2. In the drippings, saute tomato and garlic for 1-2 minutes or until heated through. Stir in the bacon, lemon juice, salt and pepper.
3. Drain linguine; add to the skillet. Sprinkle with cheese and parsley; toss to coat.

FAST FIX

EASY CHICKEN PICCATA

My chicken dish is ready to serve in a half hour. It takes just a few minutes in the oven to bake to tender perfection.
—**HANNAH WILLIAMS** MALIBU, CA

START TO FINISH: 30 MIN.
MAKES: 4 SERVINGS

- **4 boneless skinless chicken breast halves (6 ounces each)**
- **½ teaspoon salt**
- **¼ teaspoon pepper**
- **½ cup all-purpose flour**
- **3 tablespoons olive oil**
- **1 cup chicken stock**
- **3 to 4 tablespoons capers, drained**
- **2 to 3 tablespoons lemon juice**
- **3 tablespoons butter**

1. Preheat oven to 350°. Cut chicken breasts in half crosswise. Pound with a meat mallet to 1/2-in. thickness; sprinkle with salt and pepper. Place the flour in a shallow bowl. Dip the chicken in flour to coat both sides; shake off excess.
2. In a large skillet, heat 1 tablespoon oil over medium-high heat. Brown chicken in batches, adding additional oil as needed. Transfer chicken to an ungreased 13x9-in. baking dish.
3. Add the stock, capers and lemon juice to pan, stirring to loosen any browned bits. Whisk in the butter, 1 tablespoon at a time, until creamy. Pour sauce over chicken. Bake for 5-10 minutes or until no longer pink.

TOP TIP

Flattening Chicken

Flatten or pound meat for quicker, more even cooking and to yield an attractive appearance. When tender cuts of meat or poultry are flattened, it's best to put them inside a heavy-duty resealable plastic bag or between two sheets of heavy plastic wrap to prevent messy splatters. Use only the smooth side of a meat mallet to gently pound them to the desired thickness to prevent the meat from shredding. When tougher cuts of meat need tenderizing, pound with the ridged side of a meat mallet to break up the connective tissue.

LASAGNA CASSEROLE, 110

TURKEY CORDON BLEU CASSEROLE, 106

TOMATO-FRENCH BREAD LASAGNA, 114

BURRITO BAKE, 115

CASSEROLE ENTREES

It's no wonder casseroles are so popular! Not only are they comfort food at its very best, they're also convenient, freezer friendly, easy to assemble in advance and often made using ingredients you already have stocked in the pantry. Dinner will be something special when the bubbly, oven-baked goodness of a lasagna, potpie, mac and cheese, stuffed shells or any of these other one-dish wonders is set on the table. Cozy up with these timeless classics for a meal you won't forget.

(5) INGREDIENTS

MASHED POTATO HOT DISH

My cousin gave me this simple savory recipe. Whenever I'm making homemade mashed potatoes, I throw in a few extra spuds so I can make this for supper the next night.

—TANYA ABERNATHY YACOLT, WA

PREP: 15 MIN. • **BAKE:** 20 MIN.
MAKES: 4 SERVINGS

- **1 pound ground beef**
- **1 can (10¾ ounces) condensed cream of chicken soup, undiluted**
- **2 cups frozen French-style green beans**
- **2 cups hot mashed potatoes (prepared with milk and butter)**
- **½ cup shredded cheddar cheese**

1. In a large skillet, cook beef over medium heat until no longer pink; drain. Stir in soup and beans.
2. Transfer to a greased 2-qt. baking dish. Top with mashed potatoes; sprinkle with cheese. Bake, uncovered, at 350° for 20-25 minutes or until bubbly and cheese is melted.

"This is a huge thumbs up in our house! I no longer make just a single batch—I always have to double it."

—ZANASMOM
FROM TASTEOFHOME.COM

TURKEY CORDON BLEU CASSEROLE

We love everything about traditional cordon bleu, but this turkey variation is a nice change of pace. It's easy to make, too.

—KRISTINE BLAUERT WABASHA, MN

PREP: 20 MIN. • **BAKE:** 25 MIN.
MAKES: 8 SERVINGS

- **2 cups uncooked elbow macaroni**
- **2 cans (10¾ ounces each) condensed cream of chicken soup, undiluted**
- **¾ cup 2% milk**
- **¼ cup grated Parmesan cheese**
- **1 teaspoon prepared mustard**
- **1 teaspoon paprika**
- **½ teaspoon dried rosemary, crushed**
- **¼ teaspoon garlic powder**
- **⅛ teaspoon rubbed sage**
- **2 cups cubed cooked turkey**
- **2 cups cubed fully cooked ham**
- **2 cups (8 ounces) shredded part-skim mozzarella cheese**
- **¼ cup crushed Ritz crackers**

1. Preheat oven to 350°. Cook the macaroni according to package directions.
2. Meanwhile, in a large bowl, whisk soup, milk, Parmesan cheese, mustard and seasonings. Stir in turkey, ham and mozzarella cheese.
3. Drain the macaroni; add to soup mixture and toss to combine. Transfer to eight greased 8-oz. ramekins. Sprinkle with crushed crackers. Bake, uncovered, 25-30 minutes or until bubbly.

FREEZE OPTION *Cover and freeze unbaked casserole. To use, partially thaw in refrigerator overnight. Remove from refrigerator 30 minutes before baking. Preheat oven to 350°. Bake as directed, increasing time as necessary to heat through and for a thermometer inserted in center to read 165°.*

FAST FIX

UNSTUFFED PEPPERS

If you like stuffed peppers, you will love a speedy version that's ready in just half an hour. Instead of cooking the instant rice, you can use 2 cups of leftover cooked rice if you have it on hand.

—**BETH DEWYER** DU BOIS, PA

START TO FINISH: 30 MIN.
MAKES: 6 SERVINGS

- **1 cup uncooked instant rice**
- **1 pound ground beef**
- **2 medium green peppers, cut into 1-inch pieces**
- **½ cup chopped onion**
- **1 jar (26 ounces) marinara sauce**
- **1½ teaspoons salt-free seasoning blend**
- **½ cup shredded Italian cheese blend**
- **½ cup seasoned bread crumbs**
- **1 tablespoon olive oil**

1. Preheat oven to 350°. Cook rice according to package directions.
2. Meanwhile, in a large skillet, cook beef, green peppers and onion over medium-high heat until meat is no longer pink; drain. Stir in the rice, marinara sauce and seasoning blend. Stir in cheese.
3. Transfer to a greased 2-qt. baking dish. Toss the bread crumbs and olive oil; sprinkle over the top. Bake for 8-10 minutes or until heated through and topping is golden brown.

TOP TIP

Stuffed Peppers Substitute

For a quick substitute for rice in this recipe or traditional stuffed peppers or cabbage rolls, try leftover cooked barley or whole kernel corn. Adding a tablespoon or two of quick-cooking oats will help keep the dishes from getting too saucy after baking.

FIVE-CHEESE JUMBO SHELLS

Using five cheeses in one recipe doesn't usually translate to a dish that's considered light, but this meatless meal is proof that it can be done with great success (and flavor!). The shells freeze beautifully, so leftovers are a cinch to save for another quick dinner.

—LISA RENSHAW KANSAS CITY, MO

PREP: 45 MIN. • **BAKE:** 50 MIN. + STANDING • **MAKES:** 8 SERVINGS

- **24 uncooked jumbo pasta shells**
- **1 tablespoon olive oil**
- **1 medium zucchini, shredded and squeezed dry**
- **½ pound baby portobello mushrooms, chopped**
- **1 medium onion, finely chopped**
- **2 cups reduced-fat ricotta cheese**
- **½ cup shredded part-skim mozzarella cheese**
- **½ cup shredded provolone cheese**
- **½ cup grated Romano cheese**
- **1 large egg, lightly beaten**
- **1 teaspoon Italian seasoning**
- **½ teaspoon crushed red pepper flakes**
- **1 jar (24 ounces) meatless spaghetti sauce**
- **¼ cup grated Parmesan cheese**

1. Preheat oven to 350°. Cook shells according to package directions for al dente; drain and rinse in cold water.

2. In a large skillet, heat oil over medium-high heat. Add vegetables; cook and stir until tender. Remove from heat. In a bowl, combine ricotta, mozzarella, provolone and Romano cheeses; stir in egg, seasonings and vegetables.

3. Spread 1 cup sauce into a 13x9-in. baking dish coated with cooking spray. Fill pasta shells with cheese mixture; place in baking dish. Top with remaining sauce. Sprinkle with Parmesan cheese.

4. Bake, covered, 40 minutes. Bake, uncovered, 10 minutes longer or until cheese is melted. Let stand for 10 minutes before serving.

FREEZE OPTION *Cool unbaked casserole; cover and freeze. To use, partially thaw in refrigerator overnight. Remove from refrigerator 30 minutes before baking. Preheat oven to 350°. Cover casserole with foil; bake 50 minutes. Uncover; bake 15-20 minutes longer or until heated through and a thermometer inserted in center reads 165°.*

5 INGREDIENTS

RAVIOLI LASAGNA

When people sample this, they think it's a from-scratch recipe. But the lasagna actually starts with frozen ravioli and requires just three other ingredients.

—**PATRICIA SMITH** ASHEBORO, NC

PREP: 25 MIN. • **BAKE:** 40 MIN. • **MAKES:** 6-8 SERVINGS

- **1 pound ground beef**
- **1 jar (28 ounces) spaghetti sauce**
- **1 package (25 ounces) frozen sausage or cheese ravioli**
- **1½ cups (6 ounces) shredded part-skim mozzarella cheese**

1. In a large skillet, cook beef over medium heat until no longer pink; drain. In a greased 2½-qt. baking dish, layer a third of the spaghetti sauce, half of the ravioli and beef, and ½ cup cheese; repeat layers. Top with the remaining sauce and cheese.

2. Cover and bake at 400° for 40-45 minutes or until heated through.

OVEN STEW AND BISCUITS

Here's a stick-to-the-ribs stew that's sure to warm up any day. The recipe came from my brother, who was a wonderful cook.

—**BERTHA BROOKMEIER** EL CAJON, CA

PREP: 20 MIN. • **BAKE:** 45 MIN. • **MAKES:** 6-8 SERVINGS

- **⅓ cup all-purpose flour**
- **1 teaspoon salt**
- **½ teaspoon pepper**
- **2 pounds beef top sirloin, cut into 1-inch cubes**
- **¼ cup canola oil**
- **1 can (14½ ounces) stewed tomatoes**
- **1 jar (4½ ounces) sliced mushrooms, drained**
- **1 large onion, thinly sliced**
- **3 tablespoons soy sauce**
- **3 tablespoons molasses**
- **1 medium green pepper, cut into 1-inch pieces**
- **1 tube (12 ounces) refrigerated buttermilk biscuits**
- **1 teaspoon butter, melted**
- **Sesame seeds**

1. In a large resealable plastic bag, combine the flour, salt and pepper. Add beef in batches; shake to coat. In a large skillet, brown beef in batches in oil over medium heat. Return all to the pan; stir in tomatoes, mushrooms, onion, soy sauce and molasses.

2. Transfer to a greased 13x9-in. baking dish. Cover and bake at 375° for 20 minutes. Stir in the green pepper. Cover and bake 10 minutes longer.

3. Uncover; top with biscuits. Brush biscuits with butter; sprinkle with sesame seeds. Bake 15-18 minutes more or until the biscuits are golden brown.

STACKED ENCHILADA

Here's my easy stacked version of a classic Tex-Mex dish. Loaded with chicken, black beans and green pepper, this tortilla pie is both delicious and simple to prepare.

—**REBECCA PEPSIN** LONGMONT, CO

PREP: 20 MIN. • **BAKE:** 20 MIN. • **MAKES:** 4 SERVINGS

- **⅔ cup chopped green pepper**
- **2 teaspoons canola oil**
- **1 garlic clove, minced**
- **1 cup shredded cooked chicken**
- **1 cup canned black beans, rinsed and drained**
- **⅓ cup thinly sliced green onions**
- **½ cup enchilada sauce**
- **½ cup picante sauce**
- **4 corn tortillas (6 inches)**
- **1 cup shredded cheddar cheese**
- **Sour cream and shredded lettuce, optional**

1. In a large skillet, saute pepper in oil for 3 minutes. Add garlic and cook 2 minutes longer or until pepper is crisp-tender. Stir in the chicken, beans and onions; heat through. Transfer to a bowl and keep warm.

2. In the same skillet, combine enchilada and picante sauces. Coat both sides of one tortilla with sauce mixture; place in a greased 9-in. pie plate. Top with a third of the chicken mixture and ¼ cup cheese. Repeat layers twice. Top with remaining tortilla, sauce and cheese.

3. Cover and bake at 350° for 18-22 minutes or until heated through. Remove to a serving plate and cut into wedges. Serve with sour cream and lettuce if desired.

LASAGNA CASSEROLE

Growing up, this was the meal I always wanted on my birthday. Mother made the sauce from scratch, but I use store-bought spaghetti sauce to save time. Replace the ground beef with Italian sausage for more spice.
—DEB MORRISON SKIATOOK, OK

PREP: 15 MIN. • **BAKE:** 1 HOUR + STANDING
MAKES: 6-8 SERVINGS

- **1 pound ground beef**
- **¼ cup chopped onion**
- **½ teaspoon salt**
- **½ teaspoon pepper, divided**
- **1 pound medium pasta shells, cooked and drained**
- **4 cups (16 ounces) shredded part-skim mozzarella cheese, divided**
- **3 cups (24 ounces) 4% cottage cheese**
- **2 large eggs, lightly beaten**
- **⅓ cup grated Parmesan cheese**
- **2 tablespoons dried parsley flakes**
- **1 jar (24 ounces) meatless pasta sauce**

1. In a large skillet, cook beef and onion over medium heat until meat is no longer pink; drain. Sprinkle with salt and 1/4 teaspoon pepper; set aside.
2. In a large bowl, combine the pasta, 3 cups mozzarella cheese, cottage cheese, eggs, Parmesan cheese, parsley and remaining pepper. Transfer to a greased shallow 3-qt. baking dish. Top with beef mixture and spaghetti sauce (dish will be full).
3. Cover and bake at 350° for 45 minutes. Sprinkle with remaining mozzarella cheese. Bake, uncovered, 15 minutes longer or until bubbly and cheese is melted. Let stand for 10 minutes before serving.
FREEZE OPTION *Sprinkle casserole with remaining mozzarella cheese. Cover and freeze unbaked casserole. To use, partially thaw in refrigerator overnight. Remove from refrigerator 30 minutes before baking. Preheat oven to 350°. Bake casserole as directed, increasing time as necessary to heat through and for a thermometer inserted in center to read 165°.*

CREAMY HAM & CHEESE CASSEROLE

Leftover ham, convenient cooking creme and garlic-herb seasoning make this pasta toss so simple and delicious. I was so proud when I came up with the recipe!

—BETSY L. HOWARD KIRKWOOD, MO

PREP: 15 MIN. • **BAKE:** 20 MIN.
MAKES: 4 SERVINGS

- **8 ounces uncooked wide egg noodles**
- **3 cups cubed fully cooked ham**
- **1 can (10¾ ounces) condensed cream of chicken soup, undiluted**
- **1 carton (10 ounces) Philadelphia original cooking creme**
- **1 cup 2% milk**
- **½ teaspoon garlic-herb seasoning blend**
- **¼ teaspoon pepper**
- **2 cups (8 ounces) shredded Monterey Jack cheese**

1. Cook noodles according to package directions. Meanwhile, combine the ham, soup, cooking creme, milk and seasonings in a large bowl.
2. Drain noodles and add to ham mixture; mix well. Transfer to a 13x9-in. baking dish coated with cooking spray; sprinkle with cheese.
3. Bake, uncovered, at 350° for 20-25 minutes or until heated through.

FAST FIX

CRUNCHY TUNA SURPRISE

This recipe comes from my Grandma Mollie's kitchen. With my busy lifestyle, I appreciate quick and easy family-pleasers like this.

—LISA LE SAGE WAUWATOSA, WI

START TO FINISH: 30 MIN.
MAKES: 4 SERVINGS

- **1 can (12 ounces) tuna, drained and flaked**
- **1½ cups cooked rice**
- **1 can (10¾ ounces) condensed cream of mushroom soup, undiluted**
- **½ cup 2% milk**
- **¼ cup minced fresh parsley**
- **¾ cup crushed cornflakes**
- **2 tablespoons butter, melted**

1. In a large bowl, combine the first five ingredients. Transfer to a greased shallow 1½-qt. baking dish.
2. Combine the cornflake crumbs and butter; sprinkle over the top. Bake, uncovered, at 350° for 25-30 minutes or until bubbly.

BAKED ZITI

I enjoy making this dish for family and friends. It's easy to prepare, and I like to get creative with the sauce. For example, sometimes I might add my home-canned tomatoes, mushrooms or vegetables.

—ELAINE ANDERSON NEW GALILEE, PA

PREP: 20 MIN. • **BAKE:** 45 MIN. + STANDING
MAKES: 6-8 SERVINGS

- **12 ounces uncooked ziti or small tube pasta**
- **2 pounds ground beef**
- **1 jar (24 ounces) spaghetti sauce**
- **2 large eggs, beaten**
- **1 carton (15 ounces) ricotta cheese**
- **2½ cups (10 ounces) shredded mozzarella cheese, divided**
- **½ cup grated Parmesan cheese**

1. Cook pasta according to package directions.
2. Meanwhile, preheat oven to 350°. In a large skillet, cook beef over medium heat until no longer pink; drain. Stir in spaghetti sauce.
3. In a large bowl, combine eggs, ricotta cheese, 1½ cups mozzarella cheese and the Parmesan cheese. Drain pasta; add to cheese mixture and stir until blended.
4. Spoon a third of the meat sauce into a greased 13x9-in. baking dish; top with half of the pasta mixture. Repeat layers. Top with remaining meat sauce.
5. Cover and bake 40 minutes or until a thermometer reads 160°. Uncover; sprinkle with remaining mozzarella cheese. Bake 5-10 minutes longer or until the cheese is melted. Let stand for 15 minutes before serving.

5 INGREDIENTS

HAM & CHEESE POTATO CASSEROLE

This hammed-up spin on cheesy hash browns makes two hearty casseroles you can use as a main or side dish. Serve one today and save the other for a crazy school night.

—**KARI ADAMS** FORT COLLINS, CO

PREP: 15 MIN. • **BAKE:** 50 MIN. + STANDING
MAKES: 2 CASSEROLES (5 SERVINGS EACH)

- **2 cans (10¾ ounces each) condensed cream of celery soup, undiluted**
- **2 cups (16 ounces) sour cream**
- **½ cup water**
- **½ teaspoon pepper**
- **2 packages (28 ounces each) frozen O'Brien potatoes**
- **1 package (16 ounces) process cheese (Velveeta), cubed**
- **2½ cups cubed fully cooked ham**

1. Preheat oven to 375°. In a large bowl, mix soup, sour cream, water and pepper until blended. Stir in potatoes, cheese and ham.

2. Transfer to two greased 11x7-in. baking dishes. Bake, covered, 40 minutes. Uncover; bake 10-15 minutes longer or until bubbly. Let stand 10 minutes before serving.

FREEZE OPTION *Cover and freeze unbaked casseroles. To use, partially thaw in refrigerator overnight. Remove from refrigerator 30 minutes before baking. Preheat oven to 375°. Bake casseroles as directed, increasing time as necessary to heat through and for a thermometer inserted in center to read 165°.*

THREE-CHEESE MEATBALL MOSTACCIOLI

When my husband travels for work, I make a special dinner for our kids to keep their minds off missing Daddy. This tasty mostaccioli is meatball magic.

—**JENNIFER GILBERT** BRIGHTON, MI

PREP: 15 MIN. • **BAKE:** 35 MIN. • **MAKES:** 10 SERVINGS

- **1 package (16 ounces) mostaccioli**
- **2 large eggs, lightly beaten**
- **1 carton (15 ounces) part-skim ricotta cheese**
- **1 pound ground beef**
- **1 medium onion, chopped**
- **1 tablespoon brown sugar**
- **1 tablespoon Italian seasoning**
- **1 teaspoon garlic powder**
- **¼ teaspoon pepper**
- **2 jars (24 ounces each) pasta sauce with meat**
- **½ cup grated Romano cheese**
- **1 package (12 ounces) frozen fully cooked Italian meatballs, thawed**
- **¾ cup shaved Parmesan cheese**
- **Fresh baby arugula**

1. Preheat oven to 350°. Cook mostaccioli according to package directions for al dente; drain. Meanwhile, in a small bowl, mix eggs and ricotta cheese.

2. In a 6-qt. stockpot, cook beef and onion 6-8 minutes or until beef is no longer pink, breaking up beef into crumbles; drain. Stir in brown sugar and seasonings. Add pasta sauce and mostaccioli; toss to combine.

3. Transfer half of the pasta mixture to a greased 13x9-in. baking dish. Layer with ricotta mixture and remaining pasta mixture; sprinkle with Romano cheese. Top with meatballs and Parmesan cheese.

4. Bake, uncovered, 35-40 minutes or until heated through. If desired, top with arugula.

BAKED SPAGHETTI

This satisfying pasta bake pleases young and old, family and friends! Add a tossed green salad and breadsticks to round out a memorable menu.

—BETTY RABE MAHTOMEDI, MN

PREP: 20 MIN. • **BAKE:** 30 MIN. + STANDING • **MAKES:** 6-8 SERVINGS

- **8 ounces uncooked spaghetti, broken into thirds**
- **1 large egg**
- **½ cup milk**
- **½ teaspoon salt**
- **½ pound ground beef**
- **½ pound bulk Italian sausage**
- **1 small onion, chopped**
- **¼ cup chopped green pepper**
- **1 jar (14 ounces) meatless spaghetti sauce**
- **1 can (8 ounces) tomato sauce**
- **1 to 2 cups (4 to 8 ounces) shredded part-skim mozzarella cheese**

1. Preheat oven to 350°. Cook spaghetti according to package directions.

2. Meanwhile, in a large bowl, beat egg, milk and salt. Drain spaghetti; add to egg mixture and toss to coat. Transfer to a greased 13x9-in. baking dish.

3. In a large skillet, cook beef, sausage, onion and green pepper over medium heat until meat is no longer pink; drain. Stir in spaghetti sauce and tomato sauce. Spoon over the spaghetti mixture.

4. Bake, uncovered, 20 minutes. Sprinkle with the cheese. Bake 10 minutes longer or until cheese is melted. Let stand 10 minutes before cutting.

FREEZE OPTION *Cool spaghetti completely before tossing with egg mixture. Transfer to baking dish; cover and refrigerate. Meanwhile, prepare meat sauce and cool completely before spooning over spaghetti mixture. Cover and freeze unbaked casserole. To use, partially thaw in refrigerator overnight. Remove 30 minutes before baking. Preheat oven to 350°. Bake as directed, increasing time as necessary to heat through and for a thermometer inserted in center to read 165°.*

HOME-STYLE CHICKEN POTPIE

I served this potpie along with chili for a bowl game. No one ate the chili. In fact, one of my husband's friends called the next day and asked for the leftover pie.

—DARLENE CLAXTON BRIGHTON, MI

PREP: 1 HOUR + CHILLING • **BAKE:** 25 MIN. + STANDING
MAKES: 10-12 SERVINGS

- **¾ cup cold butter, cubed**
- **2 cups all-purpose flour**
- **1 cup (4 ounces) shredded cheddar cheese**
- **¼ cup cold water**

FILLING

- **2½ cups halved baby carrots**
- **3 celery ribs, sliced**
- **6 tablespoons butter, cubed**
- **7 tablespoons all-purpose flour**
- **1 teaspoon salt**
- **¼ teaspoon coarsely ground pepper**
- **2½ cups chicken broth**
- **1 cup heavy whipping cream**
- **4 cups cubed cooked chicken**
- **1 cup frozen pearl onions, thawed**
- **1 cup frozen peas, thawed**
- **3 tablespoons minced chives**
- **3 tablespoons minced fresh parsley**
- **2 teaspoons minced fresh thyme or ½ teaspoon dried thyme**
- **1 large egg, lightly beaten**

1. In a large bowl, cut butter into flour until crumbly. Stir in cheese. Gradually add water, tossing with a fork until dough forms a ball. Cover and refrigerate for at least 1 hour.

2. In a large saucepan, cook carrots and celery in a small amount of water until crisp-tender; drain and set aside.

3. In another saucepan, melt butter. Whisk in the flour, salt and pepper until smooth. Gradually whisk in broth and cream. Bring to a boil; cook and stir for 2 minutes or until thickened. Stir in the carrot mixture, chicken, onions, peas, chives, parsley and thyme; heat through. Transfer to a greased 13x9-in. baking dish.

4. On a floured surface, roll out dough to fit top of dish; cut out vents. Place dough over filling; trim and flute edges. Brush with egg. Bake at 400° for 25-30 minutes or until bubbly and crust is golden brown. Let stand for 10 minutes before serving.

FAST FIX

COMPANY MAC AND CHEESE

I'm not usually a fan of homemade macaroni and cheese, but when a friend served this, I had to have the recipe. This is by far the creamiest, tastiest and utterly best macaroni and cheese I have ever tried. Since it's simple to make and well received, it's a terrific potluck dish.
—CATHERINE OGDEN MIDDLEGROVE, NY

START TO FINISH: 30 MIN.
MAKES: 6-8 SERVINGS

- **1 package (7 ounces) elbow macaroni**
- **6 tablespoons butter, divided**
- **3 tablespoons all-purpose flour**
- **2 cups milk**
- **1 package (8 ounces) cream cheese, cubed**
- **2 cups (8 ounces) shredded cheddar cheese**
- **2 teaspoons spicy brown mustard**
- **½ teaspoon salt**
- **¼ teaspoon pepper**
- **¾ cup dry bread crumbs**
- **2 tablespoons minced fresh parsley**

1. Preheat oven to 400°. Cook macaroni according to package directions. Meanwhile, melt 4 tablespoons butter in a large saucepan. Stir in flour until smooth. Gradually add milk. Bring to a boil; cook and stir for 2 minutes.
2. Reduce heat; add cheeses, mustard, salt and pepper. Stir until cheese is melted and sauce is smooth. Drain macaroni; add to cheese sauce and stir to coat.
3. Transfer to a greased shallow 3-qt. baking dish. Melt remaining butter; toss with bread crumbs and parsley. Sprinkle over macaroni. Bake, uncovered, 15-20 minutes or until golden brown.

TOMATO-FRENCH BREAD LASAGNA

This makes a great main dish along with your favorite side salad and a special dessert. I sometimes serve it as a side dish to accompany veal cutlets or a roast.
—PATRICIA COLLINS IMBLER, OR

PREP: 30 MIN. • **BAKE:** 40 MIN.
MAKES: 8-10 SERVINGS

- **1 pound ground beef**
- **⅓ cup chopped onion**
- **⅓ cup chopped celery**
- **2 garlic cloves, minced**
- **14 slices French bread (½ inch thick)**
- **4 large tomatoes, sliced ½ inch thick**
- **1 teaspoon dried basil**
- **1 teaspoon dried parsley flakes**
- **1 teaspoon dried oregano**
- **1 teaspoon dried rosemary, crushed**
- **1 teaspoon garlic powder**
- **¾ teaspoon salt**
- **½ teaspoon pepper**
- **2 teaspoons olive oil, divided**
- **3 tablespoons butter**
- **3 tablespoons all-purpose flour**
- **1½ cups milk**
- **⅓ cup grated Parmesan cheese**
- **2 cups (8 ounces) shredded mozzarella cheese**

1. In a skillet, cook beef, onion, celery and garlic over medium heat until beef is no longer pink; drain and set aside. Toast bread; line the bottom of an ungreased 13x9-in. baking dish with 10 slices. Top with half of the meat mixture and half of the tomatoes.
2. Combine seasonings; sprinkle half over tomatoes. Drizzle with 1 teaspoon oil. Crumble remaining bread over top. Repeat layers of meat, tomatoes, seasonings and oil.
3. In a saucepan over medium heat, melt the butter; stir in flour until smooth. Gradually stir in milk; bring to a boil. Cook and stir until thickened and bubbly, about 2 minutes. Remove from the heat; stir in Parmesan. Pour over casserole. Top with the shredded mozzarella. Bake, uncovered, at 350° for 40-45 minutes or until bubbly and cheese is golden brown.

BURRITO BAKE

Years ago when I was in college, my roommate would frequently make this economical casserole. It's so easy to put together, and one pan serves several.
—CINDEE NESS HORACE, ND

PREP: 25 MIN. • **BAKE:** 30 MIN.
MAKES: 6 SERVINGS

- **1 pound ground beef**
- **1 can (16 ounces) refried beans**
- **¼ cup chopped onion**
- **1 envelope taco seasoning**
- **1 tube (8 ounces) refrigerated crescent rolls**
- **2 cups (8 ounces) shredded cheddar cheese**
- **2 cups (8 ounces) shredded part-skim mozzarella cheese**
- **Optional toppings: chopped green pepper, shredded lettuce, chopped tomatoes and sliced ripe olives**

1. Preheat oven to 350°. In a large skillet, cook beef over medium heat until no longer pink; drain. Add beans, onion and taco seasoning.
2. Unroll crescent roll dough. Press onto the bottom and up the sides of a greased 13x9-in. baking dish; seal seams and perforations.
3. Spread beef mixture over crust; sprinkle with the cheeses. Bake, uncovered, for 30 minutes or until golden brown. Sprinkle with toppings of your choice.

TOP TIP

Ground Beef Basics

Ground beef is often labeled using the cut of meat that it is ground from, such as ground chuck or ground round. (Ground beef comes from a combination of beef cuts.) Ground beef can also be labeled according to the fat content of the ground mixture or the percentage of lean meat to fat, such as 85% or 90% lean. The higher the percentage, the leaner the meat. Select ground beef that is bright red in color and is in a tightly sealed package. Purchase before the "sell by" date. Handle the mixture as little as possible when shaping hamburgers, meat loaves or meatballs to keep the final product light in texture.

“I usually substitute refrigerated biscuits or a refrigerated pie crust for the crescent rolls. My family loves when I make it!”
—MRS._WHITE FROM TASTEOFHOME.COM

CHICKEN RANCH MAC & CHEESE

Prep once, feed the family twice when you double this recipe and freeze half. I created it for the people I love most, using the ingredients they love best.
—ANGELA SPENGLER TAMPA, FL

PREP: 15 MIN. • **BAKE:** 30 MIN.
MAKES: 8 SERVINGS

- **3 cups uncooked elbow macaroni**
- **3 tablespoons butter**
- **2 tablespoons all-purpose flour**
- **½ teaspoon salt**
- **¼ teaspoon pepper**
- **1 cup 2% milk**
- **1½ cups (6 ounces) shredded cheddar cheese**
- **½ cup grated Parmesan cheese**
- **½ cup shredded Swiss cheese**
- **¾ cup ranch salad dressing**
- **1 cup coarsely chopped cooked chicken**

TOPPING

- **⅓ cup seasoned bread crumbs**
- **2 tablespoons butter, melted**
- **10 bacon strips, cooked and crumbled**
- **1 tablespoon minced fresh parsley**

1. Preheat oven to 350°. In a 6-qt. stockpot, cook macaroni according to package directions for al dente; drain and return to pot.
2. Meanwhile, in a medium saucepan, melt butter over medium heat. Stir in flour, salt and pepper until smooth; gradually whisk in milk. Bring to a boil, stirring constantly; cook and stir 1-2 minutes or until thickened. Stir in cheeses until blended. Stir in dressing.
3. Add the cooked chicken and cheese sauce to the macaroni, tossing to combine. Transfer to a greased 13x9-in. baking dish.
4. Toss bread crumbs with melted butter; sprinkle over macaroni. Top with bacon. Bake, uncovered, 30-35 minutes or until topping is golden brown. Sprinkle with parsley.

HAMBURGER CASSEROLE

This "oldie but goodie" is such a hit it's traveled all over the country! My mother originated the recipe in Pennsylvania, I brought it to Texas when I married, I'm still making it in California, and my daughter treats her friends to it in Colorado.

—HELEN CARMICHALL SANTEE, CA

PREP: 20 MIN. • **COOK:** 45 MIN.
MAKES: 10 SERVINGS

- **2 pounds lean ground beef (90% lean)**
- **4 pounds potatoes, peeled and sliced ¼ inch thick**
- **1 large onion, sliced**
- **1 teaspoon salt**
- **½ teaspoon pepper**
- **1 teaspoon beef bouillon granules**
- **1 cup boiling water**
- **1 can (28 ounces) diced tomatoes, undrained**
- **Minced fresh parsley, optional**

In a Dutch oven, layer half of the meat, potatoes and onion. Sprinkle with half of the salt and pepper. Repeat layers. Dissolve bouillon in water; pour over all. Top with tomatoes. Cover and cook over medium heat for 45-50 minutes or until potatoes are tender. Garnish with parsley if desired.

EASY BEEF-STUFFED SHELLS

Here's a rich, comforting dish that's terrific right away or made ahead and baked the next day. Pesto makes a surprising filling for these cheesy, satisfying shells.

—BLAIR LONERGAN ROCHELLE, VA

PREP: 45 MIN. + CHILLING • **BAKE:** 45 MIN.
MAKES: 10 SERVINGS

- **20 uncooked jumbo pasta shells**
- **1 pound ground beef**
- **1 large onion, chopped**
- **1 carton (15 ounces) ricotta cheese**
- **2 cups (8 ounces) shredded Italian cheese blend, divided**
- **½ cup grated Parmesan cheese**
- **¼ cup prepared pesto**
- **1 large egg**
- **1 jar (26 ounces) spaghetti sauce, divided**

1. Cook pasta shells according to package directions to al dente; drain and rinse in cold water. In a large skillet, cook beef and onion over medium heat until meat is no longer pink; drain. In a large bowl, combine the ricotta cheese, 1½ cups Italian cheese blend, Parmesan cheese, pesto, egg and half of the beef mixture.

2. Spread ¾ cup spaghetti sauce into a greased 13x9-in. baking dish. Spoon cheese mixture into pasta shells; place in baking dish. Combine remaining beef mixture and spaghetti sauce; pour over shells. Sprinkle with remaining cheese. Cover and refrigerate overnight.

3. Remove from the refrigerator 30 minutes before baking. Cover and bake at 350° for 40 minutes. Uncover; bake 5-10 minutes longer or until cheese is melted.

BAKED ORANGE ROUGHY AND RICE

It might sound too good to be true, but believe us when we say that this delectable fish and rice dinner will leave you with just one dish in the sink to wash. Your brood will be lining up to dig in once they see (and smell) the results!

—*TASTE OF HOME* TEST KITCHEN

PREP: 10 MIN. • **BAKE:** 30 MIN.
MAKES: 4 SERVINGS

- **2 cups uncooked instant rice**
- **1 package (16 ounces) frozen broccoli-cauliflower blend, thawed**
- **4 orange roughy fillets (6 ounces each)**
- **1 can (14½ ounces) chicken broth**
- **1 can (14½ ounces) fire-roasted diced tomatoes, undrained**
- **1 teaspoon garlic powder**
- **1 teaspoon lemon-pepper seasoning**
- **¼ to ½ teaspoon cayenne pepper**
- **½ cup shredded cheddar cheese**

1. Place rice in a greased 13x9-in. baking dish. Layer with the vegetables and fish. Pour the broth and tomatoes over the top; sprinkle with seasonings.

2. Cover and bake at 375° for 25-30 minutes or until fish flakes easily with a fork and rice is tender. Sprinkle with cheese; bake 5 minutes longer or until cheese is melted.

SPINACH BEEF PIE

I stumbled upon this recipe many years ago, and it's still one I turn to today. If you like meat pies, it's a nice variation from traditional chicken or turkey.
—**MEG STANKIEWICZ** GARFIELD HEIGHTS, OH

PREP: 25 MIN. • **BAKE:** 30 MIN. • **MAKES:** 6-8 SERVINGS

- **1 cup all-purpose flour**
- **⅓ cup old-fashioned oats**
- **7 tablespoons cold butter**
- **2 to 3 tablespoons cold water**
- **1 pound ground beef**
- **1 medium onion, chopped**
- **1 medium green pepper, chopped**
- **1 garlic clove, minced**
- **¼ cup ketchup**
- **1 teaspoon salt**
- **1 teaspoon dried oregano**
- **½ teaspoon dried basil**
- **½ teaspoon dried marjoram**
- **¼ teaspoon pepper**
- **1 package (10 ounces) frozen chopped spinach, thawed and squeezed dry**
- **3 large eggs, lightly beaten**
- **2 cups (8 ounces) shredded cheddar cheese, divided**
- **1 large tomato, seeded and diced**

1. In a large bowl, combine flour and oats; cut in the butter until crumbly. Gradually add water, tossing with a fork until dough forms a ball. Roll out dough to fit a 9-in. pie plate. Transfer to plate; trim and flute edges.
2. In a skillet, cook the beef, onion, green pepper and garlic over medium heat until meat is no longer pink; drain. Stir in ketchup and seasonings. Fold in spinach; cool slightly. Stir in eggs and 1 cup cheese until combined; spoon into crust.
3. Bake at 400° for 25-30 minutes or until the center is set. Sprinkle tomato and remaining cheese around edge of pie. Bake 5-10 minutes longer or until cheese is melted. Let stand for 5-10 minutes before cutting.

CABBAGE ROLL CASSEROLE

I layer cabbage with tomato sauce and beef to create a hearty casserole that tastes like cabbage rolls but without all the work.
—**DOREEN MARTIN** KITIMAT, BC

PREP: 20 MIN. • **BAKE:** 55 MIN. • **MAKES:** 12 SERVINGS

- **2 pounds ground beef**
- **1 large onion, chopped**
- **3 garlic cloves, minced**
- **2 cans (15 ounces each) tomato sauce, divided**
- **1 teaspoon dried thyme**
- **½ teaspoon dill weed**
- **½ teaspoon rubbed sage**
- **¼ teaspoon salt**
- **¼ teaspoon pepper**
- **¼ teaspoon cayenne pepper**
- **2 cups cooked rice**
- **4 bacon strips, cooked and crumbled**
- **1 medium head cabbage (2 pounds), shredded**
- **1 cup (4 ounces) shredded part-skim mozzarella cheese**

1. Preheat oven to 375°. In a large skillet, cook beef and onion over medium heat until meat is no longer pink. Add garlic; cook 1 minute longer. Drain. Stir in one can of tomato sauce and seasonings. Bring to a boil. Reduce heat; cover and simmer 5 minutes. Stir in rice and bacon; heat through. Remove from heat.
2. Layer a third of the cabbage in a greased 13x9-in. baking dish. Top with half of the meat mixture. Repeat layers; top with remaining cabbage. Pour remaining tomato sauce over top.
3. Cover and bake 45 minutes. Uncover; sprinkle with cheese. Bake 10 minutes longer or until cheese is melted. Let stand 5 minutes before serving.

TOP TIP

Cabbage 101

When buying cabbage, look for those with crisp-looking leaves that are firmly packed. The head should feel heavy for its size. Store cabbage tightly wrapped in a plastic bag in the refrigerator for up to 2 weeks. Remove the core, rinse and blot dry just before using. A 1½-pound cabbage will yield 8 cups shredded.

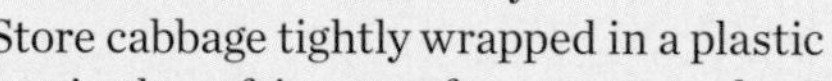

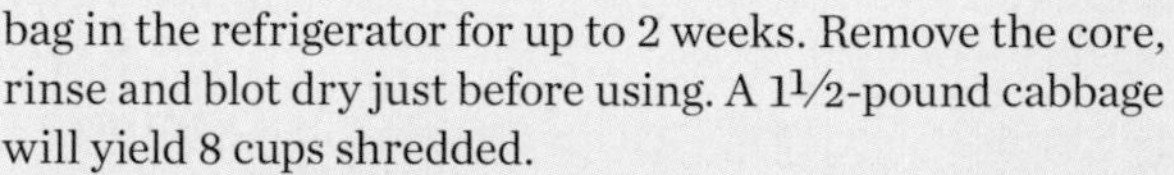

To shred cabbage by hand, cut cabbage into wedges. Place cut side down on a cutting board. With a large sharp knife, cut into thin slices, as shown above.

"I've made this dish twice. It's one of my favorites of all the *Taste of Home* recipes that I've tried. I add a little hot sauce on mine. Great recipe!"

—**SUMMERJEWL** FROM TASTEOFHOME.COM

PEPPER JACK MAC

I go with this dish when I want something hearty, creamy and cheesy. It's comfort food at its finest.

—**RIANNA STYX** LIBERTYVILLE, IL

PREP: 35 MIN. • **BAKE:** 20 MIN.
MAKES: 6 SERVINGS

- **2 cups uncooked elbow macaroni**
- **¼ cup butter, cubed**
- **¼ cup all-purpose flour**
- **½ teaspoon salt**
- **½ teaspoon ground mustard**
- **½ teaspoon pepper**
- **½ teaspoon Worcestershire sauce**
- **1½ cups milk**
- **½ cup heavy whipping cream**
- **3 cups (12 ounces) shredded pepper Jack cheese**
- **1 package (8 ounces) cream cheese, cubed**
- **1 cup (4 ounces) shredded sharp cheddar cheese**
- **½ cup shredded Asiago cheese**

TOPPING

- **¾ cup panko (Japanese) bread crumbs**
- **4 bacon strips, cooked and crumbled**
- **¼ cup grated Parmesan cheese**
- **1 cup cheddar french-fried onions, crushed**

1. Cook the macaroni according to package directions; drain and set aside.

2. In a large saucepan, melt butter. Stir in the flour, salt, mustard, pepper and Worcestershire sauce until smooth; gradually add milk and cream. Bring to a boil; cook and stir for 1 minute or until thickened. Stir in cheeses until melted. Stir macaroni into cheese mixture.

3. Transfer to a greased 2-qt. baking dish. Sprinkle with the panko bread crumbs, bacon, Parmesan cheese and onions. Bake, uncovered, at 350° for 20-25 minutes or until bubbly and golden brown.

BEST LASAGNA

For a casual meal, you can't go wrong with this rich and meaty lasagna. My grown sons and daughter-in-law still request it for their birthdays.

—**PAM THOMPSON** GIRARD, IL

PREP: 1 HOUR • **BAKE:** 50 MIN. + STANDING
MAKES: 12 SERVINGS

- **9 lasagna noodles**
- **1¼ pounds bulk Italian sausage**
- **¾ pound ground beef**
- **1 medium onion, diced**
- **3 garlic cloves, minced**
- **2 cans (one 28 ounces, one 15 ounces) crushed tomatoes**
- **2 cans (6 ounces each) tomato paste**
- **⅔ cup water**
- **2 to 3 tablespoons sugar**
- **3 tablespoons plus ¼ cup minced fresh parsley, divided**
- **2 teaspoons dried basil**
- **¾ teaspoon fennel seed**
- **¾ teaspoon salt, divided**
- **¼ teaspoon coarsely ground pepper**
- **1 large egg, lightly beaten**
- **1 carton (15 ounces) ricotta cheese**
- **4 cups (16 ounces) shredded part-skim mozzarella cheese**
- **¾ cup grated Parmesan cheese**

1. Cook noodles according to package directions; drain. Meanwhile, in a Dutch oven, cook sausage, beef and onion over medium heat 8-10 minutes or until meat is no longer pink, breaking up meat into crumbles. Add garlic; cook 1 minute longer. Drain.

2. Stir in tomatoes, tomato paste, water, sugar, 3 tablespoons parsley, basil, fennel, ½ teaspoon salt and pepper; bring to a boil. Reduce heat; simmer, uncovered, 30 minutes, stirring occasionally.

3. In a small bowl, mix egg, ricotta cheese, and remaining parsley and salt.

4. Preheat oven to 375°. Spread 2 cups meat sauce into an ungreased 13x9-in. baking dish. Layer with three noodles and a third of the ricotta mixture. Sprinkle with 1 cup mozzarella cheese and 2 tablespoons Parmesan cheese. Repeat the layers twice. Top with remaining meat sauce and cheeses (dish will be full).

5. Bake, covered, for 25 minutes. Bake, uncovered, 25 minutes longer or until bubbly. Let stand for 15 minutes before serving.

CHICKEN & EGG NOODLE CASSEROLE

I made this for my friend Michelle and her family after they experienced a fire at their home. Loaded with oodles of noodles and sprinkled with crumbs, it's the perfect way to spread a little love.
—LIN KRANKEL OXFORD, MI

PREP: 20 MIN. • **BAKE:** 30 MIN.
MAKES: 8 SERVINGS

- **6 cups uncooked egg noodles (about 12 ounces)**
- **2 cans (10¾ ounces each) condensed cream of chicken soup, undiluted**
- **1 cup (8 ounces) sour cream**
- **¾ cup 2% milk**
- **¼ teaspoon salt**
- **¼ teaspoon pepper**
- **3 cups cubed cooked chicken breasts**
- **1 cup crushed butter-flavored crackers (about 20 crackers)**
- **¼ cup butter, melted**

1. Preheat oven to 350°. Cook noodles according to package directions for al dente; drain.
2. In a large bowl, whisk soup, sour cream, milk, salt and pepper until blended. Stir in chicken and noodles. Transfer to a greased 13x9-in. baking dish. In a small bowl, mix crushed crackers and butter; sprinkle over top. Bake 30-35 minutes or until bubbly.

EASY TACO CASSEROLE

Your family is sure to enjoy this mildly spicy one-dish meal that boasts Southwestern flair. It's quick to make and fun to serve.
—FLO BURTNETT GAGE, OK

PREP: 15 MIN. • **BAKE:** 20 MIN.
MAKES: 6 SERVINGS

- **1 pound ground beef**
- **1 cup salsa**
- **½ cup mayonnaise**
- **2 teaspoons chili powder**
- **2 cups crushed tortilla chips**
- **1 cup (4 ounces) shredded Colby cheese**
- **1 cup (4 ounces) shredded Monterey Jack cheese**
- **1 medium tomato, chopped**
- **2 cups shredded lettuce**

1. In a large saucepan, cook beef over medium heat until no longer pink; drain. Add the salsa, mayonnaise and chili powder.
2. In an ungreased 2-qt. baking dish, layer half of the meat mixture, chips and cheeses. Repeat layers. Bake, uncovered, at 350° for 20-25 minutes or until heated through. Just before serving, top with tomato and lettuce.

BEEF NOODLE CASSEROLE

This casserole is perfect when there's a busy day coming up because you can prepare it in advance and store in the freezer. The ingredients blend together to create a delicious flavor combination.
—GRACE LEMA WINTON, CA

PREP: 20 MIN. • **BAKE:** 45 MIN.
MAKES: 8-10 SERVINGS

- **1 package (8 ounces) egg noodles**
- **2 pounds ground beef**
- **1 large onion, chopped**
- **1 medium green pepper, chopped**
- **1 can (14¾ ounces) cream-style corn**
- **1 can (10¾ ounces) condensed tomato soup, undiluted**
- **1 can (8 ounces) tomato sauce**
- **1 jar (2 ounces) sliced pimientos, drained**
- **2 tablespoons chopped jalapeno pepper**
- **1½ teaspoons salt**
- **½ teaspoon chili powder**
- **¼ teaspoon ground mustard**
- **¼ teaspoon pepper**
- **1 jar (4½ ounces) sliced mushrooms, drained**
- **1½ cups (6 ounces) shredded cheddar cheese**

1. Cook noodles according to package directions.
2. Meanwhile, in a large skillet, cook the beef, onion and green pepper over medium heat until the meat is no longer pink and vegetables are tender; drain. Add the next 10 ingredients. Drain noodles; stir into mixture.
3. Transfer to a greased 13x9-in. baking dish. Sprinkle with shredded cheese. Bake, uncovered, at 350° for 45 minutes or until heated through.
FREEZE OPTION *Cool unbaked casserole; cover and freeze. To use, partially thaw in refrigerator overnight. Remove from refrigerator 30 minutes before baking. Preheat oven to 350°. Bake casserole as directed, increasing time as necessary to heat through and for a thermometer inserted in center to read 165°.*
NOTE *Wear disposable gloves when cutting hot peppers; the oils can burn skin. Avoid touching your face.*

GRILLED CHEESE & TOMATO SOUP BAKE

This superstar of a casserole unites two classic comfort foods: grilled cheese sandwiches and tomato soup. There's no need for hands to get messy dipping into a bowl of hot soup. Best of all, my picky-eater husband devours every bite.
—**MEGAN KUNS** PERRYSBURG, OH

PREP: 25 MIN. • **BAKE:** 25 MIN. + STANDING
MAKES: 6 SERVINGS

- **3 ounces reduced-fat cream cheese**
- **1½ teaspoons dried basil, divided**
- **12 slices Italian, sourdough or rye bread (½ inch thick)**
- **6 slices part-skim mozzarella cheese**
- **6 tablespoons butter, softened**
- **½ cup tomato paste**
- **1 garlic clove, minced**
- **¼ teaspoon salt**
- **¼ teaspoon pepper**
- **1¾ cups 2% milk**
- **2 large eggs**
- **1 cup (4 ounces) shredded Italian cheese blend or part-skim mozzarella cheese**

1. Preheat oven to 350°. In a small bowl, mix the cream cheese and 1 teaspoon basil until blended; spread onto six bread slices. Top with the mozzarella cheese and remaining bread. Spread outsides of sandwiches with butter. Arrange in a greased 13x9-in. baking dish.
2. In a small saucepan, combine tomato paste, garlic, salt, pepper and remaining basil; cook and stir over medium heat 1 minute. Gradually whisk in milk; bring to a boil. Reduce heat; simmer, uncovered, 4-5 minutes or until thickened, stirring frequently. Remove from heat.
3. Whisk the eggs in a large bowl; gradually whisk in a third of the milk mixture. Stir in remaining milk mixture; pour over sandwiches. Sprinkle with Italian cheese blend.
4. Bake, uncovered, for 25-30 minutes or until golden brown and cheese is melted. Let stand for 10 minutes before serving.

BROCCOLI-HAM HOT DISH

One of my friends gave me this recipe. My family loves it because it includes broccoli, one of our favorite vegetables. I love that it's a colorful addition to the table and a delicious way to use up leftover ham.

—MARGARET ALLEN ABINGDON, VA

PREP: 20 MIN. • **BAKE:** 30 MIN.
MAKES: 8 SERVINGS

- **2 packages (10 ounces each) frozen cut broccoli**
- **2 cups cooked rice**
- **6 tablespoons butter, cubed**
- **2 cups fresh bread crumbs (about 2½ slices)**
- **1 medium onion, chopped**
- **3 tablespoons all-purpose flour**
- **1 teaspoon salt**
- **¼ teaspoon pepper**
- **3 cups milk**
- **1½ pounds fully cooked ham, cubed**
- **Shredded cheddar or Swiss cheese**

1. Preheat oven to 350°. Cook broccoli according to package directions; drain. Spoon rice into a 13x9-in. baking pan. Place broccoli over rice.

2. Melt the butter in a large skillet. Sprinkle 2 tablespoons of melted butter over the bread crumbs and set aside. In remaining butter, saute onion until soft. Add flour, salt and pepper, stirring constantly until blended; stir in milk. Bring to a boil; cook and stir 2 minutes or until thickened. Add ham.

3. Pour over rice and broccoli. Sprinkle with crumbs. Bake 30 minutes or until heated through. Sprinkle with cheese; let stand 5 minutes before serving.

WINTER DAY DINNER

I rely on this recipe to warm us up during the cold-weather months. When it comes to casseroles, my husband doesn't care for noodles. So I look for creative recipes that call for potatoes.

—LINDA HAGEDORN ROCKVILLE, MD

PREP: 25 MIN. • **BAKE:** 1½ HOURS
MAKES: 8 SERVINGS

- **1½ pounds ground beef**
- **1 medium onion, chopped**
- **2 tablespoons Worcestershire sauce**
- **1 teaspoon salt**
- **½ teaspoon pepper**
- **8 medium potatoes, sliced**
- **1 package (16 ounces) frozen peas, thawed**

CHEESE SAUCE

- **¼ cup butter, cubed**
- **⅓ cup all-purpose flour**
- **½ teaspoon salt**
- **¼ teaspoon pepper**
- **2 cups milk**
- **4 ounces process cheese (Velveeta), cubed**

1. In a large skillet, cook the beef and onion over medium heat until meat is no longer pink; drain. Stir in the Worcestershire sauce, salt and pepper.

2. Place half of the potatoes in a greased 13x9-in. baking dish; layer with meat mixture, peas and remaining potatoes. Set aside.

3. In a large saucepan, melt butter over medium heat. Stir in the flour, salt and pepper until smooth. Gradually stir in milk. Bring to a boil; cook and stir for 2 minutes or until thickened. Stir in cheese until melted. Pour over potatoes.

4. Cover and bake at 350° for 1½ hours or until potatoes are tender.

CHIPOTLE SHREDDED BEEF, 132

SLOW COOKER BEEF AU JUS, 139

EASY SLOW COOKER MAC & CHEESE, 129

MANGO-PINEAPPLE CHICKEN TACOS, 134

SLOW COOKER DINNERS

Slow cookers put you on the fast track to fixing dinner. All it takes is a few minutes of prep in the morning plus the flip of a switch. When you come home from your busy day, a hearty dinner awaits. Dig in to this unbeatable mix-it-and-forget-it convenience with any of these tantalizing entrees.

SLOW COOKER PIZZA CASSEROLE

A comforting casserole with mass appeal is just what you need when cooking for a crowd. For added convenience, it stays warm in a slow cooker.

—VIRGINIA KRITES CRIDERSVILLE, OH

PREP: 20 MIN. • **COOK:** 2 HOURS
MAKES: 12-14 SERVINGS

- **1 package (16 ounces) rigatoni or large tube pasta**
- **1½ pounds ground beef**
- **1 small onion, chopped**
- **4 cups (16 ounces) shredded part-skim mozzarella cheese**
- **2 cans (15 ounces each) pizza sauce**
- **1 can (10¾ ounces) condensed cream of mushroom soup, undiluted**
- **1 package (8 ounces) sliced pepperoni**

1. Cook the pasta according to package directions. Meanwhile, in a skillet, cook beef and onion over medium heat until meat is no longer pink; drain.

2. Drain the pasta; place in a 5-qt. slow cooker. Stir in the beef mixture, shredded cheese, pizza sauce, soup and pepperoni. Cover and cook on low for 2-3 hours or until heated through.

TOP-RATED ITALIAN POT ROAST

I'm always collecting recipes from newspapers and magazines, and this one just sounded too good not to try. You'll love the blend of wholesome ingredients and aromatic spices.

—KAREN BURDELL LAFAYETTE, CO

PREP: 30 MIN. • **COOK:** 6 HOURS
MAKES: 8 SERVINGS

- **1 cinnamon stick (3 inches)**
- **6 whole peppercorns**
- **4 whole cloves**
- **3 whole allspice berries**
- **2 teaspoons olive oil**
- **1 boneless beef chuck roast (2 pounds)**
- **2 celery ribs, sliced**
- **2 medium carrots, sliced**
- **1 large onion, chopped**
- **4 garlic cloves, minced**
- **1 cup dry sherry or reduced-sodium beef broth**
- **1 can (28 ounces) crushed tomatoes**
- **¼ teaspoon salt**
- **Hot cooked egg noodles and minced parsley, optional**

1. Place cinnamon stick, peppercorns, cloves and allspice berries on a double thickness of cheesecloth. Gather corners of cloth to enclose spices; tie securely with string.

2. In a large skillet, heat olive oil over medium-high heat. Brown roast on all sides; transfer to a 4-qt. slow cooker. Add celery, carrots and spice bag.

3. Add onion to same skillet; cook and stir until tender. Add the garlic; cook 1 minute longer. Add sherry, stirring to loosen browned bits from pan. Bring to a boil; cook and stir until liquid is reduced to ⅔ cup. Stir in tomatoes and salt; pour over roast and vegetables.

4. Cook, covered, on low 6-7 hours or until meat and vegetables are tender. Remove roast from slow cooker; keep warm. Discard spice bag; skim fat from sauce. Serve roast and sauce with noodles and parsley, if desired.

FREEZE OPTION *Place sliced pot roast in freezer containers; top with sauce. Cool and freeze. To use, partially thaw in refrigerator overnight. Heat through in a covered saucepan, stirring gently and adding a little broth if necessary.*

SLOW-COOKED STUFFED PEPPERS

I use the slow cooker more than anyone I know. I love the convenience of walking in the door and having a meal ready to go. My stuffed peppers are a favorite because they're healthy and easy. Unlike other stuffed pepper recipes, there's no need to parboil the peppers.

—MICHELLE GURNSEY LINCOLN, NE

PREP: 15 MIN. • **COOK:** 3 HOURS
MAKES: 4 SERVINGS

- **4 medium sweet red peppers**
- **1 can (15 ounces) black beans, rinsed and drained**
- **1 cup (4 ounces) shredded pepper jack cheese**
- **¾ cup salsa**
- **1 small onion, chopped**
- **½ cup frozen corn**
- **⅓ cup uncooked converted long grain rice**
- **1¼ teaspoons chili powder**
- **½ teaspoon ground cumin**
- **Reduced-fat sour cream, optional**

1. Cut and discard tops from peppers; remove seeds. In a large bowl, mix beans, cheese, salsa, onion, corn, rice, chili powder and cumin; spoon into peppers. Place in a 5-qt. slow cooker coated with cooking spray.

2. Cook, covered, on low 3-4 hours or until peppers are tender and filling is heated through. If desired, serve with sour cream.

TOP TIP

Make-Ahead Peppers

Stuffed peppers are my specialty for fall potlucks. Peppers are abundant in summer in both the garden and at farmers markets, so that's when I stock up and freeze them. To prepare the peppers for freezing, wash well; remove seeds and stem. Blanch for 3 minutes; drain well and freeze on a waxed paper-lined cookie sheet. Once frozen, place them in plastic freezer bags and enjoy them all fall and winter long.

—RUTH J. ALBUQUERQUE, NM

SLOW-COOKED BARBECUED PORK SANDWICHES

These saucy sandwiches are great for a hungry crowd and easy to prepare. The tender pulled barbecued pork has an unexpected, pleasant hint of lemon. Once the meat is cooked, transfer it to a slow cooker to keep it warm until it's time to serve.
—KIMBERLY WALLACE DENNISON, OH

PREP: 20 MIN. • **COOK:** 9 HOURS • **MAKES:** 10 SERVINGS

- **1 medium onion, chopped**
- **1 tablespoon butter**
- **1 can (15 ounces) tomato puree**
- **½ cup packed brown sugar**
- **¼ cup steak sauce**
- **2 tablespoons lemon juice**
- **½ teaspoon salt**
- **1 boneless pork shoulder butt roast (3 pounds)**
- **10 hard rolls, split**
- **Coleslaw, optional**

1. In a large skillet, saute onion in butter until tender. Stir in the tomato puree, brown sugar, steak sauce, lemon juice and salt. Cook over medium heat until sugar is dissolved and heated through.
2. Place roast in a 5-qt. slow cooker; pour sauce over the top. Cover and cook on low for 7-9 hours or until meat is tender. Remove roast; cool slightly. Skim fat from cooking juices. Shred meat with two forks and return to the slow cooker; heat through. Serve on rolls. Top with coleslaw if desired.

HERBED SLOW COOKER CHICKEN

I use my slow cooker to prepare these well-seasoned chicken breasts that cook up moist and tender. My daughter, who has young kids to keep up with, shared this great recipe with me several years ago. I've since made it repeatedly.
—SUNDRA HAUCK BOGALUSA, LA

PREP: 5 MIN. • **COOK:** 4 HOURS • **MAKES:** 4 SERVINGS

- **1 tablespoon olive oil**
- **1 teaspoon paprika**
- **½ teaspoon garlic powder**
- **½ teaspoon seasoned salt**
- **½ teaspoon dried thyme**
- **½ teaspoon dried basil**
- **½ teaspoon pepper**
- **½ teaspoon browning sauce, optional**
- **4 bone-in chicken breast halves (8 ounces each)**
- **½ cup chicken broth**

In a small bowl, combine the first eight ingredients; rub over chicken. Place in a 5-qt. slow cooker; add broth. Cover and cook on low for 4-5 hours or until chicken is tender.

TOP TIP

Shredding Meat for Sandwiches

Remove cooked meat from pan or slow cooker with a slotted spoon if necessary. Reserve cooking liquid if called for. Place meat in a shallow pan to catch drippings. With two forks, pull meat into thin shreds. Return shredded meat to the pan or slow cooker to warm or use as the recipe directs.

EASY SLOW COOKER MAC & CHEESE

My sons always cheer, "You're the best mom in the world!" whenever I make this creamy mac and cheese perfection. You can't beat a response like that!

—HEIDI FLEEK HAMBURG, PA

PREP: 25 MIN. • **COOK:** 1 HOUR • **MAKES:** 8 SERVINGS

- **2 cups uncooked elbow macaroni**
- **1 can (10¾ ounces) condensed cheddar cheese soup, undiluted**
- **1 cup 2% milk**
- **½ cup sour cream**
- **¼ cup butter, cubed**
- **½ teaspoon onion powder**
- **¼ teaspoon white pepper**
- **⅛ teaspoon salt**
- **1 cup (4 ounces) shredded cheddar cheese**
- **1 cup (4 ounces) shredded fontina cheese**
- **1 cup (4 ounces) shredded provolone cheese**

1. Cook macaroni according to package directions for al dente. Meanwhile, in a large saucepan, combine soup, milk, sour cream, butter and seasonings; cook and stir over medium-low heat until blended. Stir in cheeses until melted.

2. Drain macaroni; transfer to a greased 3-qt. slow cooker. Stir in cheese mixture. Cook, covered, on low 1-2 hours or until heated through.

CHICKEN & MUSHROOM ALFREDO

Everyone in my family loves when I make this dinner, even my kids! My favorite advantage of this recipe is that I can add whatever vegetables I have on hand to make it heartier. I usually toss in corn, peas or diced red bell pepper.

—MONICA WERNER ONTARIO, CA

PREP: 20 MIN. • **COOK:** 4 HOURS • **MAKES:** 4 SERVINGS

- **4 bone-in chicken breast halves (12 to 14 ounces each), skin removed**
- **2 tablespoons canola oil**
- **1 can (10¾ ounces) condensed cream of chicken soup, undiluted**
- **1 can (10¾ ounces) condensed cream of mushroom soup, undiluted**
- **1 cup chicken broth**
- **1 small onion, chopped**
- **1 jar (6 ounces) sliced mushrooms, drained**
- **¼ teaspoon garlic salt**
- **¼ teaspoon pepper**
- **8 ounces fettuccine**
- **1 package (8 ounces) cream cheese, softened and cubed**
- **Shredded Parmesan cheese, optional**

1. In a large skillet, brown the chicken in oil in batches. Transfer to a 4- or 5-qt. slow cooker. In a large bowl, combine the soups, broth, onion, mushrooms, garlic salt and pepper; pour over meat. Cover and cook on low for 4-5 hours or until chicken is tender.

2. Cook fettuccine according to package directions; drain. Remove chicken from slow cooker and keep warm. Turn the slow cooker off and stir in cream cheese until melted. Serve chicken and sauce with fettucine. Top with Parmesan cheese if desired.

SPICY COWBOY CHILI

Toasting the peppers for this chili releases their earthy flavors, but wear gloves when handling dried peppers and seeds.
—RACHEL SPRINKEL HILO, HI

PREP: 45 MIN. • **COOK:** 7 HOURS • **MAKES:** 14 SERVINGS (3½ QUARTS)

- **1 whole garlic bulb**
- **2 to 3 tablespoons olive oil, divided**
- **2 dried ancho chilies**
- **2 dried chipotle chilies**
- **1 bottle (12 ounces) dark beer**
- **3 pounds beef stew meat, cut into ¾-inch pieces**
- **2 large onions, chopped**
- **3 cans (16 ounces each) kidney beans, rinsed and drained**
- **3 cans (14½ ounces each) diced tomatoes, undrained**
- **2 cans (8 ounces each) tomato sauce**
- **2 tablespoons Worcestershire sauce**
- **1 tablespoon chili powder**
- **1 teaspoon pepper**
- **½ teaspoon salt**
- **Shredded cheddar cheese, optional**

1. Preheat oven to 425°. Remove papery outer skin from garlic bulb, but do not peel or separate the cloves. Cut off top of garlic bulb, exposing individual cloves. Brush cut cloves with 1 teaspoon oil. Wrap in foil. Bake 30-35 minutes or until cloves are soft. Unwrap and cool slightly. Squeeze garlic from skins; mash with a fork.
2. Meanwhile, in a large dry skillet over medium-high heat, toast chilies on both sides until puffy, about 3-6 minutes. (Do not blacken.) Cool. Remove stems and seeds; coarsely chop chilies. Place in a small bowl; cover with beer. Let stand to soften, about 30 minutes.
3. In the same skillet, heat 1 tablespoon oil over medium-high heat. Brown beef in batches, adding additional oil if needed; transfer to a 6-qt. slow cooker. In the skillet, heat 2 teaspoons oil over medium heat. Add onions; cook and stir until tender. Add to beef.
4. Stir in the remaining ingredients, mashed garlic and dried chilies mixture. Cover and cook on low 7-9 hours or until meat is tender. If desired, serve with cheese.
NOTE *One-half teaspoon ground chipotle pepper may be substituted for the dried chipotle chilies; add ground chipotle with mashed garlic and beer mixture to slow cooker.*

EASY CITRUS HAM

I created this recipe many years ago with items I already had on hand. The succulent ham has a mild citrus flavor. It was so popular at a church social that I knew I had a winner!
—SHEILA CHRISTENSEN SAN MARCOS, CA

PREP: 15 MIN. • **COOK:** 4 HOURS + STANDING
MAKES: 10-12 SERVINGS

- **1 boneless fully cooked ham (3 to 4 pounds)**
- **½ cup packed dark brown sugar**
- **1 can (12 ounces) lemon-lime soda, divided**
- **1 medium navel orange, thinly sliced**
- **1 medium lemon, thinly sliced**
- **1 medium lime, thinly sliced**
- **1 tablespoon chopped crystallized ginger**

1. Cut ham in half; place in a 5-qt. slow cooker. In a small bowl, combine brown sugar and 1/4 cup soda; rub over ham. Top with orange, lemon and lime slices. Add candied ginger and remaining soda to the slow cooker.
2. Cover and cook on low for 4-5 hours or until a thermometer reads 140°, basting occasionally with cooking juices. Let stand for 10 minutes before slicing.

(5) INGREDIENTS

HAWAIIAN SAUSAGE SUBS

If you are looking for a different way to use kielbasa, the sweet and mildly spicy flavor of these sandwiches is a nice change of pace. These are great for birthday parties or potlucks.
—JUDY DAMES BRIDGEVILLE, PA

PREP: 15 MIN. • **COOK:** 3 HOURS • **MAKES:** 12 SERVINGS

- **3 pounds smoked kielbasa or Polish sausage, cut into 3-inch pieces**
- **2 bottles (12 ounces each) chili sauce**
- **1 can (20 ounces) pineapple tidbits, undrained**
- **¼ cup packed brown sugar**
- **12 hoagie buns, split**

Place kielbasa in a 3-qt. slow cooker. Combine the chili sauce, pineapple and brown sugar; pour over kielbasa. Cover and cook on low for 3-4 hours or until heated through. Serve on buns.

SLOW-COOKED PORK ROAST

Here's a tasty meal that's wonderful for the hot, sticky months of summer, when you don't want to turn on the oven. But it's so good, it will end up a favorite you'll serve all year long.
—MARION LOWERY MEDFORD, OR

PREP: 20 MIN. • **COOK:** 6 HOURS + STANDING • **MAKES:** 12 SERVINGS

- **2 cans (8 ounces each) unsweetened crushed pineapple, undrained**
- **1 cup barbecue sauce**
- **2 tablespoons unsweetened apple juice**
- **1 tablespoon minced fresh rosemary or 1 teaspoon dried rosemary, crushed**
- **1 teaspoon minced garlic**
- **2 teaspoons grated lemon peel**
- **1 teaspoon liquid smoke, optional**
- **½ teaspoon salt**
- **¼ teaspoon pepper**
- **1 boneless pork loin roast (3 to 4 pounds)**

1. In a large saucepan, combine the first nine ingredients. Bring to a boil. Reduce heat; simmer, uncovered, for 3 minutes.
2. Meanwhile, cut roast in half. In a nonstick skillet coated with cooking spray, brown pork roast on all sides.
3. Place roast in a 5-qt. slow cooker. Pour sauce over roast and turn to coat. Cover and cook on low for 6-7 hours or until meat is tender. Let stand for 10 minutes before slicing.

GREAT NORTHERN BEAN CHILI

My easy version of Southwestern chicken chili uses just a few ingredients. I like to serve it with tortilla chips, sour cream and a dash of hot sauce on top. It's a great alternative to traditional chili.
—MAMESMOM FROM TASTE OF HOME.COM.

PREP: 20 MIN. • **COOK:** 4 HOURS • **MAKES:** 8 SERVINGS

- **2 pounds boneless skinless chicken breasts, cut into 1-inch cubes**
- **1 tablespoon canola oil**
- **1 jar (48 ounces) great northern beans, rinsed and drained**
- **1 jar (16 ounces) salsa**
- **1 can (14½ ounces) chicken broth**
- **1 teaspoon ground cumin, optional**
- **2 cups (8 ounces) shredded Monterey Jack cheese**

In a large skillet, brown chicken in oil. In a 4- or 5-qt. slow cooker, combine the beans, salsa, broth, cumin if desired and chicken. Cover and cook on low for 4-6 hours or until chicken is tender. Serve with cheese.

CHIPOTLE SHREDDED BEEF

This beef is delicious all rolled up in a tortilla, served with corn salsa and eaten as a burrito. You could also serve it over rice or mashed potatoes or in buns—so many possibilities!

—**DARCY WILLIAMS** OMAHA, NE

PREP: 25 MIN. • **COOK:** 8 HOURS • **MAKES:** 10 SERVINGS

- **1 teaspoon canola oil**
- **1 small onion, chopped**
- **1 can (28 ounces) diced tomatoes, undrained**
- **¼ cup cider vinegar**
- **¼ cup chopped chipotle peppers in adobo sauce plus 2 teaspoons sauce**
- **6 garlic cloves, minced**
- **2 tablespoons brown sugar**
- **2 bay leaves**
- **½ teaspoon ground cumin**
- **½ teaspoon paprika**
- **½ teaspoon pepper**
- **¼ teaspoon ground cinnamon**
- **1 boneless beef chuck roast (2½ pounds)**
- **5 cups cooked brown rice**
- **Shredded reduced-fat cheddar cheese and reduced-fat sour cream, optional**

1. In a large skillet coated with cooking spray, heat oil over medium-high heat. Add onion; cook and stir 2-3 minutes or until tender. Stir in tomatoes, vinegar, peppers with sauce, garlic, brown sugar, bay leaves and spices. Bring to a boil. Reduce heat; simmer, uncovered, 4-6 minutes or until thickened.

2. Place roast in a 5-qt. slow cooker; add tomato mixture. Cook, covered, on low 8-10 hours or until meat is tender.

3. Discard bay leaves. Remove roast; cool slightly. Skim fat from cooking juices. Shred beef with two forks. Return beef and cooking juices to slow cooker; heat through. Serve with rice. If desired, top with cheese and sour cream.

FREEZE OPTION *Freeze cooled meat mixture and juices in freezer containers. To use, partially thaw in refrigerator overnight. Heat through in a saucepan, stirring occasionally and adding a little water if necessary.*

SLOW COOKER LIME CHICKEN CHILI

Lime juice gives this chili a zesty twist, while canned tomatoes and beans make preparation a breeze. It's fun to top with homemade toasted tortilla strips.

—**DIANE RANDAZZO** SINKING SPRING, PA

PREP: 25 MIN. • **COOK:** 4 HOURS • **MAKES:** 6 SERVINGS (2 QUARTS)

- **1 medium onion, chopped**
- **1 each medium sweet yellow, red and green peppers, chopped**
- **2 tablespoons olive oil**
- **3 garlic cloves, minced**
- **1 pound ground chicken**
- **2 cans (14½ ounces each) diced tomatoes, undrained**
- **1 can (15 ounces) white kidney or cannellini beans, rinsed and drained**
- **¼ cup lime juice**
- **1 tablespoon all-purpose flour**
- **1 tablespoon baking cocoa**
- **1 tablespoon ground cumin**
- **1 tablespoon chili powder**
- **2 teaspoons ground coriander**
- **1 teaspoon grated lime peel**
- **½ teaspoon salt**
- **½ teaspoon garlic pepper blend**
- **¼ teaspoon pepper**
- **2 flour tortillas (8 inches), cut into ¼-inch strips**
- **6 tablespoons reduced-fat sour cream**

1. In a large skillet, saute onion and peppers in oil for 7-8 minutes or until crisp-tender. Add garlic; cook 1 minute longer. Add chicken; cook and stir over medium heat for 8-9 minutes or until meat is no longer pink.

2. Transfer to a 3-qt. slow cooker. Stir in the tomatoes, beans, lime juice, flour, cocoa, cumin, chili powder, coriander, lime peel, salt, garlic pepper and pepper.

3. Cover and cook on low 4-5 hours or until heated through.

4. Place tortilla strips on a baking sheet coated with cooking spray. Bake at 400° for 8-10 minutes or until crisp. Serve chili with sour cream and tortilla strips.

"Delicious! I added an extra ½ teaspoon of salt and used prepackaged tortilla strips that you use for salads. I also added some hot sauce to my portion to give it a little more kick."

—**IMMANDA** FROM TASTEOFHOME.COM

MANGO-PINEAPPLE CHICKEN TACOS

I lived in the Caribbean when I was growing up, and the fresh tropical fruits in this delectable chicken entree bring me back to my childhood.

—LISSA NELSON PROVO, UT

PREP: 25 MIN. • **COOK:** 5 HOURS
MAKES: 16 SERVINGS

- **2 medium mangoes, peeled and chopped**
- **1½ cups cubed fresh pineapple or canned pineapple chunks, drained**
- **2 medium tomatoes, chopped**
- **1 medium red onion, finely chopped**
- **2 small Anaheim peppers, seeded and chopped**
- **2 green onions, finely chopped**
- **1 tablespoon lime juice**
- **1 teaspoon sugar**
- **4 pounds bone-in chicken breast halves, skin removed**
- **3 teaspoons salt**
- **¼ cup packed brown sugar**
- **32 taco shells, warmed**
- **¼ cup minced fresh cilantro**

1. In a large bowl, combine the first eight ingredients. Place chicken in a 6-qt. slow cooker; sprinkle with salt and brown sugar. Top with mango mixture. Cover and cook on low for 5-6 hours or until chicken is tender.

2. Remove chicken; cool slightly. Strain cooking juices, reserving mango mixture and ½ cup juices. Discard remaining juices. When cool enough to handle, remove chicken from bones; discard bones.

3. Shred chicken with two forks. Return chicken and reserved mango mixture and cooking juices to slow cooker; heat through. Serve in taco shells; sprinkle with cilantro.

FREEZE OPTION *Freeze cooled meat mixture in freezer containers. To use, partially thaw in refrigerator overnight. Heat through in a saucepan, stirring occasionally and adding a little broth if necessary.*

CREAMY CHICKEN & BROCCOLI STEW

No one will ever guess how easy it is to make this recipe. My husband, who doesn't like many chicken dishes, requests this one regularly.

—MARY WATKINS LITTLE ELM, TX

PREP: 15 MIN. • **COOK:** 6 HOURS
MAKES: 8 SERVINGS

- **8 bone-in chicken thighs, skin removed (about 3 pounds)**
- **1 cup Italian salad dressing**
- **½ cup white wine or chicken broth**
- **6 tablespoons butter, melted, divided**
- **1 tablespoon dried minced onion**
- **1 tablespoon garlic powder**
- **1 tablespoon Italian seasoning**
- **¾ teaspoon salt, divided**
- **¾ teaspoon pepper, divided**
- **1 can (10¾ ounces) condensed cream of mushroom soup, undiluted**
- **1 package (8 ounces) cream cheese, softened**
- **2 cups frozen broccoli florets, thawed**
- **2 pounds red potatoes, quartered**

1. Place chicken in a 4-qt. slow cooker. Combine the salad dressing, wine, 4 tablespoons butter, onion, garlic powder, Italian seasoning, ½ teaspoon salt and ½ teaspoon pepper in a small bowl; pour over chicken.

2. Cover and cook on low for 5 hours. Skim fat. Combine the soup, cream cheese and 2 cups of liquid from slow cooker in a small bowl until blended; add to slow cooker.

3. Cover and cook 45 minutes longer or until chicken is tender, adding the broccoli during the last 30 minutes of cooking.

4. Meanwhile, place potatoes in a large saucepan and cover with water. Bring to a boil. Reduce heat; cover and simmer for 15-20 minutes or until tender. Drain and return to pan. Mash potatoes with the remaining butter, salt and pepper. Serve with chicken and broccoli mixture.

MELT-IN-YOUR-MOUTH CHUCK ROAST

We like well-seasoned foods in our house, so this recipe is perfect for our palates. You'll love how flavorful and tender this roast turns out.

—BETTE MCCUMBER SCHENECTADY, NY

PREP: 20 MIN. • **COOK:** 5 HOURS
MAKES: 6 SERVINGS

- **1 large onion, sliced**
- **1 medium green pepper, sliced**
- **1 celery rib, chopped**
- **1 boneless beef chuck roast (2 to 3 pounds)**
- **1 can (14½ ounces) Italian stewed tomatoes**
- **½ cup beef broth**
- **½ cup ketchup**
- **3 tablespoons brown sugar**
- **2 tablespoons Worcestershire sauce**
- **4½ teaspoons prepared mustard**
- **3 garlic cloves, minced**
- **1 tablespoon soy sauce**
- **2 teaspoons pepper**
- **¼ teaspoon crushed red pepper flakes**
- **3 tablespoons cornstarch**
- **¼ cup cold water**

1. Place the onion, green pepper and celery in a 5-qt. slow cooker; add the roast. In a large bowl, combine the tomatoes, broth, ketchup, brown sugar, Worcestershire sauce, mustard, garlic, soy sauce, pepper and pepper flakes; pour over meat. Cover and cook on low for 5-6 hours or until meat is tender.

2. Remove meat and vegetables; keep warm. Skim fat from cooking juices if necessary; transfer to a small saucepan. Combine cornstarch and cold water until smooth; stir into cooking juices. Bring to a boil; cook and stir for 2 minutes or until thickened. Serve with roast.

FREEZE OPTION *Cool beef and gravy mixture. Freeze in freezer containers. To use, partially thaw in refrigerator overnight. Heat through slowly in a covered skillet until a thermometer inserted in beef reads 165°, stirring occasionally and adding a little broth or water if necessary.*

GREEN CHILI SHREDDED PORK

Slow cooker pork with green chilies always makes my hungry clan happy. I look forward to the creative possibilities for using up the leftovers.

—**MARY SHIVERS** ADA, OK

PREP: 10 MIN. • **COOK:** 6 HOURS
MAKES: 8 SERVINGS

- **1 boneless pork loin roast (3 to 4 pounds)**
- **1½ cups apple cider or juice**
- **1 can (4 ounces) chopped green chilies, drained**
- **3 garlic cloves, minced**
- **1½ teaspoons salt**
- **1½ teaspoons hot pepper sauce**
- **1 teaspoon chili powder**
- **1 teaspoon pepper**
- **½ teaspoon ground cumin**
- **½ teaspoon dried oregano**
- **16 flour tortillas (8 inches)**
- **Optional toppings: chopped peeled mango, shredded lettuce, chopped fresh cilantro and lime wedges**

1. Place pork in a 5- or 6-qt. slow cooker. In a small bowl, mix cider, green chilies, garlic, salt, pepper sauce, chili powder, pepper, cumin and oregano; pour over pork. Cook, covered, on low 6-8 hours or until meat is tender.

2. Remove roast; cool slightly. Shred pork with two forks. Return to slow cooker; heat through. Using tongs, serve pork in tortillas with toppings as desired.

FREEZE OPTION *Place shredded pork in freezer containers; top with cooking juices. Cool and freeze. To use, partially thaw in refrigerator overnight. Heat through in a saucepan, stirring occasionally.*

SLOW-COOKED SHEPHERD'S PIE

Shepherd's pie is to the British what meat loaf is to Americans, so as a young child living in the U.K., the mashed potato-topped dish was a weekly staple. This is my go-to recipe when I'm longing for the sights and smells of my mother's kitchen.
—MARI SITKIEWICZ DOWNERS GROVE, IL

PREP: 35 MIN. • **COOK:** 5¼ HOURS
MAKES: 5 SERVINGS

- **2 pounds medium Yukon Gold potatoes, peeled and quartered**
- **2 tablespoons butter**
- **¼ to ⅓ cup 2% milk**
- **¾ teaspoon salt, divided**
- **½ teaspoon pepper, divided**
- **1 pound ground beef**
- **1 large onion, chopped**
- **2 garlic cloves, minced**
- **3 tablespoons tomato paste**
- **1¾ cups sliced fresh mushrooms**
- **2 medium carrots, chopped**
- **1 cup beef broth**
- **¼ cup dry white wine**
- **2 teaspoons Worcestershire sauce**
- **½ teaspoon dried thyme**
- **⅓ cup frozen peas**
- **½ cup shredded Monterey Jack cheese**
- **1 tablespoon minced fresh parsley**

1. Place potatoes in a large saucepan and cover with water. Bring to a boil. Reduce the heat; cover and cook for 10-15 minutes or until tender. Drain, then shake over low heat for 1 minute to dry. Mash potatoes, gradually adding butter and enough milk to reach the desired consistency. Stir in ½ teaspoon salt and ¼ teaspoon pepper.
2. Meanwhile, in a large skillet, cook the beef, onion, and garlic over medium heat until meat is no longer pink; drain.
3. Add tomato paste; cook 2 minutes. Add the mushrooms, carrots, broth, wine, Worcestershire sauce and thyme. Bring to a boil. Reduce heat; simmer, uncovered, until most of the liquid is evaporated. Stir in peas. Season with remaining salt and pepper.
4. Transfer beef mixture to a greased 4-qt. slow cooker. Spread mashed potatoes over top. Cover and cook on low for 5-6 hours or until bubbly. Sprinkle with cheese. Cover and cook 10 minutes longer or until cheese is melted. Just before serving, sprinkle with parsley.

BAKE OPTION *Transfer cooked beef mixture to a greased 8-in. square baking dish. Spread mashed potatoes over top. Sprinkle with cheese. Bake, uncovered, at 350° for 30-40 minutes or until bubbly and topping is lightly browned. Sprinkle with parsley.*

(5) INGREDIENTS

MAPLE MUSTARD CHICKEN

This recipe is one of my husband's top picks. It only calls for five ingredients, and we try to have them on hand all the time for a delicious and cozy dinner.
—JENNIFER SEIDEL MIDLAND, MI

PREP: 5 MIN. • **COOK:** 3 HOURS
MAKES: 6 SERVINGS

- **6 boneless skinless chicken breast halves (6 ounces each)**
- **½ cup maple syrup**
- **⅓ cup stone-ground mustard**
- **2 tablespoons quick-cooking tapioca**
- **Hot cooked brown rice**

Place the chicken in a 3-qt. slow cooker. In a small bowl, combine the syrup, mustard and tapioca; pour over chicken. Cover and cook on low 3-4 hours or until tender. Serve with rice.

FREEZE OPTION *Cool chicken in sauce. Freeze in freezer containers. To use, partially thaw in refrigerator overnight. Heat through slowly in a covered skillet until a thermometer inserted in chicken reads 165°, stirring occasionally and adding a little broth or water if necessary.*

SLOW-COOKED STROGANOFF

I've been preparing Stroganoff in my slow cooker for more years than I can count. Once you've done it this way, you'll never cook it on the stovetop again. It's a great meal for family or company.

—**KAREN HERBERT** PLACERVILLE, CA

PREP: 20 MIN. • **COOK:** 5 HOURS
MAKES: 8-10 SERVINGS

- **2 beef top round steaks (about ¾ inch thick and 1½ pounds each)**
- **½ cup all-purpose flour**
- **1½ teaspoons salt**
- **½ teaspoon ground mustard**
- **⅛ teaspoon pepper**
- **1 medium onion, sliced and separated into rings**
- **1 can (8 ounces) mushroom stems and pieces, drained**
- **1 can (10½ ounces) condensed beef broth, undiluted**
- **1½ cups (12 ounces) sour cream**
- **Hot cooked noodles**

1. Cut round steaks into 3x½-in. strips. In a shallow bowl, mix flour, salt, mustard and pepper. Add beef in batches; toss to coat.

2. In a 5-qt. slow cooker, layer the onion, mushrooms and beef. Pour broth over top. Cook, covered, on low 5-7 hours or until meat is tender. Just before serving, stir in sour cream. Serve with noodles.

SLOW COOKER BUFFALO CHICKEN LASAGNA

When I make this tasty chicken lasagna, I use a whole bottle of Buffalo wing sauce because my family likes it extra spicy. Feel free to increase the pasta sauce and use less wing sauce if you prefer.

—**HEIDI PEPIN** SYKESVILLE, MD

PREP: 25 MIN.
COOK: 4 HOURS + STANDING
MAKES: 8 SERVINGS

- **1½ pounds ground chicken**
- **1 tablespoon olive oil**
- **1 bottle (12 ounces) Buffalo wing sauce**
- **1½ cups meatless spaghetti sauce**
- **1 carton (15 ounces) ricotta cheese**
- **2 cups (8 ounces) shredded part-skim mozzarella cheese**
- **9 no-cook lasagna noodles**
- **2 medium sweet red peppers, chopped**
- **½ cup crumbled blue cheese or feta cheese**
- **Chopped celery and additional crumbled blue cheese, optional**

1. In a Dutch oven, cook chicken in oil over medium heat until no longer pink; drain. Stir in wing sauce and spaghetti sauce. In a small bowl, mix ricotta and mozzarella cheeses.

2. Spread 1 cup sauce onto the bottom of an oval 6-qt. slow cooker. Layer with three noodles (breaking noodles to fit), 1 cup sauce, a third of the peppers and a third of the cheese mixture. Repeat layers twice. Top with remaining sauce; sprinkle with blue cheese.

3. Cover and cook on low for 4-5 hours or until noodles are tender. Let stand 15 minutes before serving. Top with chopped celery and additional blue cheese if desired.

(5) INGREDIENTS

SLOW COOKER BEEF AU JUS

It's easy to fix this roast, which has lots of onion flavor. Sometimes I also add cubed potatoes and baby carrots to the slow cooker to make a terrific meal with plenty of leftovers.

—**CAROL HILLE** GRAND JUNCTION, CO

PREP: 20 MIN.
COOK: 6 HOURS + STANDING
MAKES: 10 SERVINGS

- **1 beef rump roast or bottom round roast (3 pounds)**
- **1 large onion, sliced**
- **¾ cup reduced-sodium beef broth**
- **1 envelope (1 ounce) au jus gravy mix**
- **2 garlic cloves, halved**
- **¼ teaspoon pepper**

1. Cut roast in half. In a large nonstick skillet coated with cooking spray, brown meat on all sides over medium-high heat.

2. Place onion in a 5-qt. slow cooker. Top with meat. Combine the broth, gravy mix, garlic and pepper; pour over meat. Cover and cook on low for 6-7 hours or until meat is tender.

3. Remove meat to a cutting board. Let stand for 10 minutes. Thinly slice meat and return to the slow cooker to keep warm; serve with cooking juices and onion.

"This was so simple and very rich and flavorful. I added two cups of baby carrots and four diced potatoes and only used a 1.5 pound roast. Definitely a keeper."

—**DANIELLEYLEE**
FROM TASTEOFHOME.COM

SLOW COOKER POT ROAST

I work full time but love to make home-cooked meals for my husband and son. It's a comfort to walk in and smell this roast that will be fall-apart tender and delicious.

—GINA JACKSON OGDENSBURG, NY

PREP: 15 MIN. • **COOK:** 6 HOURS • **MAKES:** 6 SERVINGS

- **1 cup warm water**
- **1 tablespoon beef base**
- **½ pound sliced fresh mushrooms**
- **1 large onion, coarsely chopped**
- **3 garlic cloves, minced**
- **1 boneless beef chuck roast (3 pounds)**
- **½ teaspoon pepper**
- **1 tablespoon Worcestershire sauce**
- **¼ cup butter, cubed**
- **⅓ cup all-purpose flour**
- **¼ teaspoon salt**

1. In a 5- or 6-qt. slow cooker, whisk water and beef base; add mushrooms, onion and garlic. Sprinkle roast with pepper; transfer to slow cooker. Drizzle with Worcestershire sauce. Cook, covered, on low 6-8 hours or until meat is tender.

2. Remove roast to a serving platter; tent with foil. Strain cooking juices, reserving vegetables. Skim fat from cooking juices. In a large saucepan, melt butter over medium heat. Stir in flour and salt until smooth; gradually whisk in cooking juices. Bring to a boil, stirring constantly; cook and stir 1-2 minutes or until thickened. Stir in cooked vegetables. Serve with roast.

NOTE *Look for beef base near the broth and bouillon.*

SLOW-COOKED LAMB CHOPS

Chops are without a doubt the cut of lamb we like best. I usually simmer them on low for hours in a slow cooker. The aroma is irresistible, and they come out so tender they practically melt in your mouth.

—SANDY MCKENZIE BRAHAM, MN

PREP: 10 MIN. • **COOK:** 4 HOURS • **MAKES:** 4 SERVINGS

- **1 medium onion, sliced**
- **1 teaspoon dried oregano**
- **½ teaspoon dried thyme**
- **½ teaspoon garlic powder**
- **¼ teaspoon salt**
- **⅛ teaspoon pepper**
- **8 lamb loin chops (about 1¾ pounds)**
- **2 garlic cloves, minced**

Place onion in a 3-qt. slow cooker. Combine the oregano, thyme, garlic powder, salt and pepper; rub over the lamb chops. Place chops over onion. Top with garlic. Cover and cook on low for 4-6 hours or until the meat is tender.

TOP TIP

Lamb Chops

A lamb chop is a tender bone-in cut of lamb that comes from the loin, rib and sirloin. It is often prepared by seasoning or marinating with herbs, then by cooking with a dry-heat method of baking, broiling or grilling. If you're not partial to the strong flavor of lamb, try domestic grain-fed lamb, which has a milder flavor than grass-fed lamb. Also look for lamb rather than mutton, which has a stronger flavor.

POLYNESIAN HAM SANDWICHES

The sweetness of the brown sugar and pineapple combined with the tanginess of the Dijon mustard are a perfect match in the tasty sandwich filling.

—JACKIE SMULSKI LYONS, IL

PREP: 20 MIN. • **COOK:** 3 HOURS • **MAKES:** 12 SERVINGS

- **2 pounds fully cooked ham, finely chopped**
- **1 can (20 ounces) crushed pineapple, undrained**
- **¾ cup packed brown sugar**
- **⅓ cup chopped green pepper**
- **¼ cup Dijon mustard**
- **1 green onion, chopped**
- **1 tablespoon dried minced onion**
- **12 hamburger buns or kaiser rolls, split**

In a 3-qt. slow cooker, combine the first seven ingredients. Cover and cook on low for 3-4 hours or until heated through. Using a slotted spoon, place ½ cup on each bun.

SLOW-COOKED CURRY CHICKEN

We adopted three children from Thailand. We all love the spicy flavors found in this dish. Add more or less curry depending on your taste preferences.

—HELEN TOULANTIS WANTAGH, NY

PREP: 25 MIN. • **COOK:** 4½ HOURS • **MAKES:** 6 SERVINGS

- **6 boneless skinless chicken breast halves (6 ounces each)**
- **1¼ teaspoons salt**
- **1 can (13.66 ounces) light coconut milk**
- **1 teaspoon curry powder**
- **½ teaspoon ground turmeric**
- **½ teaspoon cayenne pepper**
- **3 green onions, sliced, divided**
- **2 tablespoons cornstarch**
- **2 tablespoons cold water**
- **1 to 2 tablespoons lime juice**
- **3 cups hot cooked rice**

1. Sprinkle chicken with salt. In a large nonstick skillet coated with cooking spray, brown chicken on both sides. Place in a 5-qt. slow cooker.
2. Combine the coconut milk, curry, turmeric and cayenne; pour over chicken. Sprinkle with half of the onions. Cover and cook on low for 4-5 hours or until chicken is tender.
3. Combine cornstarch and water until smooth; stir into slow cooker. Cover and cook on high for 30 minutes or until sauce is thickened. Stir in lime juice. Serve chicken with rice and sauce; sprinkle with remaining onions.

5 INGREDIENTS

PICANTE BEEF ROAST

I created Picante Beef Roast because I love the flavor of taco seasoning and think it shouldn't be reserved just for tacos! My recipe couldn't be easier, and it works great with a pork roast, too.

—MARGARET THIEL LEVITTOWN, PA

PREP: 15 MIN. • **COOK:** 8 HOURS • **MAKES:** 8 SERVINGS

- **1 beef rump roast or bottom round roast (3 pounds), trimmed**
- **1 jar (16 ounces) picante sauce**
- **1 can (15 ounces) tomato sauce**
- **1 envelope taco seasoning**
- **3 tablespoons cornstarch**
- **¼ cup cold water**

1. Cut roast in half; place in a 5-qt. slow cooker. In a large bowl, combine the picante sauce, tomato sauce and taco seasoning; pour over roast. Cover and cook on low for 8-9 hours or until meat is tender.
2. Remove meat to a serving platter; keep warm. Skim fat from cooking juices; transfer 3 cups to a small saucepan. Bring liquid to a boil. Combine cornstarch and water until smooth. Gradually stir into the pan. Bring to a boil; cook and stir for 2 minutes or until thickened. Serve with roast.

SLOW COOKER CHICKEN DINNER

This meal-in-one, which includes juicy chicken and tasty veggies in a creamy sauce, is ready to eat when I get home from the office.

—JENET CATTAR NEPTUNE BEACH, FL

PREP: 10 MIN. • **COOK:** 8 HOURS
MAKES: 4 SERVINGS

- **6 medium red potatoes, cut into chunks**
- **4 medium carrots, cut into ½-inch pieces**
- **4 boneless skinless chicken breast halves**
- **1 can (10¾ ounces) condensed cream of chicken soup, undiluted**
- **1 can (10¾ ounces) condensed cream of mushroom soup, undiluted**
- **⅛ teaspoon garlic salt**
- **2 to 4 tablespoons mashed potato flakes, optional**

1. Place potatoes and carrots in a 5-qt. slow cooker. Top with chicken. Combine soups and garlic salt; pour over chicken.

2. Cover and cook on low for 8 hours or until the meat and vegetables are tender. To thicken, stir potato flakes into the gravy and cook 30 minutes longer, if desired.

SHORT RIBS IN RED WINE

These ribs are an easy alternative to traditionally braised short ribs. I love that I can turn my attention to other tasks while they simmer in the slow cooker.

—REBEKAH BEYER SABETHA, KS

PREP: 30 MIN. • **COOK:** 6¼ HOURS
MAKES: 6 SERVINGS

- **3 pounds bone-in beef short ribs**
- **½ teaspoon salt**
- **½ teaspoon pepper**
- **1 tablespoon canola oil**
- **4 medium carrots, cut into 1-inch pieces**
- **1 cup beef broth**
- **4 fresh thyme sprigs**
- **1 bay leaf**
- **2 large onions, cut into ½-inch wedges**
- **6 garlic cloves, minced**
- **1 tablespoon tomato paste**
- **2 cups dry red wine or beef broth**
- **4 teaspoons cornstarch**
- **3 tablespoons cold water**
- **Salt and pepper to taste**

1. Sprinkle ribs with 1/2 teaspoon each salt and pepper. In a large skillet, heat oil over medium heat. In batches, brown ribs on all sides; transfer to a 4- or 5-qt. slow cooker. Add carrots, broth, thyme and bay leaf to ribs.

2. Add onions to the same skillet; cook and stir over medium heat 8-9 minutes or until tender. Add garlic and tomato paste; cook and stir 1 minute longer. Stir in wine. Bring to a boil; cook for 8-10 minutes or until liquid is reduced by half. Add to the slow cooker. Cook, covered, on low 6-8 hours or until meat is tender.

3. Remove ribs and vegetables; keep warm. Transfer cooking juices to a small saucepan; skim fat. Discard thyme and bay leaf. Bring juices to a boil. In a small bowl, mix cornstarch and water until smooth; stir into cooking juices. Return to a boil; cook and stir 1-2 minutes or until thickened. Season with salt and pepper to taste. Serve with ribs and vegetables.

(5) INGREDIENTS

SLOW-COOKED SWISS STEAK

This recipe is a favorite because I can flour and season the steaks the night before and refrigerate them overnight. The next morning, I put everything in the slow cooker, and I have a delicious dinner waiting when I arrive home from work.

—SARAH BURKS WATHENA, KS

PREP: 10 MIN. • **COOK:** 6 HOURS
MAKES: 6 SERVINGS

- **2 tablespoons all-purpose flour**
- **½ teaspoon salt**
- **¼ teaspoon pepper**
- **1½ pounds beef round steak, cut into six pieces**
- **1 medium onion, cut into ¼-inch slices**
- **1 celery rib, cut into ½-inch slices**
- **2 cans (8 ounces each) tomato sauce**

1. In a large resealable plastic bag, combine the flour, salt and pepper. Add steak; seal bag and shake to coat.
2. Place the onion in a greased 3-qt. slow cooker. Top with steak, celery and tomato sauce. Cover and cook on low for 6-8 hours or until meat is tender.

TOP TIP

Slow Cooker Tips

Here are a few easy tips that will make using your slow cooker a cinch.

- Choose the correct size slow cooker for your recipe. A slow cooker should be from half to two-thirds full.
- Be sure the lid is sealed properly, not tilted or askew. The steam creates a seal.
- Remove food from the slow cooker within 1 hour after it's finished cooking. Promptly refrigerate any leftovers.
- Choose the proper size slow cooker for the amount of food you are making. For example, to serve a small amount of dip, smaller slow cookers are ideal. To entertain or cook for a crowd, larger slow cookers work best.

LEMON BREAD

You'll often find me baking this sunshiny-sweet bread in the kitchen when company is coming. It has a texture similar to a pound cake and it tastes just as rich, with a slight hint of lemon.
—KATHY SCOTT LINGLE, WY

PREP: 10 MIN. • **BAKE:** 45 MIN. + COOLING
MAKES: 1 LOAF (12 SLICES)

- **½ cup butter, softened**
- **1 cup sugar**
- **2 large eggs**
- **2 tablespoons lemon juice**
- **1 tablespoon grated lemon peel**
- **1½ cups all-purpose flour**
- **1 teaspoon baking powder**
- **⅛ teaspoon salt**
- **½ cup 2% milk**

GLAZE

- **½ cup confectioners' sugar**
- **2 tablespoons lemon juice**

1. In a large bowl, cream butter and sugar until light and fluffy. Beat in the eggs, lemon juice and peel. Combine the flour, baking powder and salt; gradually stir into creamed mixture alternately with milk, beating well after each addition.
2. Pour into a greased 8x4-in. loaf pan. Bake at 350° for 45 minutes or until a toothpick inserted near the center comes out clean.
3. Combine glaze ingredients. Remove bread from pan; immediately drizzle with glaze. Cool on a wire rack. Serve warm.

AUNT BETTY'S BLUEBERRY MUFFINS

My Aunt Betty bakes many items each Christmas, but I look forward to these mouthwatering muffins the most.
—SHEILA RALEIGH KECHI, KS

PREP: 15 MIN. • **BAKE:** 20 MIN.
MAKES: ABOUT 1 DOZEN

- **½ cup old-fashioned oats**
- **½ cup orange juice**
- **1 large egg**
- **½ cup canola oil**
- **½ cup sugar**
- **1½ cups all-purpose flour**
- **1¼ teaspoons baking powder**
- **½ teaspoon salt**
- **¼ teaspoon baking soda**
- **1 cup fresh or frozen blueberries**

TOPPING

- **2 tablespoons sugar**
- **½ teaspoon ground cinnamon**

1. In a large bowl, combine oats and orange juice; let stand for 5 minutes. Beat in the egg, oil and sugar until blended. Combine the flour, baking powder, salt and baking soda; stir into oat mixture just until moistened. Fold in blueberries.
2. Fill greased or paper-lined muffin cups two-thirds full. Combine topping ingredients; sprinkle over batter. Bake at 400° for 20-25 minutes or until a toothpick inserted near the center comes out clean. Cool for 5 minutes before removing from pan to a wire rack. Serve warm.

NOTE *If using frozen blueberries, use without thawing to avoid discoloring the batter.*

SUN-DRIED TOMATO PROVOLONE BREAD

My mother passed down the recipe for this savory quick bread that's packed with goodness. It goes well with soups and chowders, and it also makes a delicious accompaniment to beef and chicken entrees.

—**MARIE RIZZIO** INTERLOCHEN, MI

PREP: 30 MIN. • **BAKE:** 40 MIN. + COOLING
MAKES: 3 MINI LOAVES (6 SLICES EACH)

- **⅓ cup oil-packed sun-dried tomatoes**
- **2¼ cups all-purpose flour**
- **2 teaspoons baking powder**
- **2 teaspoons sugar**
- **1¼ teaspoons dried basil**
- **1 teaspoon salt**
- **½ teaspoon baking soda**
- **½ teaspoon coarsely ground pepper**
- **2 large eggs**
- **1¼ cups buttermilk**
- **3 tablespoons canola oil**
- **1 cup (4 ounces) shredded provolone cheese**
- **¼ cup minced fresh parsley**

1. Preheat oven to 350°. Drain tomatoes, reserving 2 tablespoons oil. Chop tomatoes and set aside.

2. In a large bowl, combine flour, baking powder, sugar, basil, salt, baking soda and pepper. In a small bowl, whisk eggs, buttermilk, oil and reserved sun-dried tomato oil. Stir into dry ingredients just until moistened. Fold in cheese, parsley and sun-dried tomatoes.

3. Transfer batter to three greased 5¾x3x2-in. loaf pans. Bake for 40-45 minutes or until a toothpick inserted in center comes out clean. Cool 10 minutes before removing from pans to wire racks.

TOP TIP

Quick Bread Basics

Bake quick breads in a light aluminum pan rather than a dark nonstick pan. (If you use a glass pan, lower the oven temperature by 25°.) Position the oven rack so the top of the loaf is in the center of the oven. Bake and cool as directed. Tightly wrap cooled bread and wait a day to enjoy it—the flavor will mellow and the sides will soften.

BREAD MACHINE PUMPKIN MONKEY BREAD

I love making this pumpkin bread for fall and winter brunches. Leftovers reheat well on busy weekdays, and any extra sauce makes an excellent pancake or waffle syrup.

—EMILY MAIN TONOPAH, AZ

PREP: 45 MIN. + RISING • **BAKE:** 20 MIN. + COOLING
MAKES: 18 SERVINGS

- **1 cup warm 2% milk (70° to 80°)**
- **¾ cup canned pumpkin**
- **2 tablespoons butter, softened**
- **¼ cup sugar**
- **1 teaspoon salt**
- **1 teaspoon ground cinnamon**
- **½ teaspoon ground ginger**
- **¼ teaspoon ground cloves**
- **¼ teaspoon ground nutmeg**
- **4 to 4¼ cups all-purpose flour**
- **2 teaspoons active dry yeast**

SAUCE

- **1 cup butter, cubed**
- **1 cup packed brown sugar**
- **1 cup dried cranberries**
- **¼ cup canned pumpkin**
- **1 teaspoon ground cinnamon**
- **½ teaspoon ground ginger**
- **¼ teaspoon ground nutmeg**
- **¼ teaspoon ground cloves**

1. In bread machine pan, place the first 11 ingredients in order suggested by manufacturer. Select dough setting. Check dough after 5 minutes of mixing; add 1-2 tablespoons of water or flour if needed.
2. Meanwhile, in a large saucepan, combine the sauce ingredients; cook and stir until blended. Remove from heat.
3. When dough cycle is completed, turn dough onto a lightly floured surface. Divide into 36 portions; shape into balls.
4. Arrange half of the balls in a greased 10-in. fluted tube pan; cover with half of the sauce. Repeat, being sure to thoroughly coat the top layer with sauce.
5. Let rise in a warm place until doubled, about 30 minutes. Preheat oven to 375°. Bake 20-25 minutes or until golden brown. Cover loosely with foil if top browns too quickly.
6. Cool in pan 10 minutes before inverting onto a serving plate. Serve warm.

HERB-HAPPY GARLIC BREAD

You'll love the fresh garlic and herbs in this recipe. The mild goat cheese that's sprinkled on top makes this heavenly garlic bread extra rich and wonderful.

—*TASTE OF HOME* TEST KITCHEN

START TO FINISH: 15 MIN. • **MAKES:** 12 SERVINGS

- **½ cup butter, softened**
- **¼ cup grated Romano cheese**
- **2 tablespoons minced fresh basil or 2 teaspoons dried basil**
- **1 tablespoon minced fresh parsley**
- **3 garlic cloves, minced**
- **1 French bread baguette**
- **4 ounces crumbled goat cheese**

1. In a small bowl, mix the first five ingredients until blended. Cut baguette crosswise in half; cut each piece lengthwise in half. Spread cut sides with butter mixture. Place on an ungreased baking sheet.

2. Bake, uncovered, at 425° for 7-9 minutes or until lightly toasted. Sprinkle with goat cheese; bake 1-2 minutes longer or until goat cheese is softened. Cut into slices.

EMPIRE STATE MUFFINS

These muffins are loaded with fruit and nuts. They're perfect to share when the apple harvest is abundant.

—BEVERLY COLLINS NORTH SYRACUSE, NY

PREP: 15 MIN. • **BAKE:** 20 MIN. • **MAKES:** 18 MUFFINS.

- **2 cups shredded tart apples**
- **1⅓ cups sugar**
- **1 cup chopped fresh or frozen cranberries**
- **1 cup shredded carrots**
- **1 cup chopped walnuts or pecans**
- **2½ cups all-purpose flour**
- **1 tablespoon baking powder**
- **2 teaspoons baking soda**
- **½ teaspoon salt**
- **2 teaspoons ground cinnamon**
- **2 large eggs, lightly beaten**
- **½ cup canola oil**

1. In a large bowl, combine apples and sugar. Gently fold in cranberries, carrots and nuts. Combine dry ingredients; add to bowl. Mix well to moisten dry ingredients. Combine eggs and oil; stir into apple mixture.

2. Fill 18 greased muffin cups two-thirds full. Bake at 375° for 20-25 minutes. Cool 5 minutes before removing from tins.

CINNAMON-SUGAR SCONES

I turn to these lighter-than-air scones whenever I need to bake something for an event. They're a hit with kids and moms alike.

—KATHY MONAHAN JACKSONVILLE, FL

PREP: 20 MIN. • **BAKE:** 20 MIN. • **MAKES:** 8 SCONES

- **3 cups biscuit baking mix**
- **¼ cup sugar**
- **½ cup vanilla yogurt**
- **⅓ cup 2% milk**
- **1 tablespoon vanilla extract**
- **1 cup cinnamon baking chips or semisweet chocolate chips**
- **Cinnamon sugar or coarse sugar**

1. Preheat oven to 375°. In a bowl, mix baking mix and sugar. In another bowl, whisk yogurt, milk and vanilla; stir into dry ingredients just until moistened. Stir in chips. Turn onto a lightly floured surface; knead gently 10 times.

2. Pat into a 9-in. circle. Sprinkle with cinnamon sugar. Cut into eight wedges. Place wedges on an ungreased baking sheet. Bake 20-25 minutes or until golden brown. Serve warm.

CHEDDAR CHEESE BATTER BREAD

My cheesy bread—a proven winner at our state fair—tastes wonderful either fresh from the oven or cooled and sliced. Best of all, the recipe makes two loaves!

—**JEANNE KEMPER** BAGDAD, KY

PREP: 30 MIN. + RISING
BAKE: 25 MIN. + COOLING
MAKES: 2 LOAVES (16 SLICES EACH)

- **2 packages (¼ ounce each) active dry yeast**
- **¾ cup warm water (110° to 115°)**
- **3 cups (12 ounces) shredded cheddar cheese**
- **¾ cup shredded Parmesan cheese**
- **2 cups warm 2% milk (110° to 115°)**
- **3 tablespoons sugar**
- **1 tablespoon butter, melted**
- **2 teaspoons salt**
- **6 to 6½ cups all-purpose flour**
- **1 large egg white, beaten**
- **1 tablespoon water**

TOPPING

- **½ cup finely shredded cheddar cheese**
- **1 garlic clove, minced**
- **½ teaspoon sesame seeds**
- **½ teaspoon poppy seeds**
- **½ teaspoon paprika**
- **¼ teaspoon celery seed**

1. In a large bowl, dissolve yeast in warm water. Add cheeses, milk, sugar, butter, salt and 3 cups flour. Beat on medium speed for 3 minutes. Stir in enough remaining flour to form a firm dough.

2. Do not knead. Cover and let rise in a warm place until doubled, about 1½ hours.

3. Stir dough down; transfer to two greased 9x5-in. loaf pans. Cover and let rise until doubled, about 30 minutes.

4. Preheat oven to 375°. In a small bowl, combine egg white and water. In another bowl, combine topping ingredients. Brush loaves with egg white mixture; sprinkle with topping. Bake 25-30 minutes or until golden brown. Remove from pans to wire racks to cool.

DELICIOUS ALMOND BRAIDS

Similar to an almond crescent, this coffee cake is light and flaky, with a rich almond center. It's so versatile you can serve it for dessert, breakfast or brunch. It will taste as if it was made from scratch at a bakery, yet the packaged puff pastry makes the recipe quick and easy.

—**GINA IDONE** STATEN ISLAND, NY

PREP: 25 MIN. • **BAKE:** 30 MIN. + COOLING
MAKES: 2 BRAIDS (6 SLICES EACH)

- **1 package (7 ounces) almond paste**
- **½ cup butter**
- **½ cup sugar**
- **1 large egg**
- **2 tablespoons all-purpose flour**
- **1 package (17.3 ounces) frozen puff pastry, thawed**

GLAZE

- **¾ cup plus 1 tablespoon confectioners' sugar**
- **2 tablespoons 2% milk**
- **½ teaspoon almond extract**
- **¼ cup sliced almonds, toasted**

1. Place the almond paste, butter and sugar in a food processor; cover and pulse until chopped. Add egg and flour; process until smooth.

2. Unfold puff pastry sheets onto a greased baking sheet. Spread half of the filling mixture down the center third of one pastry sheet. On each side, cut eight strips about 3½ in. into the center. Starting at one end, fold alternating strips at an angle across filling. Pinch ends to seal. Repeat with remaining pastry and filling. Bake at 375° for 30-35 minutes or until golden brown. Remove to a wire rack.

3. Combine the confectioners' sugar, milk and almond extract. Drizzle over braids; sprinkle with toasted almonds. Cut into slices.

“My husband and I practically devoured this in one sitting. This will be made over and over.”

—**PAMHILL** FROM TASTEOFHOME.COM

5 INGREDIENTS

PULL-APART GARLIC BREAD

People go wild over this golden, garlicky loaf whenever I serve it. There's intense flavor in every bite.

—**CAROL SHIELDS** SUMMERVILLE, PA

PREP: 10 MIN. + RISING • **BAKE:** 30 MIN.
MAKES: 1 LOAF

- **¼ cup butter, melted**
- **1 tablespoon dried parsley flakes**
- **1 teaspoon garlic powder**
- **¼ teaspoon garlic salt**
- **1 loaf (1 pound) frozen white bread dough, thawed**

1. In a small bowl, combine the butter, parsley, garlic powder and garlic salt. Cut dough into 1-in. pieces; dip into butter mixture. Layer in a greased 9x5-in. loaf pan. Cover and let rise until doubled, about 1 hour.

2. Bake at 350° for 30 minutes or until golden brown.

BERRY CREAM MUFFINS

If you can't decide which berries to use in these muffins, you can't go wrong using half raspberries and half blueberries!

—**LINDA GILMORE** HAMPSTEAD, MD

PREP: 15 MIN. • **BAKE:** 20 MIN.
MAKES: ABOUT 2 DOZEN

- **4 cups all-purpose flour**
- **2 cups sugar**
- **1¼ teaspoons baking powder**
- **1 teaspoon baking soda**
- **1 teaspoon salt**
- **3 cups fresh raspberries or frozen raspberries or blueberries**
- **4 large eggs, lightly beaten**
- **2 cups (16 ounces) sour cream**
- **1 cup canola oil**
- **1 teaspoon vanilla extract**

1. In a large bowl, combine the flour, sugar, baking powder, baking soda and salt; add berries and toss gently. Combine the eggs, sour cream, oil and vanilla; mix well. Stir into dry ingredients just until moistened.

2. Fill greased muffin cups two-thirds full. Bake at 400° for 20-25 minutes or until a toothpick inserted near the center comes out clean. Cool for 5 minutes before removing from pans to a wire rack. Serve warm.

(5) INGREDIENTS

VIRGINIA BOX BREAD

When I lived in the South, I was given this melt-in-your-mouth recipe. Cutting the dough in the baking pan lets you easily separate the rolls for serving. My family devours these tender treats as soon as they come out of the oven!

—**THELMA RICHARDSON** LA CROSSE, WI

PREP: 20 MIN. + RISING • **BAKE:** 20 MIN. • **MAKES:** 16 SERVINGS

- **1 package (¼ ounce) active dry yeast**
- **⅔ cup warm water (110° to 115°)**
- **2 large eggs, lightly beaten**
- **5 tablespoons butter, melted and cooled**
- **2 tablespoons sugar**
- **1 teaspoon salt**
- **3¼ to 3¾ cups all-purpose flour**

1. In a large bowl, dissolve yeast in warm water. Add eggs, butter, sugar, salt and 2 cups flour; beat until smooth. Add enough remaining flour to form a soft dough.

2. Turn onto a floured surface; knead until smooth and elastic, about 6-8 minutes. Place in a greased bowl, turning once to grease top. Cover and let rise in a warm place until doubled, about 1½ hours.

3. Punch dough down. On a lightly floured surface, roll dough into a 13x9-in. rectangle. Transfer to a greased 13x9-in. baking pan. Using a sharp knife, cut dough into 16 pieces. Cover and let rise until doubled, about 30 minutes. Preheat oven to 375°.

4. Bake 20 minutes or until golden brown. To serve, separate into rolls.

BLUEBERRY BANANA BREAD

These three fruity loaves combine some of my favorite flavors. Whether you enjoy a slice as a snack or for breakfast, this bread is so flavorful, you won't need butter.

—**SANDY FLICK** TOLEDO, OH

PREP: 10 MIN. • **BAKE:** 30 MIN. + COOLING • **MAKES:** 3 MINI LOAVES

- **½ cup shortening**
- **1 cup sugar**
- **2 large eggs**
- **2 teaspoons vanilla extract**
- **2 cups all-purpose flour**
- **1 teaspoon baking soda**
- **½ teaspoon salt**
- **2 medium ripe bananas, mashed**
- **1 cup fresh blueberries**

1. In a large bowl, cream the shortening and sugar until light and fluffy. Beat in eggs and vanilla. Combine the flour, baking soda and salt; gradually add creamed mixture, beating just until combined. Stir in mashed bananas. Fold in blueberries.

2. Pour into three greased 5¾x3x2-in. loaf pans. Bake at 350° for 30-35 minutes or until a toothpick inserted near the center comes out clean. Cool for 10 minutes before removing from pans to wire racks.

APPLE PULL-APART BREAD

Drizzled with icing, each finger-licking piece of this bread has a yummy filling of apples and pecans. I think you'll agree that the recipe is well worth the bit of extra effort.
—CAROLYN GREGORY HENDERSONVILLE, TN

PREP: 40 MIN. + RISING • **BAKE:** 35 MIN. + COOLING • **MAKES:** 1 LOAF

- **1 package (¼ ounce) active dry yeast**
- **1 cup warm milk**
- **½ cup butter, melted, divided**
- **1 large egg**
- **⅔ cup plus 2 tablespoons sugar, divided**
- **1 teaspoon salt**
- **3 to 3½ cups all-purpose flour**
- **1 medium tart apple, peeled and chopped**
- **½ cup finely chopped pecans**
- **½ teaspoon ground cinnamon**

ICING

- **1 cup confectioners' sugar**
- **3 to 4½ teaspoons hot water**
- **½ teaspoon vanilla extract**

1. In a large bowl, dissolve yeast in milk. Add 2 tablespoons butter, egg, 2 tablespoons sugar, salt and 3 cups flour; beat until smooth. Add enough remaining flour to form a stiff dough. Turn onto a floured surface; knead until smooth and elastic, 6-8 minutes. Place in a greased bowl, turning once to grease top. Cover and let rise in a warm place until doubled, about 1 hour.
2. Combine the apple, pecans, cinnamon and remaining sugar; set aside. Punch dough down; divide in half. Cut each half into 16 pieces. On a lightly floured surface, pat or roll out each piece into a 2½-in. circle. Place 1 teaspoon apple mixture in center of circle; pinch edges together and seal, forming a ball. Dip in remaining butter.
3. In a greased 10-in. tube pan, place 16 balls, seam side down; sprinkle with ¼ cup apple mixture. Layer remaining balls; sprinkle with remaining apple mixture. Cover and let rise until nearly doubled, about 45 minutes.
4. Bake at 350° for 35-40 minutes or until golden brown. Cool for 10 minutes; remove from pan to a wire rack. Combine icing ingredients; drizzle over warm bread.

RHUBARB SCONES

My grandfather grows rhubarb and gives us a generous supply of his harvest. With tartness similar to that of a cranberry, rhubarb is perfect for tossing into a scone.
—DANIELLE ULAM HOOKSTOWN, PA

PREP: 30 MIN. • **BAKE:** 20 MIN. • **MAKES:** 16 SCONES

- **1¼ cups whole wheat pastry flour**
- **1¼ cups all-purpose flour**
- **½ cup sugar**
- **1 tablespoon baking powder**
- **1 teaspoon ground cardamom**
- **½ teaspoon salt**
- **½ cup unsalted butter, cubed**
- **1½ cups finely chopped fresh or frozen rhubarb, thawed (3-4 stalks)**
- **½ cup heavy whipping cream**
- **¼ cup fat-free milk**
- **1 teaspoon vanilla extract**
- **Coarse sugar**

1. Preheat oven to 400°. In a large bowl, whisk the first six ingredients. Cut in butter until mixture resembles coarse crumbs. Add rhubarb; toss to coat.
2. In another bowl, whisk cream, milk and vanilla; stir into crumb mixture just until moistened.
3. Turn onto a floured surface; knead gently 4-5 times. Divide dough in half; pat into two 6-in. circles. Cut each circle into eight wedges. Place wedges on parchment paper-lined baking sheets; sprinkle with coarse sugar. Bake 18-22 minutes or until golden brown. Serve warm.
NOTE *If using frozen rhubarb, measure rhubarb while still frozen, then thaw completely. Drain in a colander, but do not press liquid out.*

CINNAMON-WALNUT STICKY BUNS

The sweet honey-walnut topping and tender texture make these sticky rolls a surefire crowd-pleaser.
—**DEBBIE BROEKER** ROCKY MOUNT, MO

PREP: 1 HOUR + RISING • **BAKE:** 30 MIN. • **MAKES:** 2 DOZEN

- **2 packages (¼ ounce each) active dry yeast**
- **1½ cups warm water (110° to 115°)**
- **1 cup mashed potatoes (without added milk and butter)**
- **½ cup sugar**
- **½ cup butter, softened**
- **2 large eggs**
- **2 teaspoons salt**
- **6 to 6½ cups all-purpose flour**

TOPPING

- **¼ cup butter**
- **1 cup packed brown sugar**
- **1 cup honey**
- **1 teaspoon ground cinnamon**
- **1 cup chopped walnuts**

FILLING

- **½ cup sugar**
- **2 teaspoons ground cinnamon**
- **2 tablespoons butter, melted**

1. In a small bowl, dissolve yeast in warm water. In a large bowl, combine mashed potatoes, sugar, butter, eggs, salt, yeast mixture and 2 cups flour; beat on medium speed until smooth. Stir in enough remaining flour to form a soft dough.
2. Turn dough onto a floured surface; knead until smooth and elastic, about 6-8 minutes. Place in a greased bowl, turning once to grease the top. Cover with plastic wrap and let rise in a warm place until doubled, about 1 hour.
3. For topping, in a small saucepan, melt butter. Stir in brown sugar, honey and cinnamon. Divide mixture among three greased 9-in. round baking pans, spreading evenly. Sprinkle with walnuts.
4. For filling, in a small bowl, mix sugar and cinnamon. Punch down dough. Turn onto a lightly floured surface; divide in half. Roll one portion into an 18x12-in. rectangle. Brush with 1 tablespoon melted butter to within ½ in. of edges; sprinkle with ¼ cup sugar mixture.
5. Roll up jelly-roll style, starting with a long side; pinch seam to seal. Cut into 12 slices. Repeat with remaining dough, butter and sugar mixture. Place eight slices in each pan, cut side down. Cover with kitchen towels; let rise until doubled, about 30 minutes. Preheat oven to 350°.
6. Bake 30-35 minutes or until golden brown. Immediately invert onto serving plates. Serve warm.

(5) INGREDIENTS

BASIC HOMEMADE BREAD

I enjoy the aroma of fresh homemade bread in my kitchen. Here's a simple yeast version that bakes up golden brown.
—**SANDRA ANDERSON** NEW YORK, NY

PREP: 20 MIN. + RISING • **BAKE:** 30 MIN. + COOLING
MAKES: 2 LOAVES (16 SLICES EACH)

- **1 package (¼ ounce) active dry yeast**
- **2¼ cups warm water (110° to 115°)**
- **3 tablespoons sugar**
- **1 tablespoon salt**
- **2 tablespoons canola oil**
- **6¼ to 6¾ cups all-purpose flour**

1. In a large bowl, dissolve yeast in warm water. Add the sugar, salt, oil and 3 cups flour. Beat until smooth. Stir in enough remaining flour to form a soft dough.
2. Turn onto a floured surface; knead until smooth and elastic, about 8-10 minutes. Place in a greased bowl, turning once to grease the top. Cover and let rise in a warm place until doubled, about 1½ hours.
3. Punch dough down. Turn onto a lightly floured surface; divide dough in half. Shape each into a loaf. Place in two greased 9x5-in. loaf pans. Cover and let rise until doubled, about 30-45 minutes.
4. Bake at 375° for 30-35 minutes or until golden brown and bread sounds hollow when tapped. Remove from pans to wire racks to cool.

TOP TIP

Lasting Goodness

Heat and humidity cause homemade bread to mold, and storing it in the refrigerator turns it stale. For best storage, keep homemade bread at room temperature in a cool, dry place for up to 3 days. To keep it soft, store it in an airtight plastic bag. You might want to try storing bread in the freezer, where it will keep fresh for up to 3 months. Slice it before freezing, then just thaw out slices as you need them.

"I used honey instead of sugar and half whole wheat flour, half all-purpose flour. Delish!"
—MARLAINED FROM TASTEOFHOME.COM

CINNAMON RAISIN QUICK BREAD

Cinnamon and raisins bring a familiar heartwarming flavor to these mildly sweet loaves. Slices are ideal for on-the-go breakfasts or quick snacks.

—**FLO BURTNETT** GAGE, OK

PREP: 15 MIN. • **BAKE:** 55 MIN. + COOLING
MAKES: 2 LOAVES (12 SLICES EACH)

- **4 cups all-purpose flour**
- **2 cups sugar, divided**
- **2 teaspoons baking soda**
- **1 teaspoon salt**
- **2 large eggs**
- **2 cups buttermilk**
- **½ cup canola oil**
- **½ cup raisins**
- **3 teaspoons ground cinnamon**

1. Preheat oven to 350°. In a large bowl, combine flour, 1½ cups sugar, soda and salt. In a small bowl, whisk eggs, buttermilk and oil. Stir into dry ingredients just until moistened. Fold in raisins. Combine cinnamon and remaining sugar; set aside.

2. Spoon half the batter into two greased 8x4-in. loaf pans. Sprinkle with half of the reserved cinnamon-sugar; repeat layers. Cut through batter with a knife to swirl.

3. Bake 55-60 minutes or until a toothpick inserted in center comes out clean. Cool for 10 minutes before removing from pans to wire racks.

FREEZE OPTION *Wrap cooled bread in foil and freeze for up to 3 months. To use, thaw at room temperature.*

> "I've made this cinnamon raisin bread 3 or 4 times now. It's perfect with a cup of coffee or tea on a brisk fall or winter day."
>
> —**VICTORIA ELAINE**
> FROM TASTEOFHOME.COM

ALMOND & CRANBERRY COCONUT BREAD

This is an all-around great bread for any season, but the red bursts of cranberry lend a special holiday look.

—**ROSEMARY JOHNSON** IRONDALE, AL

PREP: 20 MIN. • **BAKE:** 1 HOUR + COOLING
MAKES: 2 LOAVES (16 SLICES EACH)

- **2 cups flaked coconut**
- **1 cup slivered almonds**
- **1 cup butter, softened**
- **1 cup sugar**
- **4 large eggs**
- **1 cup (8 ounces) vanilla yogurt**
- **1 teaspoon almond extract**
- **4½ cups all-purpose flour**
- **3 teaspoons baking powder**
- **½ teaspoon salt**
- **½ teaspoon baking soda**
- **1 can (15 ounces) cream of coconut**
- **1 cup dried cranberries**

1. Place the coconut and almonds in an ungreased 15x10x1-in. pan. Bake at 350° for 10-15 minutes or until lightly toasted, stirring occasionally. Cool.

2. In a large bowl, cream butter and sugar until light and fluffy. Add eggs, one at a time, beating well after each addition. Beat in yogurt and extract until blended. Combine the flour, baking powder, salt and baking soda. Add to the creamed mixture alternately with cream of coconut, beating well after each addition. Fold in the cranberries, coconut and almonds.

3. Transfer to two greased and floured 9x5-in. loaf pans. Bake at 350° for 60-70 minutes or until a toothpick inserted near the center comes out clean. Cool for 10 minutes before removing from pans to wire racks to cool completely.

SOUR CREAM CHIP MUFFINS

Take one bite and you'll see why I think these rich, tender muffins are the best I've ever tasted. Mint chocolate chips make them a big hit with my family and friends.
—STEPHANIE MOON BOISE, ID

START TO FINISH: 30 MIN.
MAKES: 1 DOZEN

- **1½ cups all-purpose flour**
- **⅔ cup sugar**
- **¾ teaspoon baking powder**
- **¾ teaspoon baking soda**
- **¼ teaspoon salt**
- **1 large egg**
- **1 cup (8 ounces) sour cream**
- **5 tablespoons butter, melted**
- **1 teaspoon vanilla extract**
- **¾ cup mint or semisweet chocolate chips**

1. In a large bowl, combine the flour, sugar, baking powder, baking soda and salt. Combine the egg, sour cream, butter and vanilla. Stir into the dry ingredients just until moistened. Fold in chocolate chips.
2. Fill greased or paper-lined muffin cups three-fourths full. Bake at 350° for 18-20 minutes or until a toothpick inserted near the center comes out clean. Cool for 5 minutes before removing from pan to a wire rack.

CHOCOLATE ZUCCHINI BREAD

I shred and freeze zucchini from my garden each summer so that I can make this bread all winter long. Our family loves this chocolaty treat.
—SHARI MCKINNEY BIRNEY, MT

PREP: 15 MIN. • **BAKE:** 50 MIN. + COOLING
MAKES: 2 LOAVES (12 SLICES EACH)

- **2 cups sugar**
- **1 cup canola oil**
- **3 large eggs**
- **3 teaspoons vanilla extract**
- **2½ cups all-purpose flour**
- **½ cup baking cocoa**
- **1 teaspoon salt**
- **1 teaspoon baking soda**
- **1 teaspoon ground cinnamon**
- **¼ teaspoon baking powder**
- **2 cups shredded peeled zucchini**

1. In a large bowl, beat the sugar, oil, eggs and vanilla until well blended. Combine the flour, cocoa, salt, baking soda, cinnamon and baking powder; gradually beat into sugar mixture until blended. Stir in zucchini. Transfer to two 8x4-in. loaf pans coated with cooking spray.
2. Bake at 350° for 50-55 minutes or until a toothpick inserted near the center comes out clean. Cool for 10 minutes before removing from pans to wire racks to cool completely.

CHEESE-FILLED GARLIC ROLLS

To change up plain old dinner rolls, I added mozzarella. Now my family wants them at every gathering.
—ROSALIE FITTERY PHILADELPHIA, PA

PREP: 20 MIN. + RISING • **BAKE:** 15 MIN.
MAKES: 2 DOZEN

- **1 loaf (1 pound) frozen bread dough, thawed**
- **24 cubes part-skim mozzarella cheese (¾ inch each), about 10 ounces**
- **3 tablespoons butter, melted**
- **2 teaspoons minced fresh parsley**
- **1 garlic clove, minced**
- **½ teaspoon Italian seasoning**
- **½ teaspoon crushed red pepper flakes**
- **2 tablespoons grated Parmigiano-Reggiano cheese**

1. Divide dough into 24 portions. Shape each portion around a cheese cube to cover completely; pinch to seal. Place each roll in a greased muffin cup, seam side down. Cover with kitchen towels; let rise in a warm place until doubled, about 30 minutes. Preheat oven to 350°.
2. In a small bowl, mix butter, parsley, garlic, Italian seasoning and pepper flakes. Brush over rolls; sprinkle with cheese. Bake 15-18 minutes or until golden brown.
3. Cool 5 minutes before removing from pans. Serve warm.

WHOLE WHEAT POTATO ROLLS

My cousin gave me this recipe for classic potato rolls with a twist. If you have leftovers, go ahead and freeze them for later.
—DEVON VICKERS GODDARD, KS

PREP: 30 MIN.+ RISING • **BAKE:** 10 MIN. • **MAKES:** 24 ROLLS

- **1 package (¼ ounce) active dry yeast**
- **2 cups warm water (110° to 115°)**
- **½ cup sugar**
- **½ cup canola oil**
- **2 large eggs**
- **⅓ cup mashed potato flakes**
- **1½ teaspoons salt**
- **2 cups all-purpose flour**
- **4 to 4¾ cups whole wheat flour**
- **2 tablespoons butter, melted**
- **Quick-cooking oats, optional**

1. In a small bowl, dissolve yeast in warm water. In a large bowl, combine sugar, oil, eggs, potato flakes, salt, yeast mixture, all-purpose flour and 2½ cups whole wheat flour. Beat until smooth. Stir in enough remaining whole wheat flour to form a soft dough (dough will be sticky).
2. Turn onto a floured surface; knead until smooth and elastic, about 6-8 minutes. Place in a greased bowl, turning once to grease the top. Cover with plastic wrap and let rise in a warm place until doubled, about 1½ hours.
3. Punch down dough. Turn onto a lightly floured surface; divide and shape into 24 balls. Place 2 in. apart on greased baking sheets. Cover with kitchen towels; let rise in a warm place until doubled, about 30 minutes.
4. Preheat oven to 375°. Brush tops with melted butter; if desired, sprinkle with oats. Bake 9-11 minutes or until lightly browned. Serve warm.

HAWAIIAN DINNER ROLLS

Pineapple and coconut lend a subtly sweet flavor to these golden rolls, but you can drizzle them with honey to take the sweetness up another notch. Leftovers are perfect for sandwiches.
—KATHY KURTZ GLENDORA, CA

PREP: 35 MIN. + RISING • **BAKE:** 15 MIN. • **MAKES:** 15 ROLLS

- **1 can (8 ounces) crushed pineapple, undrained**
- **¼ cup warm pineapple juice (70° to 80°)**
- **¼ cup water (70° to 80°)**
- **1 large egg**
- **¼ cup butter, cubed**
- **¼ cup nonfat dry milk powder**
- **1 tablespoon sugar**
- **1½ teaspoons salt**
- **3¼ cups bread flour**
- **2¼ teaspoons active dry yeast**
- **¾ cup flaked coconut**

1. In bread machine pan, place the first 10 ingredients in order suggested by manufacturer. Select dough setting (check dough after 5 minutes of mixing; add 1-2 tablespoons of water or flour if needed). Just before final kneading (your machine may audibly signal this), add coconut.
2. When cycle is complete, turn dough onto a lightly floured surface. Cover with plastic wrap; let rest for 10 minutes. Divide into 15 portions; roll each into a ball. Place in a greased 13x9-in. baking pan.
3. Cover and let rise in a warm place for 45 minutes or until doubled. Bake at 375° for 15-20 minutes or until golden brown.
NOTE *We recommend you do not use a bread machine's time-delay feature for this recipe.*

CRANBERRY SWEET POTATO MUFFINS

Sweet potatoes, cranberries and cinnamon give seasonal appeal to these cheery muffins. I recommend them as a change-of-pace treat with a meal, packed into a lunch box or enjoyed as a snack.
—**DIANE MUSIL** LYONS, IL

PREP: 20 MIN. • **BAKE:** 20 MIN. + COOLING
MAKES: 1 DOZEN

- **1½ cups all-purpose flour**
- **½ cup sugar**
- **2 teaspoons baking powder**
- **¾ teaspoon salt**
- **½ teaspoon ground cinnamon**
- **½ teaspoon ground nutmeg**
- **1 large egg**
- **½ cup milk**
- **½ cup cold mashed sweet potatoes (without added butter or milk)**
- **¼ cup butter, melted**
- **1 cup chopped fresh or frozen cranberries**
- **Cinnamon-sugar**

1. In a large bowl, combine the flour, sugar, baking powder, salt, cinnamon and nutmeg. In a small bowl, combine the egg, milk, sweet potatoes and butter; stir into dry ingredients just until moistened. Fold in cranberries.

2. Fill 12 greased or paper-lined muffin cups half full. Sprinkle with cinnamon-sugar. Bake at 375° for 18-22 minutes or until a toothpick inserted in muffins comes out clean. Cool 10 minutes before removing from pan to a wire rack. Serve warm.

TOP TIP

A Stirring Story

Use a whisk or fork to combine the dry ingredients in muffin batter. This distributes the leavening and salt, and it aerates the flour. Make a well in the center of the dry ingredients. Pour the liquid mixture into the well. Stir the ingredients just until moistened; do not mix until batter is smooth. Overmixing can cause muffins to form pointy tops.

FAST FIX

BASIC BANANA MUFFINS

These muffins go over so well with kids. Not only are the treats loaded with bananas, but they're ready, start to finish, in just half an hour!

—LORNA GREENE HARRINGTON, ME

START TO FINISH: 30 MIN.
MAKES: 1 DOZEN

- **1½ cups all-purpose flour**
- **1 cup sugar**
- **1 teaspoon baking soda**
- **½ teaspoon salt**
- **3 medium ripe bananas**
- **1 large egg**
- **⅓ cup vegetable oil**
- **1 teaspoon vanilla extract**

1. In a large bowl, combine dry ingredients. In another bowl, mash the bananas. Add egg, oil and vanilla; mix well. Stir into the dry ingredients just until moistened. Fill greased or paper-lined muffin cups half full.
2. Bake at 375° for 18-22 minutes or until a toothpick inserted near the center comes out clean. Cool for 10 minutes; remove from pan to a wire rack to cool completely.

SWEET CORN BREAD

We prefer good old Southern corn bread with our beans, but we sometimes like things a bit sweeter.

—STACEY FEATHER JAY, OK

PREP: 10 MIN. • **BAKE:** 25 MIN.
MAKES: 15 SERVINGS

- **2½ cups all-purpose flour**
- **1½ cups cornmeal**
- **1 cup sugar**
- **4 teaspoons baking powder**
- **1½ teaspoons salt**
- **¾ cup shortening**
- **2 large eggs**
- **2½ cups whole milk**

1. Preheat oven to 400°. In a large bowl, combine the first five ingredients. Cut in shortening until mixture resembles coarse crumbs. In another bowl, whisk eggs and milk; stir into crumb mixture just until moistened.
2. Pour into a greased 13x9-in. baking pan. Bake 25-30 minutes or until a toothpick inserted in center comes out clean. Serve warm.

"I love this recipe. So easy. You can make these even when in a bit of a rush."
—REIZL FROM TASTEOFHOME.COM

5 INGREDIENTS

OAT DINNER ROLLS

These delicious homemade rolls make a delightful addition to any special-occasion meal. They call for only a few ingredients.

—PATRICIA RUTHERFORD WINCHESTER, IL

PREP: 30 MIN. + RISING • **BAKE:** 20 MIN.
MAKES: 2 DOZEN

- **2⅓ cups water, divided**
- **1 cup quick-cooking oats**
- **⅔ cup packed brown sugar**
- **3 tablespoons butter**
- **1½ teaspoons salt**
- **2 packages (¼ ounce each) active dry yeast**
- **5 to 5¾ cups all-purpose flour**

1. In a large saucepan, bring 2 cups water to a boil. Stir in the oats; reduce heat. Simmer, uncovered, for 1 minute. Stir in the brown sugar, butter, salt and remaining water.
2. Transfer to a large bowl; let stand until mixture reaches 110°-115°. Stir in yeast. Add 3 cups flour; beat well. Add enough remaining flour to form a soft dough.
3. Turn onto a floured surface; knead until smooth and elastic, about 6-8 minutes. Place in a greased bowl; turn once to grease top. Cover and let rise in a warm place until doubled, about 1 hour.
4. Punch dough down; shape into 24 rolls. Place on greased baking sheets. Cover and let rise until doubled, about 30 minutes.
5. Bake at 350° for 20-25 minutes or until golden brown. Remove from pan and cool on wire racks.

PUMPKIN SWIRL BREAD

This combination of pumpkin, nuts and dates makes a flavorful bread with a beautiful golden look. The surprise inside is almost like a luscious layer of cheesecake in each slice.

—CINDY MAY TROY, MI

PREP: 15 MIN. • **BAKE:** 65 MIN. + COOLING
MAKES: 3 LOAVES (16 SLICES EACH)

FILLING

- **2 packages (8 ounces each) cream cheese, softened**
- **¼ cup sugar**
- **1 large egg**
- **1 tablespoon milk**

BREAD

- **3 cups sugar**
- **1 can (15 ounces) solid-pack pumpkin**
- **4 large eggs**
- **1 cup canola oil**
- **1 cup water**
- **4 cups all-purpose flour**
- **4 teaspoons pumpkin pie spice**
- **2 teaspoons baking soda**
- **1½ teaspoons ground cinnamon**
- **1 teaspoon salt**
- **1 teaspoon baking powder**
- **1 teaspoon ground nutmeg**
- **½ teaspoon ground cloves**
- **1 cup chopped walnuts**
- **1 cup raisins**
- **½ cup chopped dates**

OPTIONAL TOPPINGS

- **1 cup confectioners' sugar**
- **¼ teaspoon vanilla extract**
- **2 to 3 tablespoons 2% milk**
- **Additional chopped walnuts**

1. Preheat oven to 350°. Grease and flour three 8x4-in. loaf pans. In a small bowl, beat filling ingredients until smooth.
2. In a large bowl, beat sugar, pumpkin, eggs, oil and water until well blended. In another bowl, whisk flour, pie spice, soda, cinnamon, salt, baking powder, nutmeg and cloves; gradually beat into pumpkin mixture. Stir in walnuts, raisins and dates.
3. Pour half of the batter into prepared pans, dividing evenly. Spoon filling over batter. Cover filling completely with remaining batter.
4. Bake 65-70 minutes or until a toothpick inserted in bread portion comes out clean. Cool 10 minutes before removing from pans to wire racks to cool completely. Wrap in foil; refrigerate until serving.
5. If desired, just before serving, in a small bowl mix confectioners' sugar, vanilla and enough milk to reach a drizzling consistency. Drizzle over bread; sprinkle with walnuts.

EASY FRESH STRAWBERRY PIE, 178

BANANA PUDDING, 181

CHOCOLATE BAVARIAN TORTE, 183

PEANUT BUTTER CREAM PIE, 182

CAKES, PIES & DESSERTS

Life is too short to pass up dessert. Surrender to the allure of gorgeous taste-tempting cakes, cheesecakes, pies, tarts and other sweet indulgences. Whether you're hosting an elegant party or simply seeking the perfect grand finale to a weeknight meal, any one of these delights is sure to impress. From old-fashioned favorites to lip-smacking novelties, each of these unforgettable pleasures testifies that—no matter how full you are—there's always room for dessert!

BUTTERMILK POUND CAKE

A true Southern classic, this cake is the one I make most often. Once people taste it, they won't go back to their other pound cake recipes.
—**GRACIE HANCHEY** DE RIDDER, LA

PREP: 10 MIN. • **BAKE:** 70 MIN. + COOLING
MAKES: 16-20 SERVINGS

- **1 cup butter, softened**
- **2½ cups sugar**
- **4 large eggs**
- **3 cups all-purpose flour**
- **¼ teaspoon baking soda**
- **1 cup buttermilk**
- **1 teaspoon vanilla extract**
- **Confectioners' sugar, optional**

1. In a large bowl, cream butter and sugar until light and fluffy. Add eggs, one at a time, beating well after each addition. Combine flour and baking soda; add alternately with buttermilk and beat well. Stir in vanilla.
2. Pour into a greased and floured 10-in. fluted tube pan. Bake at 325° for 70 minutes or until a toothpick inserted near the center comes out clean. Cool in pan for 15 minutes before removing to a wire rack to cool completely. Dust with confectioners' sugar if desired.

TOP TIP

Pound Cake Perfection

For perfect pound cake, first bring all ingredients to room temperature. Thoroughly cream the butter (no substitutes) until light and fluffy. Gradually add the sugar and continue to beat for 5-7 minutes. Add the eggs one at a time, beating 1 minute after each egg. Combine the dry ingredients and add alternately with the liquid in three stages. Beat just until blended—do not overbeat. Bake until a toothpick inserted near the center comes out clean.

CHERRY ALMOND MOUSSE PIE

Anytime is the perfect time to treat your family and guests to a luscious pie with chocolate, cherries and nuts in a creamy vanilla mousse. It's a sweet yet light dessert.

—DOROTHY PRITCHETT WILLS POINT, TX

PREP: 25 MIN. + CHILLING
MAKES: 10 SERVINGS

- **1 can (14 ounces) sweetened condensed milk, divided**
- **1 ounce unsweetened chocolate**
- **½ teaspoon almond extract, divided**
- **1 frozen pie shell (9 inches), baked**
- **1 jar (10 ounces) maraschino cherries, drained**
- **1 package (8 ounces) cream cheese, softened**
- **1 cup cold water**
- **1 package (3.4 ounces) instant vanilla pudding mix**
- **1 cup heavy whipping cream, whipped**
- **½ cup chopped toasted almonds**
- **Chopped chocolate, optional**

1. In a small saucepan over low heat, cook and stir 1/2 cup milk and chocolate until chocolate is melted and mixture is thickened, about 4 minutes. Stir in 1/4 teaspoon extract. Pour into pie shell; set aside.
2. Set aside eight whole cherries for garnish. Chop the remaining cherries; set aside. In a large bowl, beat cream cheese until fluffy. Gradually beat in water and remaining milk. Beat in pudding mix and remaining extract. Fold in whipped cream. Stir in chopped cherries and almonds.
3. Pour over pie. Chill 4 hours or until set. Garnish with whole cherries and, if desired, chopped chocolate.

ELEGANT ORANGE BLOSSOM CHEESECAKE

The aroma of orange zest hints at how heavenly this delicate cheesecake tastes. Gingersnap cookie crumbs make a distinctive crust, while glazed orange slices become a blossomlike topping.

—SHARON DELANEY-CHRONIS
SOUTH MILWAUKEE, WI

PREP: 40 MIN. • **BAKE:** 70 MIN. + CHILLING
MAKES: 16 SERVINGS

- **3 cups crushed gingersnap cookies (about 60 cookies)**
- **2 teaspoons plus 2 tablespoons grated orange peel, divided**
- **⅓ cup butter, melted**
- **1½ cups orange juice**
- **⅓ cup sliced fresh gingerroot**
- **4 packages (8 ounces each) cream cheese, softened**
- **⅔ cup sugar**
- **6 ounces white baking chocolate, melted**
- **1 tablespoon vanilla extract**
- **4 large eggs, lightly beaten**

CANDIED ORANGE SLICES

- **3 cups water**
- **1½ cups sugar**
- **2 small navel oranges, thinly sliced**

1. Place a greased 9-in. springform pan on a double thickness of heavy-duty foil (about 18 in. square). Securely wrap foil around pan.
2. In a large bowl, combine crumbs, 2 teaspoons orange peel and butter. Press onto bottom and 2 in. up sides of prepared pan.
3. In a large saucepan, combine orange juice and ginger; bring to a boil. Reduce heat and simmer, stirring occasionally, until mixture is syrupy and reduced to about 3 tablespoons. Strain; discard ginger.
4. In a large bowl, beat cream cheese and sugar until smooth. Beat in ginger syrup, melted chocolate, vanilla and remaining orange peel. Add eggs; beat on low speed just until combined. Pour into crust. Place springform pan in a large baking pan; add 1 in. of hot water to larger pan.
5. Bake at 325° for 70-80 minutes or until center is just set and top appears dull. Remove springform pan from water bath; remove foil. Cool on a wire rack for 10 minutes. Carefully run a knife around edge of pan to loosen; cool 1 hour longer. Refrigerate overnight.
6. For candied orange slices, in a large skillet, combine water and sugar. Cook and stir over medium heat until sugar is completely dissolved. Add orange slices. Bring to a boil. Reduce heat; simmer for 45 minutes or until translucent. Drain oranges on a wire rack; arrange in a single layer on waxed paper to dry.
7. Remove sides of pan. Top the cheesecake with candied orange slices. Refrigerate leftovers.

BANANA CREAM CHEESECAKE

Here is a lovely company dessert that can be made a day or two in advance. It's the perfect finale to any meal.
—MARGIE SNODGRASS WILMORE, KY

PREP: 25 MIN. + CHILLING • **MAKES:** 10 SERVINGS

- **1¾ cups graham cracker crumbs**
- **¼ cup sugar**
- **½ cup butter, melted**

FILLING

- **1 package (8 ounces) cream cheese, softened**
- **½ cup sugar**
- **1 carton (8 ounces) frozen whipped topping, thawed, divided**
- **3 to 4 medium firm bananas, sliced**
- **1¾ cups cold milk**
- **1 package (3.4 ounces) instant banana cream pudding mix**

1. In a small bowl, combine cracker crumbs and sugar; stir in butter. Set aside ½ cup for topping. Press remaining crumb mixture onto the bottom and up the sides of a greased 9-in. springform pan or 9-in. square baking pan. Bake at 350° for 5-7 minutes. Cool on wire rack.
2. In a large bowl, beat the cream cheese and sugar until smooth. Fold in 2 cups whipped topping. Arrange half of the banana slices in crust; top with half of the cream cheese mixture. Repeat layers.
3. In a small bowl, whisk the milk and pudding mix for 2 minutes. Let stand for 2 minutes or until soft-set; fold in remaining whipped topping. Pour over the cream cheese layer. Sprinkle with reserved crumb mixture. Refrigerate 1-2 hours or until set.

FAST FIX

BLUEBERRY CRUMBLE TARTS

Pop one in a lunch box, share a batch at work or wait until after dinner—these tarts are sweet anytime, anywhere. Sometimes I refrigerate prepared tarts overnight and bake them while making dinner the next day.
—CAROLE FRASER NORTH YORK, ON

START TO FINISH: 30 MIN. • **MAKES:** 6 SERVINGS

- **2 cups fresh blueberries**
- **¼ cup sugar**
- **1 tablespoon cornstarch**
- **1 package (6 count) individual graham cracker tart shells**
- **¼ cup all-purpose flour**
- **¼ cup quick-cooking oats**
- **¼ cup packed brown sugar**
- **2 tablespoons cold butter**
- **Ice cream or whipped cream, optional**

1. Preheat oven to 375°. In a bowl, toss blueberries with sugar and cornstarch; spoon into tart shells. In a small bowl, mix flour, oats and brown sugar; cut in butter until crumbly. Sprinkle over blueberries.
2. Place tarts on a baking sheet. Bake 20-25 minutes or until topping is golden brown and filling is bubbly. Serve warm or at room temperature. If desired, top with ice cream.

BUTTER PECAN LAYER CAKE

Pecans and butter give this cake the same irresistible flavor as the popular ice cream. Loads of nuts are folded into the batter, and more are sprinkled over the delectable frosting.

—**BECKY MILLER** TALLAHASSEE, FL

PREP: 40 MIN. • **BAKE:** 25 MIN. + COOLING • **MAKES:** 12-16 SERVINGS

- **2⅔ cups chopped pecans**
- **1¼ cups butter, softened, divided**
- **2 cups sugar**
- **4 large eggs**
- **2 teaspoons vanilla extract**
- **3 cups all-purpose flour**
- **2 teaspoons baking powder**
- **½ teaspoon salt**
- **1 cup milk**

FROSTING

- **1 cup butter, softened**
- **8 to 8½ cups confectioners' sugar**
- **1 can (5 ounces) evaporated milk**
- **2 teaspoons vanilla extract**

1. Place pecans and 1/4 cup butter in a baking pan. Bake at 350° for 20-25 minutes or until toasted, stirring frequently; set aside.
2. In a large bowl, cream sugar and remaining butter until light and fluffy. Add eggs, one at a time, beating well after each addition. Stir in vanilla. Combine the flour, baking powder and salt; add to the creamed mixture alternately with milk, beating well after each addition. Stir in 1⅓ cups of toasted pecans.
3. Pour into three greased and floured 9-in. round baking pans. Bake at 350° for 25-30 minutes or until a toothpick inserted near the center comes out clean. Cool for 10 minutes before removing from pans to wire racks to cool completely.
4. For frosting, cream butter and confectioners' sugar in a large bowl. Add milk and vanilla; beat until smooth. Stir in remaining toasted pecans. Spread frosting between layers and over top and sides of cake.

STRAWBERRY BANANA TRIFLE

No matter where I take this dessert, the bowl is emptied in minutes. It's fun to make because everyone oohs and aahs over how pretty it is.

—**KIM WATERHOUSE** RANDOLPH, ME

PREP: 20 MIN. + COOLING • **MAKES:** 14 SERVINGS

- **1 cup sugar**
- **¼ cup cornstarch**
- **3 tablespoons strawberry gelatin powder**
- **1 cup cold water**
- **1 pint fresh strawberries, sliced**
- **1¾ cups cold milk**
- **1 package (3.4 ounces) instant vanilla pudding mix**
- **3 medium firm bananas, sliced**
- **1 tablespoon lemon juice**
- **6 cups cubed angel food cake**
- **2 cups heavy whipping cream, whipped**
- **Additional strawberries or banana slices, optional**

1. In a saucepan, combine the sugar, cornstarch and gelatin; stir in water until smooth. Bring to a boil; cook and stir for 2 minutes or until thickened. Remove from the heat. Stir in strawberries; set aside.
2. In a large bowl, combine milk and pudding mix. Beat on low speed for 2 minutes; set aside. Toss bananas with lemon juice; drain and set aside.
3. Place half of the cake cubes in a trifle bowl or 3-qt. serving bowl. Layer with half of the pudding, bananas, strawberry sauce and whipped cream. Repeat the layers. Cover and refrigerate for at least 2 hours. Garnish with additional fruit if desired.

LEMON ORANGE CAKE

I like to bake this lovely three-layer cake instead of a traditional pumpkin or apple pie for Thanksgiving. It has that tangy Florida citrus flavor and isn't any more difficult to make than a two-layer cake.

—NORMA POOLE AUBURNDALE, FL

PREP: 20 MIN. • **BAKE:** 25 MIN. + COOLING
MAKES: 10-12 SERVINGS

- **1 cup butter, softened**
- **¼ cup shortening**
- **2 cups sugar**
- **5 large eggs**
- **3 cups all-purpose flour**
- **1 teaspoon baking powder**
- **½ teaspoon baking soda**
- **½ teaspoon salt**
- **1 cup buttermilk**
- **1 teaspoon vanilla extract**
- **½ teaspoon lemon extract**

FROSTING

- **½ cup butter, softened**
- **3 tablespoons orange juice**
- **3 tablespoons lemon juice**
- **1 to 2 tablespoons grated orange peel**
- **1 to 2 tablespoons grated lemon peel**
- **1 teaspoon lemon extract**
- **5½ to 6 cups confectioners' sugar**

1. In a bowl, cream butter, shortening and sugar until light and fluffy. Add eggs, one at a time, beating well after each addition. Combine the flour, baking powder, baking soda and salt; add to creamed mixture alternately with buttermilk, beginning and ending with dry ingredients. Beat well after each addition. Stir in extracts.
2. Pour into three greased and floured 9-in. round baking pans. Bake at 350° for 25-30 minutes or until a toothpick inserted near the center comes out clean. Cool for 10 minutes before removing from pans to wire racks to cool completely.
3. For frosting, in a bowl, cream butter until light and fluffy. Add the orange juice, lemon juice, peels and extract; beat until well blended. Gradually add confectioners' sugar, beating until frosting reaches desired spreading consistency. Spread frosting between layers and over top and sides of cake.

KEY LIME PIE CUPCAKES

I bake over 200 of these cupcakes for our church suppers, and we always run out. If you can't find Key lime juice, use regular lime juice and add a tad more sugar.

—JULIE HERRERA-LEMLER ROCHESTER, MN

PREP: 45 MIN. • **BAKE:** 20 MIN. + COOLING
MAKES: 32 CUPCAKES

- **2 packages (14.1 ounces each) refrigerated pie pastry**
- **1 cup butter, softened**
- **2½ cups sugar**
- **4 large eggs**
- **½ cup Key lime juice**
- **2 cups all-purpose flour**
- **1½ cups self-rising flour**
- **1½ cups buttermilk**

FROSTING

- **12 ounces cream cheese, softened**
- **1½ cups butter, softened**
- **1½ teaspoons vanilla extract**
- **2¾ to 3 cups confectioners' sugar**
- **6 tablespoons Key lime juice**
- **Fresh raspberries**

1. Preheat the oven to 350°. Line 32 muffin cups with foil liners. On a lightly floured work surface, unroll pastry sheets. Cut 32 circles with a floured 2¼-in. round cookie cutter (discard remaining pastry or save for another use). Press one circle into each liner. Bake 10-12 minutes or until lightly browned. Cool on wire racks.
2. In a large bowl, beat butter and sugar until crumbly. Add eggs, one at a time, beating well after each addition. Beat in lime juice. In another bowl, whisk flours; add to butter mixture alternately with buttermilk, beating well after each addition.
3. Pour batter into prepared cups. Bake for 20-22 minutes or until a toothpick inserted in center comes out clean. Cool in pans 10 minutes before removing cupcakes to wire racks to cool completely.
4. In a large bowl, beat cream cheese, butter and vanilla until blended. Beat in enough confectioners' sugar, alternately with lime juice, to reach desired consistency. Frost cupcakes; top with berries. Refrigerate leftovers.

NOTE *As a substitute for 1½ cups self-rising flour, place 2¼ teaspoons baking powder and ¾ teaspoon salt in a measuring cup. Add all-purpose flour to measure 1 cup. Combine with an additional ½ cup all-purpose flour.*

"These are excellent! My family and friends loved them. I love the cupcake texture and flavor so much I will never use a box mix again."

—MEGHARTWHITE FROM TASTEOFHOME.COM

WHITE CHOCOLATE FRUIT TART

It takes a little time to make, but this tart is absolutely marvelous, especially in summer when fresh fruit is in abundance.
—CLAIRE DARBY NEW CASTLE, DE

PREP: 30 MIN. • **BAKE:** 25 MIN. + CHILLING
MAKES: 16 SERVINGS

- **¾ cup butter, softened**
- **½ cup confectioners' sugar**
- **1½ cups all-purpose flour**

FILLING

- **1 package (10 to 12 ounces) white baking chips, melted and cooled**
- **¼ cup heavy whipping cream**
- **1 package (8 ounces) cream cheese, softened**
- **1 can (20 ounces) pineapple chunks**
- **1 pint fresh strawberries, sliced**
- **1 can (11 ounces) mandarin oranges, drained**
- **2 kiwifruit, peeled and sliced**

GLAZE

- **3 tablespoons sugar**
- **2 teaspoons cornstarch**
- **½ teaspoon lemon juice**

1. In a small bowl, cream the butter and confectioners' sugar until light and fluffy. Gradually add flour and mix well.
2. Press into an ungreased 11-in. fluted tart pan with removable bottom or a 12-in. pizza pan with sides. Bake at 300° for 25-30 minutes or until lightly browned. Cool on a wire rack.
3. For filling, in a small bowl, beat melted chips and cream. Add cream cheese; beat until smooth. Spread over crust. Refrigerate for 30 minutes.
4. Drain pineapple chunks, reserving 1/2 cup juice. Arrange the pineapple, strawberries, oranges and kiwi over the filling.
5. For glaze, in a small saucepan, combine sugar and cornstarch. Stir in lemon juice and reserved pineapple juice until smooth. Bring to a boil over medium heat; cook and stir for 2 minutes or until thickened. Cool.
6. Brush glaze over fruit. Refrigerate for 1 hour before serving. Refrigerate leftovers.

PEANUT BUTTER CUPCAKES

Peanut butter lovers can double their pleasure with these tender treats. I use the popular ingredient in the cupcakes as well as in the creamy homemade frosting.
—RUTH HUTSON WESTFIELD, IN

PREP: 20 MIN. • **BAKE:** 20 MIN. + COOLING
MAKES: ABOUT 1½ DOZEN

- **⅓ cup butter, softened**
- **½ cup peanut butter**
- **1¼ cups packed brown sugar**
- **1 large egg**
- **1 teaspoon vanilla extract**
- **2 cups all-purpose flour**
- **½ teaspoon salt**
- **½ teaspoon baking powder**
- **½ teaspoon baking soda**
- **¼ teaspoon ground cinnamon**
- **¾ cup 2% milk**

FROSTING

- **⅓ cup peanut butter**
- **2 cups confectioners' sugar**
- **2 teaspoons honey**
- **1 teaspoon vanilla extract**
- **3 to 4 tablespoons 2% milk**

1. In a large bowl, cream the butter, peanut butter and brown sugar until light and fluffy. Beat in the egg and vanilla. Combine the dry ingredients; add to creamed mixture alternately with the milk, beating well after each addition.
2. Fill paper-lined muffin cups two-thirds full. Bake at 350° for 18-22 minutes or until a toothpick inserted near the center comes out clean. Cool for 10 minutes before removing from pans to wire racks to cool completely.
3. For frosting, in a small bowl, cream peanut butter and sugar until light and fluffy. Beat in honey and vanilla. Beat in enough milk to achieve a spreading consistency. Frost cupcakes.

NOTE *Reduced-fat peanut butter is not recommended for this recipe.*

MINIATURE PEANUT BUTTER CHEESECAKES

My mother passed down the recipe for these yummy treats. With a peanut butter cup inside, they're perfect for the holidays or any special occasion.

—**MARY ANN DELL** PHOENIXVILLE, PA

PREP: 20 MIN. • **BAKE:** 15 MIN. + CHILLING
MAKES: 6 SERVINGS

- **⅓ cup graham cracker crumbs**
- **1 tablespoon sugar**
- **5 teaspoons butter, melted**

FILLING

- **4 ounces cream cheese, softened**
- **¼ cup sugar**
- **2 teaspoons all-purpose flour**
- **2 tablespoons beaten egg**
- **¼ teaspoon vanilla extract**
- **6 miniature peanut butter cups**

1. In a small bowl, combine the cracker crumbs, sugar and butter. Press onto the bottoms of six paper-lined muffin cups; set aside.
2. In a small bowl, beat the cream cheese, sugar and flour until smooth. Add egg and vanilla; beat on low speed just until combined. Place a peanut butter cup in the center of each muffin cup; fill with cream cheese mixture.
3. Bake at 350° for 15-18 minutes or until center is set. Cool on a wire rack for 10 minutes before removing from pan to a wire rack to cool completely. Refrigerate for at least 2 hours.

CHERRY CHOCOLATE COCONUT CUPCAKES

Chocolate-covered coconut candy is tucked inside each of these morsels. The fluffy white ganache frosting is complemented by sparkly coarse sugar and chocolate-covered cherries.

—**SANDY PLOY** WEST ALLIS, WI

PREP: 35 MIN. + CHILLING
BAKE: 20 MIN. + COOLING
MAKES: 2 DOZEN

- **1 package (10 to 12 ounces) vanilla or white chips**
- **½ cup butter, cubed**
- **1 cup heavy whipping cream**
- **1 teaspoon coconut extract**
- **1 can (21 ounces) cherry pie filling**
- **1 cup buttermilk**
- **2 large eggs**
- **2 cups all-purpose flour**
- **2 cups sugar**
- **¾ cup baking cocoa**
- **2 teaspoons baking soda**
- **1 teaspoon baking powder**
- **½ teaspoon salt**
- **6 packages (1.9 ounces each) chocolate-covered coconut candy bars**
- **½ cup semisweet chocolate chips**
- **1 teaspoon shortening**
- **24 maraschino cherries, well drained**
- **3¼ cups confectioners' sugar**
- **2 tablespoons coarse sugar**

1. For ganache, place vanilla chips and butter in a large bowl. In a small saucepan, bring cream just to a boil. Pour over chip mixture; whisk until smooth. Stir in extract. Cover and refrigerate for at least 4 hours, stirring occasionally.
2. In a large bowl, beat the pie filling, buttermilk and eggs until well blended. Combine the flour, sugar, cocoa, baking soda, baking powder and salt; gradually beat into pie filling mixture until blended.
3. Fill 24 paper-lined muffin cups one-third full. Cut candy bars in half; place half of a candy bar in center of each cupcake. Cover each with 2 tablespoonfuls batter.
4. Bake at 375° for 16-20 minutes or until a toothpick inserted near the center comes out clean. Cool for 10 minutes before removing from pans to wire racks to cool completely.
5. Meanwhile, in a microwave, melt chocolate chips and shortening; stir until smooth. Dip cherries in chocolate mixture; allow excess to drip off. Place on a waxed paper-lined baking sheet. Refrigerate until set.
6. Remove ganache from refrigerator; gradually beat in confectioners' sugar until frosting is light and fluffy. Pipe frosting over cupcakes; sprinkle with coarse sugar. Garnish cupcakes with chocolate-dipped cherries.

RHUBARB DREAM BARS

Dreaming of a different way to use rhubarb? Try these sweet bars. I top a tender shortbread-like crust with rhubarb, walnuts and coconut for delicious results.

—MARION TOMLINSON MADISON, WI

PREP: 15 MIN. • **BAKE:** 45 MIN. + COOLING
MAKES: 2 DOZEN

- **1¼ cups all-purpose flour, divided**
- **⅓ cup confectioners' sugar**
- **½ cup cold butter, cubed**
- **1¼ to 1½ cups sugar**
- **2 large eggs**
- **2 cups diced fresh or frozen rhubarb**
- **½ cup chopped walnuts**
- **½ cup flaked coconut**

1. In a large bowl, combine 1 cup flour and the confectioners' sugar. Cut in butter until crumbly. Pat into a lightly greased 13x9-in. baking dish. Bake at 350° for 13-15 minutes or until edges are lightly browned.
2. In a large bowl, combine sugar and remaining flour. Add eggs. Stir in the rhubarb, walnuts and coconut; pour over crust. Bake 30-35 minutes longer or until set. Cool on a wire rack. Cut into bars.

NOTE *If using frozen rhubarb, measure rhubarb while still frozen, then thaw completely. Drain in a colander, but do not press liquid out.*

"I made these for a birthday party and everyone went crazy over them. I don't even like rhubarb, and I couldn't keep my hands off of them, either."

—HAG2NUT2000
FROM TASTEOFHOME.COM

CHOCOLATE-STRAWBERRY CREAM CHEESE TART

Sure to impress, this dessert features velvety cream cheese, jewel-like strawberries and a drizzle of fudge piled on a crunchy chocolate-almond crust. It's too gorgeous to resist.
—PRISCILLA YEE CONCORD, CA

PREP: 20 MIN. • **BAKE:** 15 MIN. + CHILLING • **MAKES:** 12 SERVINGS

- **¾ cup all-purpose flour**
- **½ cup finely chopped almonds, toasted**
- **6 tablespoons butter, melted**
- **⅓ cup baking cocoa**
- **¼ cup packed brown sugar**

FILLING

- **2 packages (8 ounces each) cream cheese, softened**
- **1 cup confectioners' sugar**
- **1 teaspoon vanilla extract**
- **3 cups halved fresh strawberries**
- **3 tablespoons hot fudge ice cream topping**

1. Preheat oven to 375 °. In a small bowl, combine the first five ingredients; press onto the bottom and up the sides of an ungreased 9-in. fluted tart pan with removable bottom. Bake 12-15 minutes or until crust is set. Cool on a wire rack.
2. In another small bowl, beat cream cheese, confectioners' sugar and vanilla until smooth. Spread over bottom of prepared crust. Arrange strawberry halves, cut side down, over filling. Cover and refrigerate at least 1 hour.
3. Just before serving, drizzle fudge topping over tart. Refrigerate leftovers.

VERY BERRY CRISP

I love this recipe because it's easy, versatile and delicious. The crispy topping is flavored with graham cracker crumbs, cinnamon and almonds. Try it with frozen yogurt or whipped topping.
—SCARLETT ELROD NEWNAN, GA

PREP: 20 MIN. • **BAKE:** 25 MIN. • **MAKES:** 8 SERVINGS

- **2 cups fresh raspberries**
- **2 cups sliced fresh strawberries**
- **2 cups fresh blueberries**
- **⅓ cup sugar**
- **2 tablespoons plus ¼ cup all-purpose flour, divided**
- **⅓ cup graham cracker crumbs**
- **⅓ cup quick-cooking oats**
- **¼ cup packed brown sugar**
- **2 tablespoons sliced almonds**
- **½ teaspoon ground cinnamon**
- **1 tablespoon canola oil**
- **1 tablespoon butter, melted**
- **1 tablespoon water**

1. In a large bowl, combine the berries, sugar and 2 tablespoons flour; transfer to an 11x7-in. baking dish coated with cooking spray.
2. In a small bowl, combine the cracker crumbs, oats, brown sugar, almonds, cinnamon and remaining flour. Stir in the oil, butter and water until moistened. Sprinkle over berries.
3. Bake at 375° for 25-30 minutes or until filling is bubbly and topping is golden brown.

LEMON BARS

Basic lemon bars have been popular for years. The wonderful tangy flavor is a nice change from chocolate-laden desserts.
—ETTA SOUCY MESA, AZ

PREP: 10 MIN. • **BAKE:** 45 MIN. + COOLING • **MAKES:** 9 SERVINGS

- **1 cup all-purpose flour**
- **½ cup butter, softened**
- **¼ cup confectioners' sugar**

FILLING

- **2 large eggs**
- **1 cup sugar**
- **2 tablespoons all-purpose flour**
- **½ teaspoon baking powder**
- **2 tablespoons lemon juice**
- **1 teaspoon grated lemon peel**
- **Additional confectioners' sugar**

1. In a bowl, combine the flour, butter and confectioners' sugar. Pat into an ungreased 8-in. square baking pan. Bake at 350° for 20 minutes.
2. For filling, in a small bowl, beat eggs. Add the sugar, flour, baking powder, lemon juice and peel; beat until frothy. Pour over the crust. Bake 25 minutes longer or until light golden brown. Cool on a wire rack. Dust with confectioners' sugar. Cut into bars.

FRUIT PIZZA

This colorful dessert is a hit every time I serve it. Refrigerated sugar cookie dough makes for an easy and delicious crust. There's a wealth of nutrients in the fruit, so don't feel guilty enjoying a second piece (or two!).
—JANET O'NEAL POPLAR BLUFF, MO

PREP: 30 MIN. + CHILLING • **BAKE:** 15 MIN. + COOLING
MAKES: 16-20 SERVINGS

- **1 tube (16½ ounces) refrigerated sugar cookie dough**
- **1 package (8 ounces) cream cheese, softened**
- **¼ cup confectioners' sugar**
- **1 carton (8 ounces) frozen whipped topping, thawed**
- **2 to 3 kiwifruit, peeled and thinly sliced**
- **1 to 2 firm bananas, sliced**
- **1 can (11 ounces) mandarin oranges, drained**
- **½ cup red grape halves**
- **¼ cup sugar**
- **¼ cup orange juice**
- **2 tablespoons water**
- **1 tablespoon lemon juice**
- **1½ teaspoons cornstarch**
- **Pinch salt**

1. Pat cookie dough into an ungreased 14-in. pizza pan. Bake at 350° for 15-18 minutes or until deep golden brown; cool.
2. In a bowl, beat the cream cheese and confectioners' sugar until smooth. Fold in whipped topping. Spread over crust. Arrange fruit on top.
3. In a saucepan, bring the sugar, orange juice, water, lemon juice, cornstarch and salt to a boil, stirring constantly for 2 minutes or until thickened. Cool; brush over fruit. Chill. Store in refrigerator.

APPLE DUMPLINGS WITH SAUCE

Covered in a luscious caramel sauce, these spiced dumplings are amazing served alone or with a big scoop of vanilla ice cream.
—ROBIN LENDON CINCINNATI, OH

PREP: 1 HOUR + CHILLING • **BAKE:** 50 MIN. • **MAKES:** 8 SERVINGS

- **3 cups all-purpose flour**
- **1 teaspoon salt**
- **1 cup shortening**
- **⅓ cup cold water**
- **8 medium tart apples, peeled and cored**
- **8 teaspoons butter**
- **9 teaspoons cinnamon-sugar, divided**

SAUCE

- **1½ cups packed brown sugar**
- **1 cup water**
- **½ cup butter, cubed**

1. In a large bowl, combine flour and salt; cut in shortening until crumbly. Gradually add water, tossing with a fork until dough forms a ball. Divide into eight portions. Cover and refrigerate at least 30 minutes or until easy to handle.
2. Preheat oven to 350°. Roll each portion of dough between two lightly floured sheets of waxed paper into a 7-in. square. Place an apple on each square. Place 1 teaspoon butter and 1 teaspoon cinnamon-sugar in the center of each apple.
3. Gently bring up corners of pastry to each center; pinch edges to seal. If desired, cut out apple leaves and stems from dough scraps; attach to dumplings with water. Place in a greased 13x9-in. baking dish. Sprinkle with remaining cinnamon-sugar.
4. In a large saucepan, combine sauce ingredients. Bring just to a boil, stirring until blended. Pour over apples.
5. Bake 50-55 minutes or until apples are tender and pastry is golden brown, basting occasionally with sauce. Serve dumplings warm.

CARAMEL BROWNIES

My family can't possibly eat all of the sweets I whip up, so my co-workers are more than happy to sample them. They're especially fond of these rich, chewy brownies that are full of gooey caramel, chocolate chips and crunchy walnuts.
—CLARA BAKKE COON RAPIDS, MN

PREP: 20 MIN. • **BAKE:** 35 MIN. + COOLING • **MAKES:** 2 DOZEN

- **2 cups sugar**
- **¾ cup baking cocoa**
- **1 cup canola oil**
- **4 large eggs**
- **¼ cup 2% milk**
- **1½ cups all-purpose flour**
- **1 teaspoon salt**
- **1 teaspoon baking powder**
- **1 cup (6 ounces) semisweet chocolate chips**
- **1 cup chopped walnuts, divided**
- **1 package (14 ounces) caramels**
- **1 can (14 ounces) sweetened condensed milk**

1. In a large bowl, beat the sugar, cocoa, oil, eggs and milk. Combine the flour, salt and baking powder; gradually add to egg mixture until well blended. Fold in chocolate chips and ½ cup walnuts.
2. Spoon two-thirds of the batter into a greased 13x9-in. baking pan. Bake at 350° for 12 minutes.
3. Meanwhile, in a large saucepan, heat the caramels and condensed milk over low heat until caramels are melted. Pour over baked brownie layer. Sprinkle with remaining chopped walnuts.
4. Drop remaining batter by teaspoonfuls over caramel layer; carefully swirl brownie batter with a knife.
5. Bake for 35-40 minutes or until a toothpick inserted near the center comes out with moist crumbs (do not overbake). Cool on a wire rack.

TOP TIP

Storing Brownies

Cover a pan of uncut brownies with foil or put the pan in a large resealable plastic bag. (If made with perishable ingredients, like cream cheese, they should be covered and refrigerated.) Once the brownies are cut, store them in an airtight container. Most brownies freeze well for up to 3 months. To freeze a pan of uncut bars, place in an airtight container or resealable plastic bag. Or wrap individual bars in plastic wrap and stack in an airtight container. Thaw at room temperature before serving.

"My 14-year-old daughter first made these for Christmas four years ago. I didn't think that they would be special enough. Boy, was I wrong! They are a hit wherever we take them."

—**PEPPER6** FROM TASTEOFHOME.COM

TROPICAL CARROT CAKE

I look forward to August because that's when our clan gets together for our annual family reunion. Everyone loves this classic carrot cake with the special flair it gets from pineapple. My great-aunt gave me the recipe, and I've made it a tradition to bring it every year.
—VICTORIA CASEY ENTERPRISE, OR

PREP: 15 MIN. • **BAKE:** 45 MIN. + COOLING
MAKES: 12-16 SERVINGS

- **3 large eggs**
- **¾ cup canola oil**
- **¾ cup buttermilk**
- **2 cups all-purpose flour**
- **2 cups sugar**
- **2 teaspoons baking soda**
- **2 teaspoons ground cinnamon**
- **½ teaspoon salt**
- **2 teaspoons vanilla extract**
- **2 cups finely shredded carrots**
- **1 cup raisins**
- **1 can (8 ounces) crushed pineapple, undrained**
- **1 cup chopped walnuts**
- **1 cup flaked coconut**

FROSTING

- **1 package (8 ounces) cream cheese, softened**
- **4 to 4½ cups confectioners' sugar**
- **1 to 2 tablespoons heavy whipping cream**
- **1 teaspoon vanilla extract**

1. In a large bowl, beat eggs, oil and buttermilk. Combine flour, sugar, baking soda, cinnamon and salt; add to egg mixture and mix well. Stir in vanilla, carrots, raisins, pineapple, walnuts and coconut; mix well. Pour into a greased 13x9-in. baking pan. Bake at 350° for 45-50 minutes or until cake tests done. Cool.
2. For frosting, beat all ingredients in a bowl until smooth. Frost cake.

FAST FIX

WHITE CHOCOLATE-STRAWBERRY TIRAMISU

Here's a twist on a classic dessert that highlights another flavor combo my husband and I love: strawberries and white chocolate. Lighten it up if you'd like—I've had good luck with light nondairy whipped topping and reduced-fat cream cheese.
—ANNA GINSBERG AUSTIN, TX

START TO FINISH: 30 MIN.
MAKES: 15 SERVINGS

- **2 cups heavy whipping cream**
- **1 package (8 ounces) cream cheese, softened**
- **½ cup (4 ounces) mascarpone cheese**
- **9 ounces white baking chocolate, melted and cooled**
- **1 cup confectioners' sugar, divided**
- **1 teaspoon vanilla extract**
- **2 packages (3 ounces each) ladyfingers, split**
- **⅔ cup orange juice**
- **4 cups sliced fresh strawberries**
- **Chocolate syrup, optional**

1. In a large bowl, beat cream until soft peaks form. In another bowl, beat cheeses until light and fluffy. Beat in cooled chocolate, ½ cup confectioners' sugar and vanilla. Fold in 2 cups of the whipped cream.
2. Brush half of the ladyfingers with half of the orange juice; arrange in a 13x9-in. dish. Spread with 2 cups cream cheese mixture; top with half of the strawberries. Brush remaining ladyfingers with remaining orange juice; arrange over berries.
3. Gently stir remaining confectioners' sugar into remaining cream cheese mixture; fold in remaining whipped cream. Spread over ladyfingers. Top with the remaining strawberries. Refrigerate until serving. If desired, drizzle with chocolate syrup before serving.

CONTEST-WINNING GERMAN CHOCOLATE PIE

Thanksgiving dinner at our house averages 25 guests and a dozen different pies. This particular pie resembles a luscious German chocolate cake.
—DEBBIE CLAY FARMINGTON, NM

PREP: 40 MIN. + CHILLING
BAKE: 30 MIN. + COOLING
MAKES: 8 SERVINGS

Pastry for single-crust pie (9 inches)

FILLING

- **4 ounces German sweet chocolate, chopped**
- **1 tablespoon butter**
- **1 teaspoon vanilla extract**
- **⅓ cup sugar**
- **3 tablespoons cornstarch**
- **1½ cups whole milk**
- **2 large egg yolks**

TOPPING

- **⅔ cup evaporated milk**
- **½ cup sugar**
- **¼ cup butter, cubed**
- **1 large egg, lightly beaten**
- **1⅓ cups flaked coconut, toasted**
- **½ cup chopped pecans, toasted**

1. Preheat oven to 400°. On a lightly floured surface, roll pastry dough to a ⅛-in.-thick circle; transfer to a 9-in. pie plate. Trim pastry to ½ in. beyond rim of plate; flute edge.
2. Line unpricked pastry with a double thickness of foil. Fill with pie weights, dried beans or uncooked rice. Bake 25 minutes. Remove foil and weights; bake 4-6 minutes longer or until golden brown. Cool on a wire rack.
3. For filling, in a microwave, melt chocolate and butter; stir until smooth. Stir in vanilla. In a small heavy saucepan, mix sugar and cornstarch. Whisk in whole milk. Cook and stir over medium heat until thickened and bubbly. Reduce heat to low; cook and stir 2 minutes longer. Remove from heat.
4. In a small bowl, whisk a small amount of hot mixture into egg yolks; return all to pan, whisking constantly. Bring to a gentle boil; cook and stir 2 minutes. Remove from heat. Stir in chocolate mixture. Pour into crust.
5. For topping, in a small saucepan, combine evaporated milk, sugar and butter. Cook and stir until butter is melted and mixture just comes to a boil. Remove from heat.
6. In a small bowl, whisk a small amount of hot mixture into egg; return all to pan, whisking constantly. Bring to a gentle boil; cook and stir 2 minutes. Remove from heat. Stir in coconut and pecans. Pour over filling.
7. Cool pie 30 minutes on a wire rack. Refrigerate, covered, until cold, at least 3 hours.

EASY FRESH STRAWBERRY PIE

Guests will love the fruity flavor and signature flaky crust in this classic summer pie. I often use whole fresh strawberries and arrange them pointed side up in the pastry shell for a different presentation. This method not only yields an attractive look but also is a time-saver because I don't have to slice the berries. For a finishing touch, I add a generous dollop of sweet whipped cream in the center.

—SUE JURACK MEQUON, WI

PREP: 20 MIN. + COOLING • **BAKE:** 15 MIN. + CHILLING
MAKES: 6-8 SERVINGS

- **1 unbaked pastry shell (9 inches)**
- **¾ cup sugar**
- **2 tablespoons cornstarch**
- **1 cup water**
- **1 package (3 ounces) strawberry gelatin**
- **4 cups sliced fresh strawberries**
- **Fresh mint, optional**

1. Line unpricked pastry shell with a double thickness of heavy-duty foil. Bake at 450° for 8 minutes. Remove foil; bake 5 minutes longer. Cool on a wire rack.
2. In a small saucepan, combine the sugar, cornstarch and water until smooth. Bring to a boil; cook and stir for 2 minutes or until thickened. Remove from the heat; stir in gelatin until dissolved. Refrigerate for 15-20 minutes or until slightly cooled.
3. Meanwhile, arrange strawberries in the crust. Pour gelatin mixture over berries. Refrigerate until set. Garnish with mint if desired.

BLUE-RIBBON BUTTER CAKE

I found this recipe in an old cookbook I bought at a garage sale, and I couldn't wait to try it. I knew it had been someone's favorite because of the well-worn page.

—JOAN GERTZ PALMETTO, FL

PREP: 20 MIN. • **BAKE:** 65 MIN. + COOLING • **MAKES:** 12-16 SERVINGS

- **1 cup butter, softened**
- **2 cups sugar**
- **4 large eggs**
- **2 teaspoons vanilla extract**
- **3 cups all-purpose flour**
- **1 teaspoon baking powder**
- **½ teaspoon baking soda**
- **½ teaspoon salt**
- **1 cup buttermilk**

BUTTER SAUCE

- **1 cup sugar**
- **½ cup butter, cubed**
- **¼ cup water**
- **1½ teaspoons almond extract**
- **1½ teaspoons vanilla extract**

1. In a large bowl, cream butter and sugar until light and fluffy. Add eggs, one at a time, beating well after each addition. Beat in vanilla. Combine the flour, baking powder, baking soda and salt; add to creamed mixture alternately with buttermilk, beating well after each addition.
2. Pour into a greased and floured 10-in. tube pan. Bake at 350° for 65-70 minutes or until a toothpick inserted near the center comes out clean. Cool for 10 minutes. Run a knife around edges and center tube of pan. Invert cake onto a wire rack over waxed paper.
3. For sauce, combine the sugar, butter and water in a small saucepan. Cook over medium heat just until butter is melted and sugar is dissolved. Remove from the heat; stir in extracts.
4. Poke holes in the top of the warm cake; spoon 1/4 cup sauce over cake. Let stand until sauce is absorbed. Repeat twice. Poke holes into sides of cake; brush remaining sauce over sides. Cool completely.

FAVORITE BANANA CREAM PIE

Cream pies are my mom's specialty, and this dreamy dessert has the classic fruity flavor we all know and love. It looks so pretty topped with sliced bananas, and it cuts easily, too.

—JODI GRABLE SPRINGFIELD, MO

PREP: 10 MIN. • **COOK:** 15 MIN. + CHILLING • **MAKES:** 8 SERVINGS

- **1 cup sugar**
- **¼ cup cornstarch**
- **½ teaspoon salt**
- **3 cups 2% milk**
- **2 large eggs, lightly beaten**
- **3 tablespoons butter**
- **1½ teaspoons vanilla extract**
- **1 pastry shell (9 inches), baked**
- **2 large firm bananas**
- **1 cup heavy whipping cream, whipped**

1. In a large saucepan, combine sugar, cornstarch, salt and milk until smooth. Cook and stir over medium-high heat until thickened and bubbly. Reduce heat; cook and stir 2 minutes longer. Remove from heat. Stir a small amount of hot filling into eggs; return all to pan. Bring to a gentle boil; cook and stir 2 minutes longer.
2. Remove from heat. Gently stir in butter and vanilla. Press plastic wrap onto surface of custard; refrigerate, covered, 30 minutes.
3. Spread half of the custard into pastry shell. Slice bananas; arrange over filling. Pour remaining custard over bananas. Spread with whipped cream. Refrigerate for 6 hours or overnight. Garnish pie with additional banana slices right before serving.

APPLE PIE

I remember coming home one day feeling down because we lost our softball game. Grandma, in her wisdom, suggested, "Maybe a slice of hot apple pie will make you feel better." One bite...and Grandma sure was right.

—MAGGIE GREENE GRANITE FALLS, WA

PREP: 20 MIN. • **BAKE:** 45 MIN. • **MAKES:** 8 SERVINGS

- **½ cup sugar**
- **½ cup packed brown sugar**
- **3 tablespoons all-purpose flour**
- **1 teaspoon ground cinnamon**
- **¼ teaspoon ground ginger**
- **¼ teaspoon ground nutmeg**
- **6 to 7 cups thinly sliced peeled tart apples**
- **1 tablespoon lemon juice**
- **Pastry for double-crust pie (9 inches)**
- **1 tablespoon butter**
- **1 large egg white**
- **Additional sugar**

1. In a small bowl, combine the sugars, flour and spices; set aside. In a large bowl, toss apples with lemon juice. Add sugar mixture; toss to coat.
2. Line a 9-in. pie plate with bottom crust; trim pastry even with edge. Fill with apple mixture; dot with butter. Roll out remaining pastry to fit top of pie. Place over filling. Trim, seal and flute edges. Cut slits in pastry.
3. Beat egg white until foamy; brush over pastry. Sprinkle with sugar. Cover edges loosely with foil.
4. Bake at 375° for 25 minutes. Remove foil and bake 20-25 minutes longer or until crust is golden brown and filling is bubbly. Cool on a wire rack.

STRAWBERRY PRETZEL DESSERT

A salty pretzel crust nicely contrasts with cream cheese and gelatin layers.

—ALDENE BELCH FLINT, MI

PREP: 20 MIN. • **BAKE:** 10 MIN. + CHILLING
MAKES: 12-16 SERVINGS

- **2 cups crushed pretzels (about 8 ounces)**
- **¾ cup butter, melted**
- **3 tablespoons sugar**

FILLING

- **2 cups whipped topping**
- **1 package (8 ounces) cream cheese, softened**
- **1 cup sugar**

TOPPING

- **2 packages (3 ounces each) strawberry gelatin**
- **2 cups boiling water**
- **2 packages (16 ounces each) frozen sweetened sliced strawberries, thawed**
- **Additional whipped topping, optional**

1. In a bowl, combine the pretzels, melted butter and sugar. Press into an ungreased 13x9-in. baking dish. Bake at 350° for 10 minutes. Cool on a wire rack.
2. For filling, in a small bowl, beat the whipped topping, cream cheese and sugar until smooth. Spread over pretzel crust. Refrigerate until chilled.
3. For topping, dissolve gelatin in boiling water in a large bowl. Stir in strawberries with syrup; chill until partially set. Carefully spoon over filling. Chill for 4-6 hours or until firm. Cut into squares; serve with whipped topping if desired.

CREAM CHEESE-PINEAPPLE PIE

I've made this light and refreshing pie many times for friends, relatives, guests, church suppers and bazaars, and I'm always getting requests for the recipe. It's one of our favorite ways to complete a meal. I've lived on farms all my life, and I love the old-fashioned appeal of down-home desserts like this one.

—ELIZABETH BROWN CLAYTON, DE

PREP: 20 MIN. • **BAKE:** 1 HOUR + COOLING
MAKES: 8 SERVINGS

PINEAPPLE LAYER

- **⅓ cup sugar**
- **1 tablespoon cornstarch**
- **1 can (8 ounces) crushed pineapple with juice**

CREAM CHEESE LAYER

- **1 package (8 ounces) cream cheese, softened to room temperature**
- **½ cup sugar**
- **1 teaspoon salt**
- **2 large eggs**
- **½ cup milk**
- **½ teaspoon vanilla extract**
- **1 9-inch unbaked pie shell**
- **¼ cup chopped pecans**

1. Combine sugar, cornstarch and crushed pineapple plus juice in a small saucepan. Cook over medium heat, stirring constantly until mixture is thick and clear. Cool; set aside.
2. Blend the cream cheese, sugar and salt in mixer bowl. Add eggs, one at a time, beating after each addition. Blend in milk and vanilla. (Mixture may look slightly curdled.)
3. Spread cooled pineapple mixture over bottom of pie shell. Pour cream cheese mixture over pineapple layer; sprinkle with pecans.
4. Bake at 400° for 10 minutes; reduce heat to 325° and bake for 50 minutes. Cool completely before serving.

BANANA PUDDING

I didn't see my son, Lance Cpl. Eric Harris, for more than two years after he enlisted in the Marines after high school. The day he arrived stateside, I burst into tears of joy right there in the airport. This banana pudding was the first thing I made for him once we got back to our house. The comforts of home just can't be beat.
—STEPHANIE HARRIS MONTPELIER, VA

PREP: 35 MIN. + CHILLING
MAKES: 9 SERVINGS

¾ cup sugar
¼ cup all-purpose flour
¼ teaspoon salt
3 cups 2% milk
3 large eggs
1½ teaspoons vanilla extract
8 ounces vanilla wafers (about 60 cookies), divided
4 large ripe bananas, cut into ¼-inch slices

1. In a large saucepan, mix sugar, flour and salt. Whisk in milk. Cook and stir over medium heat until thickened and bubbly. Reduce heat to low; cook and stir 2 minutes longer. Remove from heat.
2. In a small bowl, whisk eggs. Whisk a small amount of hot mixture into eggs; return all to the pan, whisking constantly. Bring to a gentle boil; cook and stir 2 minutes. Remove from heat. Stir in the vanilla. Cool for 15 minutes, stirring occasionally.
3. In an ungreased 8-in. square baking dish, layer 25 vanilla wafers, half of the banana slices and half of the pudding. Repeat layers.
4. Press plastic wrap onto surface of pudding. Refrigerate 4 hours or overnight. Just before serving, crush remaining wafers and sprinkle over the top of pudding.

TOP TIP

Graham Cracker Topping

Whenever I make banana pudding, I crush up cinnamon graham crackers and sprinkle them on top. These spiced crumbs also make a good topping on other baked goods.
—JANET L. VANDALIA, IL

PEANUT BUTTER CREAM PIE

During the warm months, it's nice to have a fluffy, no-bake dessert that's a snap to make. Packed with peanut flavor, this pie gets gobbled up even after a big meal.
—JESSE & ANNE FOUST BLUEFIELD, WV

PREP: 10 MIN. + CHILLING
MAKES: 6-8 SERVINGS

- **1 package (8 ounces) cream cheese, softened**
- **¾ cup confectioners' sugar**
- **½ cup peanut butter**
- **6 tablespoons milk**
- **1 carton (8 ounces) frozen whipped topping, thawed**
- **1 graham cracker crust (9 inches)**
- **¼ cup chopped peanuts**

In a large bowl, beat cream cheese until fluffy. Beat in sugar and peanut butter. Gradually add milk. Fold in whipped topping; spoon into the crust. Sprinkle with peanuts. Chill overnight.

COCONUT PIE

I grew up watching my mother cook and bake from scratch. So the idea of anything being available pre-made was an almost foreign concept until I'd left home. One of Mom's best desserts is her creamy old-fashioned coconut pie. A rich slice is true comfort food.
—MARY MCGUIRE GRAHAM, NC

PREP: 10 MIN. • **BAKE:** 50 MIN. + COOLING
MAKES: 6-8 SERVINGS

- **1½ cups milk**
- **1 cup sugar**
- **¾ cup flaked coconut**
- **2 large eggs, lightly beaten**
- **3 tablespoons all-purpose flour**
- **1 tablespoon butter, melted**
- **¼ teaspoon vanilla extract**
- **1 unbaked pastry shell (9 inches)**

1. In a large bowl, combine the milk, sugar, coconut, eggs, flour, butter and vanilla. Pour into pie shell.
2. Bake at 350° for 50 minutes or until a knife inserted near the center comes out clean. Cool to room temperature. Refrigerate leftovers.

CREAMY CARAMEL FLAN

Flan is a tasty variation on custard. One warning, though—it's very filling! A small slice goes a long way.
—PAT FORETE MIAMI, FL

PREP: 25 MIN. + STANDING
BAKE: 50 MIN. + CHILLING
MAKES: 8-10 SERVINGS

- **¾ cup sugar**
- **1 package (8 ounces) cream cheese, softened**
- **5 large eggs**
- **1 can (14 ounces) sweetened condensed milk**
- **1 can (12 ounces) evaporated milk**
- **1 teaspoon vanilla extract**

1. In a heavy saucepan, cook and stir sugar over medium-low heat until melted and golden, about 15 minutes. Quickly pour into an ungreased 2-qt. round baking or souffle dish, tilting to coat the bottom; let mixture stand for 10 minutes.
2. In a bowl, beat the cream cheese until smooth. Beat in eggs, one at a time, until thoroughly combined. Add remaining ingredients; mix well. Pour over caramelized sugar.
3. Place the dish in a larger baking pan. Pour boiling water into larger pan to a depth of 1 in. Bake at 350° for 50-60 minutes or until center is just set (mixture will jiggle).
4. Remove dish from a larger pan to a wire rack; cool for 1 hour. Refrigerate overnight.
5. To unmold, run a knife around edges and invert onto a large rimmed serving platter. Cut into wedges or spoon onto dessert plates; spoon sauce over each serving.

NOTE *Pay close attention when melting sugar as it changes quickly. Be sure to find a pan for the water bath before starting to prepare the recipe.*

CHOCOLATE BAVARIAN TORTE

Whenever I take this torte to a potluck, I get so many requests for the recipe.
—EDITH HOLMSTROM MADISON, WI

PREP: 15 MIN. + CHILLING
BAKE: 30 MIN. + COOLING
MAKES: 12 SERVINGS

- **1 package devil's food cake mix (regular size)**
- **1 package (8 ounces) cream cheese, softened**
- **⅓ cup packed brown sugar**
- **1 teaspoon vanilla extract**
- **⅛ teaspoon salt**
- **2 cups heavy whipping cream, whipped**
- **2 tablespoons grated semisweet chocolate**

1. Prepare and bake cake according to package directions, using two 9-in. round baking pans. Cool in pans for 10 minutes before removing to wire racks to cool completely.
2. In a large bowl, beat the cream cheese, sugar, vanilla and salt until smooth. Fold in cream.
3. Cut each cake horizontally into two layers. Place bottom layer on a serving plate; top with a fourth of the cream mixture. Sprinkle with a fourth of the grated chocolate. Repeat layers three times. Cover torte and refrigerate for 8 hours or overnight.

ICED ORANGE COOKIES, 189

CARAMEL PRETZEL BITES, 197

CHOCOLATE MINT WAFERS, 186

RASPBERRY COCONUT COOKIES, 193

COOKIES & CANDIES

Whether you like them soft and chewy or crisp and crunchy, scrumptious homemade cookies make it nearly impossible to stop at just one! Satisfy your sweet tooth with this collection of slice and bake, sandwich, shaped, drop and thumbprint delights. Still need a sweet treat? Consider any of the tooth-tingling candies found here as well. From truffles to caramels, these no-fuss confections always get thumbs-up approval.

CHOCOLATE CHIP COOKIE MIX

These are the perfect cookies when cooking for a crowd because the mix can be prepared and stored for months. Also, you can bake a couple batches of cookies at a time and freeze them.
—**HELEN WORONIK** SALEM, CT

PREP: 15 MIN. • **BAKE:** 10 MIN./BATCH
MAKES: 5 DOZEN PER BATCH

COOKIE MIX
- **9 cups all-purpose flour**
- **4 teaspoons baking soda**
- **2 teaspoons salt**
- **3 cups packed brown sugar**
- **3 cups sugar**
- **4 cups shortening**

COOKIES
- **6 cups Cookie Mix (above)**
- **1 teaspoon vanilla extract**
- **2 large eggs, beaten**
- **2 cups (12 ounces) semisweet chocolate chips**

Thoroughly combine dry ingredients; cut in shortening until crumbly. Store in an airtight container in a cool dry place up to 6 months. Makes: 3 batches (18 cups mix).

TO MAKE COOKIES *Preheat oven to 375°. In a bowl, combine mix, vanilla and eggs. Fold in chocolate chips. Drop by tablespoonfuls ½ in. apart onto greased baking sheets. Bake 10-12 minutes or until golden brown. Remove to wire racks to cool.*

CHOCOLATE MINT WAFERS

These chocolaty treats with cool mint filling won't last long around your house. They're so pretty stacked on a glass plate.
—**ANNETTE ESAU** DURHAM, ON

PREP: 30 MIN. + CHILLING
BAKE: 5 MIN./BATCH + COOLING
MAKES: ABOUT 7½ DOZEN

- **⅔ cup butter, softened**
- **½ cup sugar**
- **½ cup packed brown sugar**
- **¼ cup whole milk**
- **1 large egg**
- **2 cups all-purpose flour**
- **¾ cup baking cocoa**
- **1 teaspoon baking powder**
- **½ teaspoon baking soda**
- **¼ teaspoon salt**

FILLING
- **2¾ cups confectioners' sugar**
- **¼ cup half-and-half cream**
- **¼ teaspoon peppermint extract**
- **¼ teaspoon salt**
- **Green food coloring**

1. In a large bowl, cream butter and sugars until light and fluffy. Beat in milk and egg. Combine the flour, cocoa, baking powder, baking soda and salt; gradually add to creamed mixture and mix well. Cover and refrigerate for 2 hours or until firm.

2. On a lightly floured surface, roll out dough to ⅛-in. thickness. Cut with a 1½-in. cookie cutter and place 1 in. apart on greased baking sheets. Bake at 375° for 5-6 minutes or until edges are lightly browned. Remove to wire racks to cool completely.

3. Combine filling ingredients; spread on bottom of half of the cookies and top with remaining cookies.

HAZELNUT BONBON COOKIES

Take hazelnuts to a whole new level. Wrap them up in cookie dough, dip in chocolate and finish with sprinkles or colored sugar.

—NANCY MUELLER
MENOMONEE FALLS, WI

PREP: 30 MIN.
BAKE: 10 MIN./BATCH + COOLING
MAKES: 3½ DOZEN

- **2 teaspoons instant espresso powder**
- **2 teaspoons hot water**
- **½ cup butter, softened**
- **¾ cup confectioners' sugar**
- **⅛ teaspoon salt**
- **3 teaspoons vanilla extract**
- **1½ cups all-purpose flour**
- **42 whole hazelnuts**

GLAZE

- **3 ounces semisweet chocolate, chopped**
- **2 tablespoons plus 1½ teaspoons butter**
- **1 tablespoon confectioners' sugar**
- **Chocolate jimmies**

1. In a small bowl, dissolve espresso powder in hot water; cool. Preheat oven to 350°. In a large bowl, cream butter, confectioners' sugar and salt until light and fluffy. Beat in vanilla and espresso mixture. Gradually beat in flour.

2. Wrap 1 heaping teaspoon of dough around each hazelnut to cover completely. Place 2 in. apart on ungreased baking sheets. Bake 8-10 minutes or until bottoms are golden brown. Remove to wire racks to cool completely.

3. For glaze, in a microwave, melt chocolate and butter; stir until smooth. Whisk in confectioners' sugar until blended. Dip tops of cookies in glaze; allow excess to drip off. Place on waxed paper; sprinkle with jimmies and let stand until set.

FREEZE OPTION *Freeze unglazed cookies, layered between waxed paper, in freezer containers. To use, thaw cookies in covered containers. Dip in glaze as directed.*

ROLL-OUT COOKIES

I collect cookie cutters (I have over 5,000!), so a good cutout recipe is a must. These cookies are crisp and buttery-tasting with just a hint of lemon, and the dough handles nicely.

—BONNIE PRICE YELM, WA

PREP: 25 MIN. • **BAKE:** 10 MIN./BATCH
MAKES: ABOUT 6 DOZEN 2¼-IN. COOKIES

- **1 cup butter, softened**
- **1 cup sugar**
- **1 large egg**
- **1 teaspoon vanilla extract**
- **½ teaspoon lemon extract**
- **3 cups all-purpose flour**
- **2 teaspoons baking powder**

GLAZE

- **1 cup confectioners' sugar**
- **2 tablespoons water**
- **1 tablespoon light corn syrup**
- **Food coloring, optional**

In a bowl, cream butter and sugar. Add the egg and extracts. Combine flour and baking powder; gradually add to creamed mixture and mix well. (Dough will be very stiff. If necessary, stir in the last cup of flour mixture by hand. Do not chill.) On a lightly floured surface, roll dough to ⅛-in. thickness. Cut out cookies into desired shapes. Place 2 in. apart on ungreased baking sheets. Bake at 400° for 6-7 minutes or until edges are lightly browned. Cool 2 minutes before removing to wire racks; cool completely. For glaze, combine the sugar, water and corn syrup until smooth. Tint with food coloring if desired. Using a small brush and stirring glaze often, brush on cookies, decorating as desired.

ORANGE COCONUT CREAMS

Originally a gift from our neighbors, this recipe has become one of our own favorites to make and give at the holidays.

—JULIE FORNSHELL BISMARK, ND

PREP: 1 HOUR + CHILLING • **MAKES:** 9 DOZEN

- **1 can (14 ounces) sweetened condensed milk**
- **½ cup butter, cubed**
- **1 package (2 pounds) confectioners' sugar**
- **1 cup flaked coconut**
- **1½ teaspoons orange extract**
- **2 cups (12 ounces) semisweet chocolate**
- **8 ounces German sweet chocolate, chopped**
- **2 tablespoons shortening**

1. In a small saucepan, combine milk and butter. Cook and stir over low heat until the butter is melted. Place the confectioners' sugar in a large bowl. Add milk mixture; beat until smooth. Add the coconut and orange extract; mix well. Roll into 1-in. balls; place on waxed paper-lined baking sheets. Refrigerate until firm, about 1 hour.

2. In a microwave, melt the chips, chocolate and shortening; stir until smooth. Dip balls into chocolate; allow excess to drip off. Place on waxed paper; let stand until set.

5 INGREDIENTS

CARAMEL TRUFFLES

My caramel-filled candies disappear as fast as I can make them. The five-ingredient microwave recipe is easy and fun to make.
—CHARLOTTE MIDTHUN GRANITE FALLS, MN

PREP: 1 HOUR + CHILLING • **MAKES:** 2½ DOZEN

- **26 caramels**
- **1 cup milk chocolate chips**
- **¼ cup heavy whipping cream**
- **1⅓ cups semisweet chocolate chips**
- **1 tablespoon shortening**

1. Line an 8-in. square dish with plastic wrap; set aside. In a microwave-safe bowl, combine the caramels, milk chocolate chips and cream. Microwave, uncovered, on high for 1 minute; stir. Microwave 1 minute longer, stirring every 15 seconds or until caramels are melted and mixture is smooth. Spread into prepared dish; refrigerate for 1 hour or until firm.
2. Using plastic wrap, lift candy out of pan. Cut into 30 pieces; roll each piece into a 1-in. ball. Cover and refrigerate for 1 hour or until firm.
3. In a microwave-safe bowl, melt semisweet chips and shortening; stir until smooth. Dip caramels in chocolate; allow excess to drip off. Place on waxed paper; let stand until set. Refrigerate until firm.
NOTE *This recipe was tested in a 1,100-watt microwave.*

ICED ORANGE COOKIES

I usually make these bite-size cookies at Christmastime, when oranges in Florida are plentiful. Every time I experience their wonderful aroma, I remember my grandmother, who shared the recipe.
—LORI DIPIETRO NEW PORT RICHEY, FL

PREP: 15 MIN. • **BAKE:** 10 MIN./BATCH + COOLING
MAKES: ABOUT 5½ DOZEN

- **½ cup shortening**
- **1 cup sugar**
- **2 large eggs**
- **½ cup orange juice**
- **1 tablespoon grated orange peel**
- **2½ cups all-purpose flour**
- **1½ teaspoons baking powder**
- **½ teaspoon salt**

ICING

- **2 cups confectioners' sugar**
- **¼ cup orange juice**
- **2 tablespoons butter, melted**
- **Orange paste food coloring, optional**

1. In a large bowl, cream the shortening and sugar until light and fluffy. Add eggs, one at a time, beating well after each addition. Beat in orange juice and peel. Combine the flour, baking powder and salt; gradually add to the creamed mixture.
2. Drop by heaping teaspoonfuls 2 in. apart onto ungreased baking sheets. Bake at 350° for 10-12 minutes or until edges begin to brown. Remove to wire racks to cool. In a small bowl, combine icing ingredients until smooth; drizzle over cooled cookies.

CREAMY ORANGE CARAMELS

Each Christmas I teach myself a new candy recipe. Last year I started with my caramel recipe and added a splash of orange extract for fun. This year I just might try buttered rum extract.
—SHELLY BEVINGTON HERMISTON, OR

PREP: 10 MIN. • **COOK:** 30 MIN.+ STANDING
MAKES: ABOUT 2½ POUNDS (80 PIECES)

- **1 teaspoon plus 1 cup butter, divided**
- **2 cups sugar**
- **1 cup light corn syrup**
- **1 can (14 ounces) sweetened condensed milk**
- **1 teaspoon orange extract**
- **1 teaspoon vanilla extract**

1. Line an 11x 7-in. dish with foil; grease the foil with 1 teaspoon butter.
2. In a large heavy saucepan, combine the sugar, corn syrup and remaining butter. Bring to a boil over medium heat, stirring constantly. Reduce heat to medium-low; boil gently, without stirring, for 4 minutes.
3. Remove from the heat; gradually stir in milk. Cook and stir until a candy thermometer reads 244° (firm-ball stage). Remove from the heat; stir in extracts. Immediately pour into prepared dish (do not scrape saucepan). Let stand until firm.
4. Using foil, lift out candy; remove foil. Using a buttered knife, cut caramel into 1x ¾-in. pieces. Wrap individually in waxed paper; twist ends.
NOTE *We recommend that you test your candy thermometer before each use by bringing water to a boil; the thermometer should read 212°. Adjust your recipe temperature up or down based on your test.*

FAVORITE MACAROON KISSES

These cookies are a holiday favorite around our house. You can top them off with cherries or chocolate—or some of each!
—ALICE MCTARNAGHAN CASTLETON, NY

PREP: 20 MIN. • **BAKE:** 10 MIN./BATCH • **MAKES:** ABOUT 4 DOZEN

- **⅓ cup butter, softened**
- **1 package (3 ounces) cream cheese, softened**
- **¾ cup sugar**
- **1 large egg yolk**
- **1½ teaspoons almond extract**
- **2 teaspoons orange juice**
- **1¼ cups all-purpose flour**
- **2 teaspoons baking powder**
- **¼ teaspoon salt**
- **5 cups coconut, divided**
- **Candied cherries and/or chocolate kisses**

1. In a large bowl, cream the butter, cream cheese and sugar until light and fluffy. Beat in the egg yolk, extract and juice. Combine the flour, baking powder and salt; gradually add to creamed mixture and mix well. Stir in 3 cups of coconut. Cover and chill for at least 1 hour.
2. Shape into 1-in. balls; roll in remaining coconut. Place 2 in. apart on ungreased baking sheets. Bake at 350° for 10-12 minutes or until lightly browned. Immediately place a cherry or chocolate kiss on top of each cookie. Cool 5 minutes; remove to a wire rack to cool completely.

GIANT LEMON SUGAR COOKIES

My wonderfully chewy cookies have a light lemon flavor from the juice and the zest. The sanding of sugar on top adds sparkle and crunch.

—MICHAEL VYSKOCIL GLEN ROCK, PA

PREP: 25 MIN. • **BAKE:** 15 MIN./BATCH • **MAKES:** 14 COOKIES

- **1 cup unsalted butter, softened**
- **1½ cups sugar**
- **½ cup packed brown sugar**
- **2 large eggs**
- **1½ teaspoons grated lemon peel**
- **2 tablespoons lemon juice**
- **3 cups all-purpose flour**
- **1 teaspoon baking soda**
- **¼ teaspoon salt**
- **¼ teaspoon cream of tartar**
- **4 teaspoons coarse sugar**

1. Preheat oven to 350°. In a large bowl, cream butter and sugars until light and fluffy. Beat in eggs. Beat in lemon peel and juice. In another bowl, whisk flour, baking soda, salt and cream of tartar; gradually beat into creamed mixture.

2. Shape 1/4 cupfuls of dough into balls. Place 6 in. apart on greased baking sheets. Flatten to ¾-in. thickness with bottom of a measuring cup. Lightly brush tops with water; sprinkle with coarse sugar.

3. Bake 12-15 minutes or until light brown. Remove from pans to wire racks to cool completely. Store in airtight containers.

BABY RUTH COOKIES

I love Baby Ruth candy bars and usually have a few on hand, so I decided to put them to good use in my favorite cookie recipe.

—ELINOR NIELD SOQUEL, CA

PREP: 15 MIN. • **BAKE:** 10 MIN./BATCH • **MAKES:** 4 DOZEN

- **½ cup butter, softened**
- **¾ cup sugar**
- **1 large egg**
- **½ teaspoon vanilla extract**
- **1⅓ cups all-purpose flour**
- **½ teaspoon baking soda**
- **½ teaspoon salt**
- **2 Baby Ruth candy bars (2.1 ounces each), chopped**

1. In a large bowl, cream butter and sugar until light and fluffy. Beat in egg and vanilla. Combine flour, baking soda and salt; gradually add to the creamed mixture. Stir in candy bars.

2. Drop by rounded teaspoonfuls 2 in. apart onto greased baking sheets. Bake at 350° for 10 minutes or until edges are lightly browned. Immediately remove to wire racks to cool.

“I made these cookies for two of my friends for Christmas and they were great!”

—MIKELSSWORD
FROM TASTEOFHOME.COM

CREAM-FILLED CHOCOLATE COOKIES

I've been making these cookies for years. My children and grandchildren gobble them up.

—**MAXINE FINN** EMMETSBURG, IA

PREP: 15 MIN. + CHILLING
BAKE: 10 MIN./BATCH + COOLING
MAKES: ABOUT 4½ DOZEN

- **1 cup butter, softened**
- **2 cups sugar**
- **2 large eggs**
- **1 teaspoon vanilla extract**
- **3 cups all-purpose flour**
- **⅔ cup baking cocoa**
- **1 teaspoon baking soda**
- **1 teaspoon salt**
- **½ cup whole milk**

FILLING

- **½ cup butter, softened**
- **1½ cups confectioners' sugar**
- **1 cup marshmallow creme**
- **1 teaspoon vanilla extract**

1. In a large bowl, cream butter and sugar until light and fluffy. Add eggs, one at a time, beating well after each addition. Beat in vanilla. Combine the flour, cocoa, baking soda and salt; gradually add to creamed mixture alternately with milk, beating well after each addition. Refrigerate for at least 2 hours.

2. Drop by rounded teaspoonfuls 2 in. apart onto greased baking sheets. Bake at 375° for 10-12 minutes or until edges are set. Remove to wire racks to cool.

3. In a small bowl, combine filling ingredients; beat until smooth. Spread on the bottoms of half of the cookies; top with remaining cookies. Store in the refrigerator.

VIENNESE COOKIES

I love to cook and bake. When I worked at a medical clinic, I became known as the "cookie lady." A Swedish friend gave me the recipe for these cookies. At Christmas I often triple or quadruple it so I have plenty to share and send.

—**BEVERLY STIRRAT** MISSION, BC

PREP: 35 MIN. + CHILLING
BAKE: 10 MIN./BATCH + COOLING
MAKES: ABOUT 3 DOZEN

- **1¼ cups butter, softened**
- **⅔ cup sugar**
- **2¼ cups all-purpose flour**
- **1⅔ cups ground almonds**
- **1 cup apricot preserves**
- **2 cups (12 ounces) semisweet chocolate chips**
- **2 tablespoons shortening**

1. In a large bowl, cream butter and sugar until light and fluffy. Combine flour and ground almonds; gradually add to creamed mixture and mix well. Cover and refrigerate 1 hour.

2. Preheat oven to 350°. On a lightly floured surface, roll dough to ¼-in. thickness. Cut with a floured 2¼-in. round cookie cutter. Place 2 in. apart on ungreased baking sheets. Bake 7-9 minutes or until edges are lightly browned. Remove to wire racks to cool completely.

3. Spread jam on the bottoms of half of the cookies; top with remaining cookies. In a microwave, melt chocolate chips and shortening; stir until smooth. Dip half of each sandwich cookie into chocolate mixture; allow excess to drip off. Place on waxed paper until set. Store in an airtight container.

RASPBERRY COCONUT COOKIES

My mother gave me the recipe for these rich, buttery cookies. Raspberry preserves and a cream filling make them doubly delicious.

—**JUNE BROWN** VENETA, OR

PREP: 20 MIN.
BAKE: 15 MIN./BATCH + COOLING
MAKES: 2½ DOZEN

- **¾ cup butter, softened**
- **½ cup sugar**
- **1 large egg**
- **1 teaspoon vanilla extract**
- **2 cups all-purpose flour**
- **½ cup flaked coconut**
- **1½ teaspoons baking powder**
- **¼ teaspoon salt**

FILLING

- **¼ cup butter, softened**
- **¾ cup confectioners' sugar**
- **2 teaspoons 2% milk**
- **½ teaspoon vanilla extract**
- **½ cup raspberry preserves**

1. In a large bowl, cream butter and sugar until light and fluffy. Beat in egg and vanilla. Combine the flour, coconut, baking powder and salt; gradually add to the creamed mixture and mix well.

2. Shape into 1-in. balls. Place 1½ in. apart on ungreased baking sheets; flatten with a glass dipped in flour.

3. Bake at 350° for 12-14 minutes or until edges begin to brown. Cool on wire racks.

4. In a small bowl, beat the butter, confectioners' sugar, milk and vanilla until smooth. Place ½ teaspoon preserves and a scant teaspoon of filling mixture on the bottom of half of the cookies; top with remaining cookies. Store in an airtight container in the refrigerator.

TOP TIP

Double-Strength Vanilla

Double-strength vanilla is twice as strong as pure or imitation vanilla. If using double-strength vanilla, add half the amount called for in a recipe. Regular-strength imitation vanilla can be used interchangeably with pure vanilla extract.

MERINGUE KISSES

There's a nice chocolate surprise inside these frothy kisses. They're my husband's top choice each Christmas.
—TAMI HENKE LOCKPORT, IL

PREP: 15 MIN. • **BAKE:** 30 MIN./BATCH + COOLING
MAKES: 44 COOKIES

- **3 large egg whites**
- **¼ teaspoon cream of tartar**
- **Pinch salt**
- **1 cup sugar**
- **1 teaspoon vanilla extract**
- **Red and green food coloring, optional**
- **44 milk chocolate kisses**
- **Baking cocoa, optional**

1. Place egg whites in a small bowl; let stand at room temperature for 30 minutes. Beat egg whites until foamy. Sprinkle with cream of tartar and salt; beat until soft peaks form. Gradually add sugar and vanilla, beating until stiff peaks form, about 5-8 minutes. If desired, divide batter in half and fold in red and green food coloring.
2. Drop by rounded tablespoonfuls 1½ in. apart onto lightly greased baking sheets. Press a chocolate kiss into the center of each cookie and cover it with meringue, using a knife.
3. Bake at 275° for 30-35 minutes or until firm to the touch. Immediately remove to a wire rack to cool. If desired, sprinkle with cocoa. Store in an airtight container.

TOP TIP

Sweet Storage Idea

Store soft cookies and crisp cookies in separate airtight containers. If cookies are stored together, the moisture from the soft ones will soften the crisp ones, making them lose their crunch.

(5) INGREDIENTS

SALTINE TOFFEE BARK

These sweet-and-salty treasures make great gifts, and their flavor is simply irresistible. The bark is like brittle, but better and with only a few ingredients. Get ready for a new family favorite!
—LAURA COX SOUTH DENNIS, MA

PREP: 25 MIN. + CHILLING • **MAKES:** 2 POUNDS

- **40 saltines**
- **1 cup butter, cubed**
- **¾ cup sugar**
- **2 cups (12 ounces) semisweet chocolate chips**
- **1 package (8 ounces) milk chocolate English toffee bits**

1. Line a 15x10x1-in. baking pan with heavy-duty foil. Arrange saltines in a single layer on foil; set aside.
2. In a large heavy saucepan over medium heat, melt butter. Stir in sugar. Bring to a boil; cook and stir for 1-2 minutes or until sugar is dissolved. Pour evenly over crackers.
3. Bake at 350° for 8-10 minutes or until bubbly. Immediately sprinkle with chocolate chips. Allow chips to soften for a few minutes, then spread over top. Sprinkle with toffee bits. Cool.
4. Cover and refrigerate for 1 hour or until set. Break into pieces. Store in an airtight container.

WYOMING WHOPPER COOKIES

I came up with this delicious recipe while trying to re-create a commercial cookie that was delicious but too crumbly to travel well. My version takes only about 30 minutes to make, which is great when you're looking for something to bring to a gathering at the last minute.

—JAMIE HIRSCH POWELL, WY

START TO FINISH: 30 MIN.
MAKES: 2 DOZEN

- **⅔ cup butter, cubed**
- **1¼ cups packed brown sugar**
- **¾ cup sugar**
- **3 large eggs, beaten**
- **1½ cups chunky peanut butter**
- **6 cups old-fashioned oats**
- **2 teaspoons baking soda**
- **1½ cups raisins**
- **2 cups (12 ounces) semisweet chocolate chips**

1. In a large saucepan, melt butter over low heat. Stir in the brown sugar, sugar, eggs and peanut butter until smooth. Add oats, baking soda, raisins and chocolate chips (dough will be sticky).

2. Drop on a greased baking sheet with an ice cream scoop or large spoon. Flatten slightly. Bake at 350° for 15 minutes. Remove cookies to a wire rack to cool.

NOTE *Reduced-fat peanut butter is not recommended for this recipe.*

OATMEAL CRISPIES

My husband, who normally isn't fond of oatmeal, thinks these old-fashioned cookies are great. With a hint of nutmeg, their aroma is wonderful as they bake...and they taste even better!

—KAREN HENSON ST. LOUIS, MO

PREP: 15 MIN. • **BAKE:** 10 MIN./BATCH • **MAKES:** 5½ DOZEN

- **1 cup shortening**
- **1 cup sugar**
- **1 cup packed brown sugar**
- **2 large eggs**
- **1 teaspoon vanilla extract**
- **3 cups quick-cooking oats**
- **1½ cups all-purpose flour**
- **1 teaspoon baking soda**
- **1 teaspoon salt**
- **¼ teaspoon ground nutmeg**
- **¼ teaspoon ground cinnamon**

1. In a large bowl, cream shortening and sugars until light and fluffy. Add eggs, one at a time, beating well after each addition. Beat in vanilla. Combine the oats, flour, baking soda, salt, nutmeg and cinnamon and mix well; gradually add to creamed mixture.

2. Drop by tablespoonfuls 2 in. apart onto ungreased baking sheets. Flatten with a fork. Bake at 350° for 10-12 minutes or until lightly browned. Remove to wire racks to cool.

WALNUT-FILLED PILLOWS

These tender cookie pillows filled with a delicious walnut mixture are my husband's favorite. He says it wouldn't be Christmas without them.

—**NANCY KOSTREJ** CANONSBURG, PA

PREP: 30 MIN. + CHILLING
BAKE: 10 MIN./BATCH
MAKES: 28 COOKIES

- **½ cup cold butter, cubed**
- **1 package (3 ounces) cold cream cheese**
- **1¼ cups all-purpose flour**
- **¾ cup ground walnuts**
- **¼ cup sugar**
- **2 tablespoons whole milk**
- **½ teaspoon vanilla or almond extract**
- **1 large egg, lightly beaten**
- **Confectioners' sugar**

1. In a large bowl, cut butter and cream cheese into flour until mixture resembles coarse crumbs. Blend mixture together until smooth dough forms, about 3 minutes. Pat into a rectangle; wrap in plastic wrap. Refrigerate for 1 hour or until firm. For filling, combine the walnuts, sugar, milk and vanilla.

2. Unwrap dough and place on a lightly floured surface. Roll into a 17½x10-in. rectangle; cut into 2½-in. squares. Place a level teaspoonful of filling in the center of each square. Moisten edges with water; fold in half and seal with a fork. Place 1 in. apart on ungreased baking sheets. Brush with egg.

3. Bake at 375° for 10-12 minutes or until edges are golden brown. Remove to wire racks to cool. Dust with confectioners' sugar.

"I enjoyed making these and the look on people's faces once they took a bite."

—**NESSIENESSA**
FROM TASTEOFHOME.COM

TOFFEE ALMOND SANDIES

Crisp and loaded with goodies, these are super yummy cookies. I used to bake them in large batches when our four sons still lived at home. Now I whip them up for our grandchildren.

—ALICE KAHNK KENNARD, NE

PREP: 35 MIN. • **BAKE:** 15 MIN./BATCH
MAKES: ABOUT 12 DOZEN

- **1 cup butter, softened**
- **1 cup sugar**
- **1 cup confectioners' sugar**
- **1 cup canola oil**
- **2 large eggs**
- **1 teaspoon almond extract**
- **3½ cups all-purpose flour**
- **1 cup whole wheat flour**
- **1 teaspoon baking soda**
- **1 teaspoon cream of tartar**
- **1 teaspoon salt**
- **2 cups chopped almonds**
- **1 package (8 ounces) milk chocolate English toffee bits**
- **Additional sugar**

1. In a large bowl, cream butter and sugars until light and fluffy. Beat in the oil, eggs and extract. Combine flours, baking soda, cream of tartar and salt; gradually add to creamed mixture and mix well. Stir in almonds and toffee bits.

2. Shape into 1-in. balls; roll in sugar. Place on ungreased baking sheets and flatten with a fork. Bake at 350° for 12-14 minutes or until lightly browned.

CARAMEL PRETZEL BITES

I created this recipe because I wanted to make my own version of a pretzel log dipped in caramel, chocolate and nuts from a popular candy store.

—MICHILENE KLAVER GRAND RAPIDS, MI

PREP: 45 MIN. + COOLING
MAKES: 6 DOZEN

- **2 teaspoons butter, softened**
- **4 cups pretzel sticks**
- **2½ cups pecan halves, toasted**
- **2¼ cups packed brown sugar**
- **1 cup butter, cubed**
- **1 cup corn syrup**
- **1 can (14 ounces) sweetened condensed milk**
- **⅛ teaspoon salt**
- **1 teaspoon vanilla extract**
- **1 package (11½ ounces) milk chocolate chips**
- **1 tablespoon plus 1 teaspoon shortening, divided**
- **⅓ cup white baking chips**

1. Line a 13x9-in. pan with foil; grease foil with softened butter. Spread pretzels and pecans on bottom of prepared pan.

2. In a large heavy saucepan, combine brown sugar, cubed butter, corn syrup, milk and salt; cook and stir over medium heat until a candy thermometer reads 240° (soft-ball stage). Remove from heat. Stir in vanilla. Pour over pretzel mixture.

3. In a microwave, melt chocolate chips and 1 tablespoon shortening; stir until smooth. Spread over caramel layer. In microwave, melt white baking chips and remaining shortening; stir until smooth. Drizzle over top. Let stand until set.

4. Using foil, lift candy out of pan; remove foil. Using a buttered knife, cut candy into bite-size pieces.

CASHEW CLUSTERS

I make this recipe for many bake sales at the local community college where I work. They are always the first to sell out.

—BETSY GRANTIER CHARLOTTESVILLE, VA

PREP: 20 MIN. + STANDING • **MAKES:** 6 DOZEN

- **1 pound white candy coating, coarsely chopped**
- **1 cup (6 ounces) semisweet chocolate chips**
- **4 ounces German sweet chocolate, chopped**
- **⅓ cup milk chocolate chips**
- **1 can (9¾ ounces) salted whole cashews**
- **1 can (9¼ ounces) salted cashew halves and pieces**

1. In a large microwave-safe bowl, combine the first four ingredients. Cover and microwave at 50% power until melted, stirring every 30 seconds.

2. Stir in cashews. Drop by tablespoonfuls onto waxed paper-lined pans. Let stand until set. Store in an airtight container.

NOTE *This recipe was tested in a 1,100-watt microwave.*

OATMEAL SANDWICH CREMES

These hearty cookies appeal to everyone whenever I take them to a family get-together or church bake sale. They're worth the little extra effort.

—LESLEY MANSFIELD MONROE, NC

PREP: 20 MIN. • **BAKE:** 15 MIN./BATCH + COOLING • **MAKES:** 3 DOZEN

- **¾ cup shortening**
- **1 cup sugar**
- **1 cup packed brown sugar**
- **1 large egg**
- **¼ cup water**
- **1 teaspoon vanilla extract**
- **1½ cups self-rising flour**
- **1 teaspoon baking soda**
- **1 teaspoon ground cinnamon**
- **3 cups quick-cooking oats**
- **¾ cup raisins**

FILLING

- **½ cup butter, softened**
- **½ cup shortening**
- **3¾ cups confectioners' sugar**
- **2 tablespoons 2% milk**
- **1 teaspoon vanilla extract**
- **Dash salt**

1. In a large bowl, cream shortening and sugars until light and fluffy. Beat in the egg, water and vanilla. Combine the flour, baking soda and cinnamon; gradually add to creamed mixture and mix well. Stir in oats and raisins.

2. Drop by tablespoonfuls 3 in. apart onto ungreased baking sheets. Flatten with a glass. Bake at 325° for 13-14 minutes or until lightly browned. Remove to wire racks to cool.

3. In a large bowl, combine filling ingredients; beat until smooth. Spread on the bottoms of half of the cookies; top with remaining cookies.

NOTE *As a substitute for each cup of self-rising flour, place 1½ teaspoons baking powder and ½ teaspoon salt in a measuring cup. Add all-purpose flour to measure 1 cup.*

PISTACHIO THUMBPRINTS

These mild pistachio-flavored cookies disappear in a wink at my house. For more pistachio flavor, roll cookies in chopped pistachios instead of pecans.

—ELIZABETH PROBELSKI PORT WASHINGTON, WI

PREP: 45 MIN. • **BAKE:** 10 MIN./BATCH • **MAKES:** ABOUT 4 DOZEN

- **1 cup butter, softened**
- **⅓ cup confectioners' sugar**
- **1 large egg**
- **1 teaspoon vanilla extract**
- **¾ teaspoon almond extract**
- **2 cups all-purpose flour**
- **1 package (3.4 ounces) instant pistachio pudding mix**
- **½ cup miniature chocolate chips**
- **2 cups finely chopped pecans**

FILLING

- **2 tablespoons butter, softened**
- **2 cups confectioners' sugar**
- **1 teaspoon vanilla extract**
- **2 to 3 tablespoons 2% milk**

GLAZE

- **½ cup semisweet chocolate chips**
- **2 teaspoons shortening**

1. In a large bowl, cream butter and sugar until smooth and fluffy. Beat in egg and extracts. Combine flour and dry pudding mix; gradually add to creamed mixture and mix well. Stir in chocolate chips.

2. Shape into 1-in. balls; roll in nuts. Place 2 in. apart on greased baking sheets; make a thumbprint in center of cookie. Bake at 350° for 10-12 minutes. Remove to a wire rack to cool.

3. For filling, beat the butter, confectioners' sugar, vanilla and enough milk to achieve desired consistency. Spoon into center of cooled cookies.

4. For glaze, if desired, melt chocolate chips and shortening; drizzle over cookies. Let stand until set.

> "These have a wonderful flavor and were well received during the holidays."
> —HOMEMADEWITHLOVE
> FROM TASTEOFHOME.COM

GINGER & MAPLE MACADAMIA NUT COOKIES

This spiced cookie has a real kick of ginger, similar to traditional German lebkuchen. If you don't have crystallized ginger, use colored sprinkles.

—**THOMAS FAGLON** SOMERSET, NJ

PREP: 45 MIN. + CHILLING • **BAKE:** 10 MIN./BATCH + COOLING
MAKES: ABOUT 7 DOZEN

- **1½ cups butter, softened**
- **½ cup sugar**
- **¾ cup maple syrup**
- **4 cups all-purpose flour**
- **3 teaspoons ground ginger**
- **3 teaspoons ground cinnamon**
- **1 teaspoon ground allspice**
- **½ teaspoon ground cloves**
- **1½ teaspoons salt**
- **1½ teaspoons baking soda**
- **1½ cups finely chopped macadamia nuts**
- **24 ounces dark chocolate candy coating, melted**
- **⅓ cup finely chopped crystallized ginger**

1. In a large bowl, cream butter and sugar until light and fluffy. Gradually beat in syrup. In another bowl, whisk flour, spices, salt and baking soda; gradually beat into creamed mixture. Stir in nuts.

2. Divide dough in half; shape each into a 12-in.-long roll. Wrap in plastic wrap; refrigerate 2 hours or until firm.

3. Preheat oven to 350°. Unwrap and cut dough crosswise into ¼-in. slices. Place 1 in. apart on ungreased baking sheets. Bake 8-10 minutes or until set. Cool on pans 2 minutes. Remove to wire racks to cool completely.

4. Dip each cookie halfway into melted candy coating; allow excess to drip off. Place on waxed paper-lined baking sheets; sprinkle with crystallized ginger. Refrigerate until set.

BLACK WALNUT COOKIES

Black walnuts have a more distinctive flavor than the traditional English walnuts. Black walnuts have a short shelf life, so it's best to store them in the freezer.

—DOUG BLACK CONOVER, NC

PREP: 20 MIN. + CHILLING • **BAKE:** 15 MIN./BATCH
MAKES: 10 DOZEN

- **1 cup butter, softened**
- **2 cups packed brown sugar**
- **2 large eggs**
- **1 teaspoon vanilla extract**
- **3½ cups all-purpose flour**
- **1 teaspoon baking soda**
- **¼ teaspoon salt**
- **2 cups chopped black walnuts or walnuts, divided**

1. In a large bowl, cream butter and brown sugar until light and fluffy. Beat in eggs and vanilla. Combine the flour, baking soda and salt; gradually add to creamed mixture. Stir in 1¼ cups walnuts. Finely chop the remaining nuts.
2. Shape dough into two 15-in. rolls. Roll in chopped nuts, pressing gently. Wrap each in plastic wrap. Refrigerate for 2 hours or until firm.
3. Unwrap dough; cut into ¼-in. slices. Place 2 in. apart on greased baking sheets. Bake at 300° for 12 minutes or until lightly browned. Remove to wire racks.

FROSTED MAPLE COOKIES

Living in New England, I've come to appreciate the unique qualities of our area. Many people here enjoy the flavor of maple in their recipes, and I love this adaptation of an old favorite.

—CONNIE BORDEN MARBLEHEAD, MA

PREP: 20 MIN. + CHILLING • **BAKE:** 10 MIN./BATCH + COOLING
MAKES: 4 DOZEN 2½-IN. COOKIES

- **½ cup shortening**
- **1½ cups packed brown sugar**
- **2 large eggs**
- **1 cup (8 ounces) sour cream**
- **1 tablespoon maple flavoring**
- **2¾ cups all-purpose flour**
- **1 teaspoon salt**
- **½ teaspoon baking soda**
- **1 cup chopped nuts**

FROSTING

- **½ cup butter**
- **2 cups confectioners' sugar**
- **2 teaspoons maple flavoring**
- **2 to 3 tablespoons hot water**

1. In a large bowl, cream shortening and brown sugar until light and fluffy. Add eggs, one at a time, beating well after each addition. Stir in sour cream and maple flavoring. Combine the flour, salt and baking soda; add to creamed mixture and mix well. Stir in nuts. Cover and refrigerate for 1 hour.
2. Drop dough by rounded tablespoonfuls 2 in. apart onto greased baking sheets. Bake at 375° for 8-10 minutes or until edges are lightly browned. Cool completely on wire racks.
3. For frosting, in a small saucepan, heat butter over low heat until golden brown. Remove from the heat; blend in confectioners' sugar, maple flavoring and enough water to achieve spreading consistency. Frost cookies.

COOKIE JAR GINGERSNAPS

My grandma kept two cookie jars in her pantry. One of the jars, which I now have, always contained these crisp and chewy gingersnaps.

—DEB HANDY POMONA, KS

PREP: 20 MIN. • **BAKE:** 15 MIN./BATCH
MAKES: 3-4 DOZEN

- **¾ cup shortening**
- **1 cup sugar**
- **1 large egg**
- **¼ cup molasses**
- **2 cups all-purpose flour**
- **2 teaspoons baking soda**
- **1½ teaspoons ground ginger**
- **1 teaspoon ground cinnamon**
- **½ teaspoon salt**
- **Additional sugar**

1. In a large bowl, cream shortening and sugar until light and fluffy. Beat in the egg and molasses. Combine the flour, baking soda, ginger, cinnamon and salt; gradually add to creamed mixture and mix well.
2. Shape rounded teaspoonfuls of dough into balls. Dip one side into sugar; place sugar side up 2 in. apart on greased baking sheets.
3. Bake at 350° for 12-15 minutes or until lightly browned and crinkly. Remove to wire racks to cool.

TOP TIP

Sticky Situation

For sticky liquids such as molasses, corn syrup or honey, spray the measuring cup with nonstick cooking spray before adding the liquid. This will make it easier to pour out the liquid and clean the cup.

5 INGREDIENTS

BUTTERSCOTCH TOFFEE COOKIES

My recipe, with its big butterscotch flavor, always stands out at events amid all the chocolate. I like to enjoy these cookies with a glass of milk or a cup of coffee. It's my fallback recipe when I'm short on time and need something delicious fast.
—ALLIE BLINDER NORCROSS, GA

PREP: 10 MIN. • **BAKE:** 10 MIN./BATCH
MAKES: 5 DOZEN

- **2 large eggs**
- **½ cup canola oil**
- **1 package butter pecan cake mix (regular size)**
- **1 package (10 to 11 ounces) butterscotch chips**
- **1 package (8 ounces) milk chocolate English toffee bits**

1. Preheat oven to 350°. In a large bowl, beat eggs and oil until blended; gradually add cake mix and mix well. Fold in chips and toffee bits.
2. Drop by tablespoonfuls 2 in. apart onto greased baking sheets. Bake 10-12 minutes or until golden brown. Cool 1 minute; remove to wire racks.

5 INGREDIENTS FAST FIX

CHOCOLATE-COVERED CHIPS

These are conversation starters. The salty-sweet combination makes them irresistible.
—MARCILLE MEYER BATTLE CREEK, NE

START TO FINISH: 25 MIN.
MAKES: ABOUT 4 POUNDS

- **1½ pounds white candy coating, coarsely chopped**
- **1 package (14 ounces) ridged potato chips**
- **1½ pounds milk chocolate or dark chocolate candy coating, coarsely chopped**

1. In a microwave, melt white coating; stir until smooth. Dip chips halfway in coating; allow excess to drip off. Place on waxed paper-lined baking sheets to set.
2. Melt milk or dark chocolate. Dip other half of chips; allow excess to drip off. Place on waxed paper to set. Store in an airtight container.

MAPLE WALNUT TRUFFLES

You'll be surprised and delighted when you bite into one of these little goodies. The velvety maple and white chocolate coating surrounds a sweet nutty center.
—ROXANNE CHAN ALBANY, CA

PREP: 45 MIN. + CHILLING
MAKES: 2 DOZEN

- **⅔ cup ground walnuts**
- **2 teaspoons maple syrup**
- **1 teaspoon brown sugar**
- **1 package (10 to 12 ounces) white baking chips**
- **4 ounces cream cheese, softened**
- **⅔ cup butter, softened**
- **¾ teaspoon maple flavoring**
- **1½ cups finely chopped walnuts, toasted**

1. Place the ground walnuts, syrup and brown sugar in a small bowl; mix well. Scoop teaspoonfuls and form into 24 balls; transfer to a waxed paper-lined baking sheet. Chill.
2. Meanwhile, in a microwave, melt chips; stir until smooth. Set aside. In a large bowl, beat cream cheese and butter until smooth. Beat in melted chips and maple flavoring; mix well. Refrigerate for 1 hour or until set.
3. Shape tablespoonfuls of cream cheese mixture around each walnut ball. Roll in chopped walnuts. Refrigerate for 2 hours or until firm. Store in an airtight container in the refrigerator.

GLAZED SPIRAL-SPICED HAM, 208
LEMON-ROASTED ASPARAGUS, 208

POTATO PUMPKIN MASH, 219

GARLIC-HERB PARMESAN ROLLS, 222

FLYING BAT PIZZAS, 216

SEASONAL SPECIALTIES

Christmas, Thanksgiving, the Fourth of July...at the heart of all special celebrations you'll find great tasting food. Family cooks know that holidays and the changing of the seasons offer an opportunity to experiment with new ingredients and flavors while getting creative in the kitchen. Here you'll find some of their most popular recipes, guaranteed to impress at festive gatherings year-round.

ST. PADDY'S IRISH BEEF DINNER

A variation on shepherd's pie, this hearty dish brings together saucy beef and mashed potatoes, parsnips and other vegetables. It's always the star of our March 17th meal.
—LORRAINE CALAND THUNDER BAY, ON

PREP: 25 MIN. • **COOK:** 35 MIN. • **MAKES:** 4 SERVINGS

- **2 medium Yukon Gold potatoes**
- **2 small parsnips**
- **¾ pound lean ground beef (90% lean)**
- **1 medium onion, chopped**
- **2 cups finely shredded cabbage**
- **2 medium carrots, halved and sliced**
- **1 teaspoon dried thyme**
- **1 teaspoon Worcestershire sauce**
- **1 tablespoon all-purpose flour**
- **¼ cup tomato paste**
- **1 can (14½ ounces) reduced-sodium chicken or beef broth**
- **½ cup frozen peas**
- **¾ teaspoon salt, divided**
- **½ teaspoon pepper, divided**
- **¼ cup 2% milk**
- **1 tablespoon butter**

1. Peel potatoes and parsnips and cut into large pieces; place in a large saucepan and cover with water. Bring to a boil. Reduce heat; cover and cook for 10-15 minutes or until tender. Drain.
2. Meanwhile, in a large skillet, cook beef and onion over medium heat until meat is no longer pink; drain. Stir in the cabbage, carrots, thyme and Worcestershire sauce.
3. In a small bowl, combine the flour, tomato paste and broth until smooth. Gradually stir into meat mixture. Bring to a boil. Reduce heat; cover and simmer for 15-20 minutes or until vegetables are tender. Stir in the peas, 1/4 teaspoon salt and 1/4 teaspoon pepper.
4. Drain potatoes and parsnips; mash with milk, butter and the remaining salt and pepper. Serve with meat mixture.

FAST FIX

REUBEN DIP

This rich, cheesy dip comes together so quickly, you can make it just before guests arrive. I often serve it with rye bread wedges.
—MARY JO HAGEY GLADWIN, MI

START TO FINISH: 15 MIN. • **MAKES:** 2½ CUPS

- **1 tablespoon butter**
- **2 green onions, chopped**
- **1½ cups (6 ounces) shredded Muenster cheese**
- **4 ounces cream cheese, cubed**
- **2 tablespoons ketchup**
- **2 teaspoons Dijon mustard**
- **¼ teaspoon pepper**
- **½ pound cooked corned beef, chopped**
- **1 cup sauerkraut, rinsed and well drained**
- **Assorted crackers**

1. Place butter in a small microwave-safe bowl and microwave on high for 20 seconds or until melted. Add onions; cover and cook 1 minute longer.
2. Stir in the cheeses, ketchup, mustard and pepper. Cover and cook on high for 1 minute; stir. Cook 45 seconds longer. Stir in beef.
3. Place sauerkraut in a microwave-safe 1-qt. dish; top with beef mixture. Cover and microwave on high for 2-3 minutes or until heated through. Serve with crackers.
NOTE *This recipe was tested in a 1,100-watt microwave.*

SAVORY DILL AND CARAWAY SCONES

These tender, tasty scones will melt in your mouth. Dill and caraway lend an old-world flavor that's comforting and delicious.
—SALLY SIBTHORPE SHELBY TOWNSHIP, MI

PREP: 20 MIN. • **BAKE:** 15 MIN. • **MAKES:** 1 DOZEN

- **2 cups all-purpose flour**
- **4½ teaspoons sugar**
- **1 tablespoon onion powder**
- **1 tablespoon snipped fresh dill or 1 teaspoon dill weed**
- **2 teaspoons caraway seeds**
- **1 teaspoon baking powder**
- **¾ teaspoon salt**
- **½ teaspoon baking soda**
- **½ teaspoon coarsely ground pepper**
- **6 tablespoons cold butter**
- **1 large egg yolk**
- **¾ cup sour cream**
- **½ cup ricotta cheese**
- **4 teaspoons heavy whipping cream**
- **Additional caraway seeds, optional**

1. In a large bowl, combine the first nine ingredients. Cut in butter until mixture resembles coarse crumbs. Combine the egg yolk, sour cream and ricotta cheese; stir into crumb mixture just until moistened. Turn onto a floured surface; knead 10 times.
2. Pat into two 6-in. circles. Cut each into six wedges. Separate wedges and place on a greased baking sheet. Brush tops with cream; sprinkle with additional caraway seeds if desired. Bake at 400° for 15-18 minutes or until golden brown. Serve warm.

IRISH CREAM CUPCAKES

If you're looking for a grown-up cupcake, give these a try. You'll have a hard time limiting yourself to one!
—JENNY LEIGHTY WEST SALEM, OH

PREP: 25 MIN. • **BAKE:** 20 MIN. + COOLING • **MAKES:** 2 DOZEN

- **½ cup butter, softened**
- **1½ cups sugar**
- **2 large eggs**
- **¾ cup unsweetened applesauce**
- **2 teaspoons vanilla extract**
- **2½ cups all-purpose flour**
- **3 teaspoons baking powder**
- **½ teaspoon salt**
- **½ cup Irish cream liqueur**

FROSTING

- **⅓ cup butter, softened**
- **4 ounces reduced-fat cream cheese**
- **6 tablespoons Irish cream liqueur**
- **4 cups confectioners' sugar**

1. In a large bowl, beat butter and sugar until crumbly, about 2 minutes. Add eggs, one at a time, beating well after each addition. Beat in applesauce and vanilla (the mixture may appear curdled). Combine the flour, baking powder and salt; add to the creamed mixture alternately with liqueur, beating well after each addition.
2. Fill paper-lined muffin cups two-thirds full. Bake at 350° for 18-22 minutes or until a toothpick inserted near the center comes out clean. Cool for 10 minutes before removing from pans to wire racks to cool completely.
3. For frosting, in a large bowl, beat the butter and cream cheese until fluffy. Beat in liqueur. Add confectioners' sugar; beat until smooth. Pipe over tops of the cupcakes. Refrigerate leftovers.

5 INGREDIENTS FAST FIX

LEMON-ROASTED ASPARAGUS

When it comes to fixing asparagus, it's hard to go wrong. The springy flavors in this easy recipe burst with every bite.

—JENN TIDWELL FAIR OAKS, CA

START TO FINISH: 20 MIN. • **MAKES:** 8 SERVINGS

- **2 pounds fresh asparagus, trimmed**
- **¼ cup olive oil**
- **4 teaspoons grated lemon peel**
- **2 garlic cloves, minced**
- **½ teaspoon salt**
- **½ teaspoon pepper**

Preheat oven to 425°. Place the asparagus in a greased 15x10x1-in. baking pan. Mix remaining ingredients; drizzle over asparagus. Toss to coat. Roast 8-12 minutes or until crisp-tender.

5 INGREDIENTS

GLAZED SPIRAL-SLICED HAM

In my mind, few foods in an Easter spread are as tempting as a big baked ham. I always hope for leftovers so we can have ham sandwiches in the following days.

—EDIE DESPAIN LOGAN, UT

PREP: 10 MIN. • **BAKE:** 1 HOUR 35 MIN. • **YIELD:** 12 SERVINGS

- **1 spiral-sliced fully cooked bone-in ham (7 to 9 pounds)**
- **½ cup pineapple preserves**
- **½ cup seedless raspberry jam**
- **¼ cup packed brown sugar**
- **¼ teaspoon ground cloves**

1. Preheat oven to 300°. Place ham directly on roasting pan, cut side down. Bake, covered, 1¼ to 1¾ hours.

2. In a bowl, mix the remaining ingredients. Spread over ham. Bake, uncovered, 20-30 minutes longer or until a thermometer reads 140° (do not overcook).

5 INGREDIENTS

FRESH FRUIT BOWL

This fruity salad boasts glorious color. Slightly sweet and chilled, it makes a nice accompaniment to a spring meal.
—MARION KIRST TROY, MI

PREP: 15 MIN. + CHILLING • **MAKES:** 3-4 QUARTS

- **8 to 10 cups fresh melon cubes**
- **1 to 2 tablespoons white corn syrup**
- **1 pint fresh strawberries**
- **2 cups fresh pineapple chunks**
- **2 oranges, sectioned**
- **Fresh mint leaves, optional**

In a large bowl, combine melon cubes and corn syrup. Cover and refrigerate overnight. Just before serving, stir in remaining fruit. Garnish with fresh mint leaves if desired.

HOT CROSS BUNS

My husband's grandma used to make these every year for Good Friday, and I carry on the tradition with my own version of her recipe. I make six dozen every year, and they all disappear.
—JILL EVELY WILMORE, KY

PREP: 45 MIN. + RISING • **BAKE:** 15 MIN./BATCH • **MAKES:** 6 DOZEN

- **4 packages (¼ ounce each) active dry yeast**
- **3 cups warm 2% milk (110° to 115°)**
- **2 cups canola oil**
- **8 large eggs**
- **4 large eggs, separated**
- **1⅓ cups sugar**
- **4 teaspoons ground cinnamon**
- **3 teaspoons salt**
- **2 teaspoons ground cardamom**
- **13 to 15 cups all-purpose flour**
- **2⅔ cups raisins**
- **2 teaspoons water**

ICING

- **3 cups confectioners' sugar**
- **2 tablespoons butter, melted**
- **4 to 5 tablespoons 2% milk**

1. In a very large bowl, dissolve yeast in warm milk. Add the oil, eggs, egg yolks, sugar, cinnamon, salt, cardamom, yeast mixture and 10 cups flour. Beat until smooth. Stir in enough remaining flour to form a firm dough. Stir in raisins.
2. Turn onto a floured surface; knead until smooth and elastic, about 6-8 minutes. Place in a greased bowl, turning once to grease the top. Cover and let rise in a warm place until doubled, about 1¼ hours.
3. Punch dough down. Turn onto a lightly floured surface. Cover and let rest 10 minutes. Divide into 72 pieces; shape each into a ball. Place 2 in. apart in four greased 15x10x1-in. baking pans. Cover and let rise in a warm place until doubled, about 40 minutes.
4. Preheat oven to 375°. Combine egg whites and water; brush over tops. Bake 12-15 minutes or until golden brown. Remove from pans to wire racks to cool. For icing, combine confectioners' sugar, butter and enough milk to achieve desired consistency. Pipe a cross on top of each bun.

FAST FIX

SWISS HAM KABOBS

With warm cheese, juicy pineapple and salty ham, these kabobs are my daughter's birthday dinner request every May. I'm happy to make them. They're a fantastic way to get into grilling season.
—HELEN PHILLIPS HORSEHEADS, NY

START TO FINISH: 20 MIN.
MAKES: 4 SERVINGS

- **1 can (20 ounces) pineapple chunks**
- **½ cup orange marmalade**
- **1 tablespoon prepared mustard**
- **¼ teaspoon ground cloves**
- **1 pound fully cooked ham, cut into 1-inch cubes**
- **½ pound Swiss cheese, cut into 1-inch cubes**
- **1 medium green pepper, cut into 1-inch pieces, optional**

1. Drain pineapple chunks, reserving 2 tablespoons juice; set pineapple aside. In a small bowl, mix the marmalade, mustard, cloves and reserved pineapple juice. On eight metal or soaked wooden skewers, alternately thread ham, cheese, pineapple and, if desired, green pepper.
2. Moisten a paper towel with cooking oil; using long-handled tongs, rub on grill rack to coat lightly. Grill kabobs, uncovered, over medium heat or broil 4 in. from heat 5-7 minutes or until heated through, turning and basting frequently with marmalade sauce. Serve with remaining sauce.

TOP TIP

Great Grill Marks

Trying to get those lovely grill marks on food, but always miss the mark? Add a little honey to your marinade or sauce. The honey caramelizes when grilled and creates the marks. A teaspoon to a tablespoon should do the trick, depending on the amount of marinade or sauce.
—LISA M. SPRING VALLEY, NY

"I doubled the recipe for both the kabobs and the sauce, but used only ½ cup marmalade, and it was still really good. A great way to use up leftover ham in a new dish!"
—GRAMMY DEBBIE FROM TASTEOFHOME.COM

FAST FIX

HEIRLOOM TOMATO & ZUCCHINI SALAD

Heirloom tomato wedges make this salad juicy in every delicious bite. It's a smart use of fresh herbs and veggies from your own garden or the farmers market.
—MATTHEW HASS FRANKLIN, WI

START TO FINISH: 25 MIN.
MAKES: 12 SERVINGS (¾ CUP EACH)

- **7 large heirloom tomatoes (about 2½ pounds), cut into wedges**
- **3 medium zucchini, halved lengthwise and thinly sliced**
- **2 medium sweet yellow peppers, thinly sliced**
- **⅓ cup cider vinegar**
- **3 tablespoons olive oil**
- **1 tablespoon sugar**
- **1½ teaspoons salt**
- **1 tablespoon each minced fresh basil, parsley and tarragon**

1. In a large bowl, combine tomatoes, zucchini and peppers. In a small bowl, whisk vinegar, oil, sugar and salt until blended. Stir in herbs.
2. Just before serving, drizzle dressing over salad; toss gently to coat.

CAMPFIRE HASH

My family loves to camp. We invented this recipe using ingredients we all love so we could cook it over the campfire. The hearty meal tastes so good after a full day of outdoor activities.
—JANET DANILOW WINKLEMAN, AZ

PREP: 15 MIN. • **COOK:** 40 MIN.
MAKES: 6 SERVINGS

- **1 large onion, chopped**
- **2 tablespoons canola oil**
- **2 garlic cloves, minced**
- **4 large potatoes, peeled and cubed (about 2 pounds)**
- **1 pound smoked kielbasa or Polish sausage, halved and sliced**
- **1 can (4 ounces) chopped green chilies**
- **1 can (15¼ ounces) whole kernel corn, drained**

1. In a large ovenproof skillet over medium heat, cook and stir onion in oil under tender. Add garlic; cook 1 minute longer. Add potatoes. Cook, uncovered, for 20 minutes, stirring occasionally.
2. Add kielbasa; cook and stir untilthe meat and potatoes are tender and browned, about 10-15 minutes. Stir in chilies and corn; heat through.

SUMMERTIME CHICKEN TACOS

The zesty flavors in this homemade marinade are a nice change of pace from the typical packet of taco seasoning.
—SUSAN SCOTT ASHEVILLE, NC

PREP: 10 MIN. + MARINATING
GRILL: 10 MIN. • **MAKES:** 6 SERVINGS

- **⅓ cup olive oil**
- **¼ cup lime juice**
- **4 garlic cloves, minced**
- **1 tablespoon minced fresh parsley or 1 teaspoon dried parsley flakes**
- **1 teaspoon ground cumin**
- **1 teaspoon dried oregano**
- **½ teaspoon salt, optional**
- **¼ teaspoon pepper**
- **4 boneless skinless chicken breast halves (1¼ pounds)**
- **6 flour tortillas (8 inches) or taco shells, warmed**
- **Toppings of your choice**

1. In a large resealable plastic bag, combine the first eight ingredients; add chicken. Seal bag and turn to coat. Refrigerate for 8 hours or overnight, turning occasionally.
2. Drain chicken discarding the marinade. Moisten a paper towel with cooking oil; using long-handled tongs, rub on grill rack to coat. Grill chicken, uncovered, over medium heat for 5-7 minutes on each side or until a thermometer reads 170°. Cut into thin strips; serve in tortillas or taco shells with desired toppings.

MARINATED PORK CHOPS

I make these tender chops all summer long, and my family never tires of them. My secret? Marinate the meat overnight.

—JEAN NEITZEL BELOIT, WI

PREP: 5 MIN. + MARINATING • **GRILL:** 10 MIN.
MAKES: 6 SERVINGS

- **¾ cup canola oil**
- **⅓ cup reduced-sodium soy sauce**
- **¼ cup white vinegar**
- **2 tablespoons Worcestershire sauce**
- **1 tablespoon lemon juice**
- **1 tablespoon prepared mustard**
- **1 teaspoon salt**
- **1 teaspoon pepper**
- **1 teaspoon dried parsley flakes**
- **1 garlic clove, minced**
- **6 bone-in pork loin chops (1 inch thick and 8 ounces each)**

1. In a large resealable plastic bag, combine the first 10 ingredients; add the pork. Seal bag and turn to coat; refrigerate overnight.

2. Drain pork, discarding the marinade. Grill, covered, over medium heat, for 4-5 minutes on each side or until a thermometer reads 145°. Let stand for 5 minutes.

FREEZE OPTION *Freeze uncooked pork in bag with marinade. To use, completely thaw in refrigerator. Grill as directed.*

5 INGREDIENTS FAST FIX

REFRESHING BEER MARGARITAS

I'm always surprised when people say they didn't know this drink existed. It's an ideal warm-weather cocktail, and it's easy to double or triple the recipe for a large crowd.

—ARIANNE BARNETT KANSAS CITY, MO

START TO FINISH: 5 MIN. • **MAKES:** 6 SERVINGS.

- **Lime slices and kosher salt, optional**
- **2 bottles (12 ounces each) beer**
- **1 can (12 ounces) frozen limeade concentrate, thawed**
- **¾ cup tequila**
- **¼ cup sweet and sour mix**
- **Ice cubes**

GARNISH

- **Lime slices**

1. If desired, use lime slices to moisten the rims of six margarita or cocktail glasses. Sprinkle salt on a plate; hold each glass upside down and dip rims into salt. Discard remaining salt on plate.

2. In a pitcher, combine the beer, concentrate, tequila and sweet and sour mix. Serve in prepared glasses over ice. Garnish with lime slices.

PATRIOTIC FROZEN DELIGHT

My husband and I pick lots of fruit at local farms, then freeze our harvest to enjoy all year long. This frozen dessert showcases both blueberries and strawberries and has a refreshing flavor.
—BERNICE RUSS BLADENBORO, NC

PREP: 10 MIN. + FREEZING • **MAKES:** 12 SERVINGS

- **1 can (14 ounces) sweetened condensed milk**
- **⅓ cup lemon juice**
- **2 teaspoons grated lemon peel**
- **2 cups (16 ounces) plain yogurt**
- **2 cups miniature marshmallows**
- **½ cup chopped pecans**
- **1 cup sliced fresh strawberries**
- **1 cup fresh blueberries**

In a bowl, combine milk, lemon juice and peel. Stir in yogurt, marshmallows and pecans. Spread half into an ungreased 11x7-in. dish. Sprinkle with half of the strawberries and blueberries. Cover with the remaining yogurt mixture; top with remaining berries. Cover and freeze. Remove from the freezer 15-20 minutes before serving.

> "Great lemony taste! I put a graham cracker crust on the bottom, and I think that made it even better!"
> **—COOKINNC**
> FROM TASTEOFHOME.COM

FAST FIX

SUMMER GARDEN COUSCOUS SALAD

This makes the most of summer's bounty. I used to prepare it with a mayonnaise dressing, but now lighten it with lemon vinaigrette.
—PRISCILLA YEE CONCORD, CA

START TO FINISH: 30 MIN. • **MAKES:** 9 SERVINGS

- **3 medium ears sweet corn, husks removed**
- **1 cup reduced-sodium chicken broth or vegetable broth**
- **1 cup uncooked couscous**
- **1 medium cucumber, halved and sliced**
- **1½ cups cherry tomatoes, halved**
- **½ cup crumbled feta cheese**
- **¼ cup chopped red onion**
- **3 tablespoons minced fresh parsley**
- **3 tablespoons olive oil**
- **3 tablespoons lemon juice**
- **1 teaspoon dried oregano**
- **¾ teaspoon ground cumin**
- **½ teaspoon salt**
- **½ teaspoon pepper**

1. Place corn in a Dutch oven; cover with water. Bring to a boil; cover and cook for 6-9 minutes or until corn is tender. Meanwhile, in a small saucepan, bring broth to a boil. Stir in couscous. Remove from the heat; cover and let stand for 5-10 minutes or until water is absorbed. Fluff with a fork and set aside to cool slightly.
2. In a large bowl, combine the cucumber, tomatoes, cheese, onion and parsley. Drain corn and immediately place in ice water. Drain and pat dry; cut the kernels from the cobs. Add to cucumber mixture. Stir in couscous.
3. In a small bowl, whisk the oil, lemon juice and seasonings. Pour over couscous mixture; toss to coat. Serve immediately, or cover and refrigerate until chilled.

PUMPKIN BREAD

I keep this deliciously spicy, pumpkin-rich quick bread stocked in my freezer along with other home-baked goodies. It's a winner with our harvest crew.

—JOYCE JACKSON BRIDGETOWN, NS

PREP: 10 MIN. • **BAKE:** 65 MIN. + COOLING
MAKES: 1 LOAF (16 SLICES)

1⅔ cups all-purpose flour
1½ cups sugar
1 teaspoon baking soda
1 teaspoon ground cinnamon
¾ teaspoon salt
½ teaspoon baking powder
½ teaspoon ground nutmeg
¼ teaspoon ground cloves
2 large eggs
1 cup canned pumpkin
½ cup canola oil
½ cup water
½ cup chopped walnuts
½ cup raisins, optional

1. In a large small bowl, combine the flour, sugar, baking soda , cinnamon, salt, baking powder, nutmeg and cloves. In a small bowl, whisk the eggs, pumpkin, oil and water. Stir into dry ingredients just until moistened. Fold in walnuts and if desired raisins.
2. Pour into a greased 9x5-in. loaf pan. Bake at 350° for 65-70 minutes or until a toothpick inserted in the center comes out clean. Cool in pan for 10 minutes before removing to a wire rack.

BUTTERNUT-SWEET POTATO PIE

If you're looking for a memorable autumn dessert, this custard-like pie is one folks won't soon forget. It's super easy to put together, and it slices like a dream.

—MARY ANN DELL PHOENIXVILLE, PA

PREP: 15 MIN. • **BAKE:** 50 MIN. + COOLING
MAKES: 8 SERVINGS

Pastry for single-crust pie (9 inches)
4 large eggs
1⅓ cups half-and-half cream
1 cup mashed cooked butternut squash
1 cup mashed cooked sweet potato (about 1 medium)
½ cup honey
1 tablespoon all-purpose flour
½ teaspoon salt
1 teaspoon ground cinnamon
½ teaspoon ground ginger
¼ teaspoon ground nutmeg
Dash ground cloves
Whipped cream, optional

1. Preheat oven to 375°. On a lightly floured surface, roll pastry dough to a ⅛-in.-thick circle; transfer to a 9-in. deep-dish pie plate. Trim pastry to ½ in. beyond rim of plate; flute edge.
2. In a large bowl, whisk eggs, cream, squash, sweet potato, honey, flour, salt and spices. Pour into pastry shell.
3. Bake 50-60 minutes or until a knife inserted near the center comes out clean. Cover edge loosely with foil during the last 15 minutes if needed to prevent overbrowning. Remove foil. Cool on a wire rack; serve within 2 hours or refrigerate and serve cold. If desired, top with whipped cream.

PASTRY FOR SINGLE-CRUST PIE (9 INCHES) *Combine 1¼ cups all-purpose flour and ¼ teaspoon salt; cut in ½ cup cold butter until crumbly. Gradually add 3-5 tablespoons ice water, tossing with a fork until dough holds together when pressed. Wrap in plastic wrap and refrigerate 1 hour.*

GOBLIN'S ORANGE POPCORN

Little goblins will love to munch this sweet, colorful, crispy popcorn.

—DONNA HIGBEE RIVERTON, UT

PREP: 25 MIN. • **BAKE:** 45 MIN. + COOLING
MAKES: 4 QUARTS

- **4 quarts popped popcorn**
- **½ cup butter, cubed**
- **1 cup sugar**
- **6 tablespoons light corn syrup**
- **Dash salt**
- **1 teaspoon vanilla extract**
- **12 drops yellow food coloring**
- **4 drops red food coloring**

1. Place popcorn in a very large bowl. In a small saucepan, melt butter. Stir in the sugar, corn syrup and salt. Cook and stir over medium heat until the mixture comes to a boil. Reduce heat to medium-low; cook 5 minutes longer, stirring occasionally.

2. Remove from the heat. Stir in the vanilla and food coloring. Pour over popcorn; toss to coat. Transfer to two 15x10x1-in. baking pans coated with cooking spray.

3. Bake at 250° for 45 minutes, stirring every 15 minutes. Spread on waxed paper to cool completely. Store in airtight containers.

5 INGREDIENTS FAST FIX

BLOOD 'N' GUTS DIP

Everyone will love this dip that gets its bold zip from the Dijon mustard. Pair it with pretzels for a perfect match.

—*TASTE OF HOME* TEST KITCHEN

START TO FINISH: 15 MIN.
MAKES: 2 CUPS

- **2 cups chopped fresh or frozen cranberries**
- **1 cup packed brown sugar**
- **½ cup honey**
- **¼ cup water**
- **1 cup Dijon mustard**

In a small saucepan, combine the cranberries, brown sugar, honey and water; bring to a boil. Cook and stir for 5 minutes or until thickened. Remove from the heat; cool slightly. Stir in mustard. Refrigerate until serving.

FAST FIX

TASTE-OF-FALL SALAD

My parents stayed with me at a friend's beautiful ranch for the holidays, and I made them this impressive salad. It turned into every night's first course!

—KRISTIN KOSSAK BOZEMAN, MT

START TO FINISH: 25 MIN.
MAKES: 6 SERVINGS

- **⅔ cup pecan halves**
- **¼ cup balsamic vinegar, divided**
- **Dash cayenne pepper**
- **Dash ground cinnamon**
- **3 tablespoons sugar, divided**
- **1 package (5 ounces) spring mix salad greens**
- **¼ cup olive oil**
- **1 teaspoon Dijon mustard**
- **⅛ teaspoon salt**
- **1 medium pear, thinly sliced**
- **¼ cup shredded Parmesan cheese**

1. In a large heavy skillet, cook the pecans, 2 tablespoons vinegar, cayenne and cinnamon over medium heat until nuts are toasted, about 4 minutes. Sprinkle with 1 tablespoon sugar. Cook and stir for 2-4 minutes or until sugar is melted. Spread pecans on foil to cool.

2. Place the salad greens in a large bowl. In a small bowl, whisk the oil, mustard, salt and remaining vinegar and sugar; drizzle over greens and toss to coat. Arrange the greens, pear slices and pecans on six salad plates. Sprinkle with cheese.

WICKED WITCH STUFFED POTATOES

These rich, cheesy potatoes are a savory way to work Halloween into your menu. They're sure to cast a spell that produces smiles on the fun-loving folks around your table.

—*TASTE OF HOME* TEST KITCHEN

PREP: 5 MIN. • **BAKE:** 65 MIN. • **MAKES:** 4 SERVINGS

- **2 large baking potatoes**
- **3 ounces Jarlsberg or Swiss cheese, shredded, divided**
- **¼ cup milk**
- **2 tablespoons butter**
- **½ teaspoon salt**
- **4 grape tomatoes, halved crosswise**
- **8 slices ripe olives**
- **4 small serrano peppers, stems removed**
- **4 green pepper strips**
- **4 blue corn chips**

1. Scrub and pierce potatoes. Bake at 375° for 1 hour or until potatoes are tender.
2. When potatoes are cool enough to handle, cut in half lengthwise. Scoop out pulp, leaving a thin shell. In a small bowl, mash the pulp. Stir in 1/2 cup cheese, milk, butter and salt. Spoon into potato shells. Sprinkle with remaining cheese.
3. Place on a baking sheet. Bake at 375° for 5-10 minutes or until cheese is melted.
4. Using the tomato halves, olive slices, serrano peppers and pepper strips, create a face on each potato half. Add corn chip hats.

NOTE *Wear disposable gloves when cutting hot peppers; the oils can burn skin. Avoid touching your face.*

FLYING BAT PIZZAS

Pizza is always a surefire way to lure little ones into the kitchen because they can help add toppings and decorate the pies before they go into the oven. These are tasty, quick and totally spooky!

—ANGELA HANKS ST. ALBANS, WV

PREP: 30 MIN. • **BAKE:** 10 MIN. • **MAKES:** 2 PIZZAS (8 SLICES EACH)

- **1 package (16 ounces) frozen corn, thawed**
- **1 can (16 ounces) kidney beans, rinsed and drained**
- **1 can (15 ounces) black beans, rinsed and drained**
- **1 medium sweet red pepper, finely chopped**
- **1 tablespoon chili powder**
- **1 tablespoon cider vinegar**
- **2 teaspoons olive oil**
- **1 teaspoon ground cumin**
- **2 prebaked 12-inch pizza crusts**
- **2 cups (8 ounces) shredded cheddar cheese**
- **2 spinach tortillas (10 inches)**
- **1 can (4¼ ounces) chopped ripe olives**
- **Sour cream, optional**

1. Preheat oven to 450°. In a large bowl, combine the first eight ingredients. Transfer half of the mixture to a food processor. Process until blended; spread over crusts. Top with remaining bean mixture; sprinkle with cheese.
2. For bats, cut three 7-in. strips from edges of each tortilla. Using kitchen shears, cut scallops along the straight edge of each strip. From each center portion, cut three bat faces. Assemble three bats on each pizza. Arrange olive pieces on bats to make eyes and mouths. Sprinkle remaining olives over pizzas.
3. Bake 10-15 minutes or until cheese is melted. If desired, serve with sour cream.

SPIDERWEB BROWNIES

I drizzle a chocolate spiderweb over the white icing to turn the brownies into a fun Halloween treat. They're so delicious and chocolatey that you may end up making them for gatherings throughout the year.

—SANDY PICHON SLIDELL, LA

PREP: 20 MIN. • **BAKE:** 25 MIN. + COOLING • **MAKES:** 2 DOZEN

- **¾ cup butter, cubed**
- **4 ounces unsweetened chocolate, chopped**
- **2 cups sugar**
- **3 large eggs, lightly beaten**
- **1 teaspoon vanilla extract**
- **1 cup all-purpose flour**
- **1 cup chopped pecans or walnuts**
- **1 jar (7 ounces) marshmallow creme**
- **1 ounce semisweet chocolate**

1. In a large microwave-safe bowl, melt the butter and unsweetened chocolate; stir until smooth. Remove from the heat; stir in sugar. Cool for 10 minutes. Whisk in eggs and vanilla. Stir in flour and nuts. Pour into a greased foil-lined 13x9-in. baking pan.

2. Bake at 350° for 25-30 minutes or until a toothpick inserted near the center comes out clean (do not overbake). Immediately drop marshmallow cream by spoonfuls over hot brownies; spread evenly. Cool on a wire rack.

3. Lift out of the pan; remove foil. For web decoration, melt semisweet chocolate in a microwave; stir until smooth. Transfer to a small resealable plastic bag. Cut a small hole in one corner of the bag; drizzle chocolate over the top in a spiderweb design. Let set before cutting into bars.

FAST FIX

SLITHERING HUMMUS BITES

Friends often ask me to make my famous hummus dip for parties. One year at Halloween, I decided to take it a step further by piping it into phyllo shells and topping it with olives and roasted red peppers to make creepy creatures.

—AMY WHITE MANCHESTER, CT

START TO FINISH: 20 MIN. • **MAKES:** 2½ DOZEN

- **1 jar (7½ ounces) roasted sweet red peppers, drained**
- **1 can (15 ounces) garbanzo beans or chickpeas, rinsed and drained**
- **1 garlic clove, halved**
- **3 tablespoons lemon juice**
- **2 tablespoons olive oil**
- **2 tablespoons tahini**
- **½ teaspoon salt**
- **2 packages (1.9 ounces each) frozen miniature phyllo tart shells**
- **30 pitted ripe olives**

1. Cut one roasted pepper into 30 strips; place remaining peppers in a food processor. Add beans and garlic; pulse until chopped. Add lemon juice, oil, tahini and salt; process until blended.

2. Pipe into shells. Stuff a strip of red pepper into each olive; press into filled shells.

COMPANY'S COMING TURKEY

This recipe accomplishes every cook's turkey wish—a bird that brings the flavor of seasonings and herbs in every bite. It's the perfect mouthwatering centerpiece for your Thanksgiving Day celebration. You'll love the ease of preparation, too.

—CAROLINE WAMELINK
CLEVELAND HEIGHTS, OH

PREP: 20 MIN.
BAKE: 3½ HOURS + STANDING
MAKES: 14 SERVINGS

- **8 tablespoons butter, softened, divided**
- **3 garlic cloves, minced**
- **1 tablespoon poultry seasoning**
- **1 tablespoon minced fresh rosemary**
- **1 tablespoon minced fresh thyme**
- **1 turkey (14 to 16 pounds)**
- **¾ teaspoon salt**
- **¾ teaspoon pepper**
- **3 large onions, quartered, divided**
- **3 garlic cloves**
- **2 fresh rosemary sprigs**
- **2 fresh thyme sprigs**
- **2 cans (14½ ounces each) chicken broth**
- **3 cups white wine or additional chicken broth**
- **3 celery ribs, cut into 2-inch pieces**
- **3 medium carrots, cut into 2-inch pieces**

1. In a small bowl, combine 5 tablespoons butter, minced garlic, poultry seasoning and minced rosemary and thyme. With fingers, carefully loosen skin from the turkey breast; rub butter mixture under the skin. Rub remaining butter over skin of turkey. Sprinkle salt and pepper over turkey and inside cavity.
2. Place two onions, garlic cloves and rosemary and thyme sprigs inside the cavity. Place turkey on a rack in a large shallow roasting pan. Pour broth and wine into pan. Add celery, carrots and remaining onion.
3. Bake turkey, uncovered, at 325° for 3½ -4 hours or until a thermometer reads 180°, basting occasionally. Cover loosely with foil if the turkey browns too quickly. Cover and let stand for 20 minutes before slicing. If desired, thicken the pan drippings for gravy.

FAST FIX

CRANBERRY-ORANGE CORDIALS

I like recipes that are elegant but quick. These refreshing cordials are just the right touch after a full meal. The contrasting fruit and cream layers make a pretty presentation in clear glasses.
—DIANE NEMITZ LUDINGTON, MI

START TO FINISH: 15 MIN.
MAKES: 6 SERVINGS

- **1 can (14 ounces) whole-berry cranberry sauce**
- **1 cinnamon stick (3 inches)**
- **1 whole star anise**
- **⅓ cup orange liqueur**
- **¾ cup plain Greek yogurt**
- **2 ounces cream cheese, softened**
- **2 tablespoons honey**
- **6 small mint sprigs**

1. In a small saucepan, combine the cranberry sauce, cinnamon stick and star anise. Bring to a boil. Reduce the heat; simmer mixture, uncovered, for 2 minutes, stirring constantly. Stir in liqueur. Set aside to cool; discard cinnamon stick and star anise.
2. In a small bowl, beat the yogurt, cream cheese and honey until blended. Divide among six shot or cordial glasses. Top with cooled cranberry mixture. Save any remaining sauce for another use. Garnish with mint sprigs.
TO MAKE AHEAD *Cranberry mixture can be made the day before serving. Cover and refrigerate.*

(5) INGREDIENTS

POTATO PUMPKIN MASH

No more plain white mashed potatoes for us! I swirl fresh pumpkin into our holiday spuds for an extra kick of flavor and color.
—MICHELLE MEDLEY DALLAS, TX

PREP: 20 MIN. • **COOK:** 25 MIN.
MAKES: 8 SERVINGS

- **8 cups cubed peeled pie pumpkin (about 2 pounds)**
- **8 medium Yukon Gold potatoes, peeled and cubed (about 2 pounds)**
- **½ to ¾ cup 2% milk, divided**
- **8 tablespoons butter, softened, divided**
- **1 teaspoon salt, divided**
- **1 tablespoon olive oil**
- **¼ teaspoon coarsely ground pepper**

1. Place pumpkin in a large saucepan; add water to cover. Bring to a boil. Reduce heat; cook, uncovered, for 20-25 minutes or until tender.
2. Meanwhile, place potatoes in another saucepan; add water to cover. Bring to a boil. Reduce heat; cook, uncovered, for 10-15 minutes or until potatoes are tender.
3. Drain the potatoes; return to pan. Mash potatoes, adding 1/4 cup milk, 4 tablespoons butter and 1/2 teaspoon salt. Add additional milk if needed to reach desired consistency. Transfer to a serving bowl; keep warm.
4. Drain pumpkin; return to pan. Mash pumpkin, gradually adding the remaining butter and salt and enough remaining milk to reach desired consistency; spoon evenly over the potatoes. Cut through mashed vegetables with a spoon or knife to swirl. Drizzle with olive oil; sprinkle with pepper. Serve immediately.

PRETZEL TURKEY TREATS

Get the kids in the Turkey Day spirit by having them help put together these festive treats. With colorful pretzel-based tails, they make clever edible favors.

—*TASTE OF HOME* TEST KITCHEN

PREP: 2 HOURS + STANDING • **MAKES:** 1 DOZEN

- **6 Fruit by the Foot fruit rolls**
- **9 circus peanut candies**
- **1 cup butterscotch chips, divided**
- **24 candy eyeballs**
- **6 chocolate-covered thin mints**
- **12 large sourdough pretzels**
- **36 milk chocolate kisses, unwrapped**
- **12 vanilla wafers**

1. Using kitchen scissors, cut feathers and 12 wattles from fruit rolls. Cut three circus peanuts crosswise in half. Cut 24 turkey feet from remaining circus peanuts.

2. Reserve 12 butterscotch chips for beaks. In a microwave, melt 1/2 cup of the remaining chips; stir until smooth. For heads, using melted chips, attach two candy eyeballs, a wattle and a beak to each thin mint. Repeat using halved circus peanuts for rest of heads.

3. Place a pretzel on a waxed paper-lined microwave-safe plate. Place a chocolate kiss in each of the three holes. Microwave on high for 15-20 seconds or until melted. While chocolate is still warm, arrange feathers in a fan shape over pretzel, pressing gently into melted chocolate to adhere. Repeat with remaining pretzels and kisses.

4. Melt remaining butterscotch chips. Using melted chips, attach a vanilla wafer to each pretzel for body; attach heads. Attach circus peanut pieces for feet. Let stand until set.

WINTER SQUASH, SAUSAGE & FETA BAKE

This special side dish is a feast for the eyes and the taste buds! The butternut and acorn squash bake up tender and golden, and the bright color looks perfect on your Thanksgiving table. It's a guaranteed hit at potlucks, too.

—CRAIG SIMPSON SAVANNAH, GA

PREP: 30 MIN. • **BAKE:** 45 MIN.
MAKES: 20 SERVINGS (3/4 CUP EACH)

- **1 pound bulk Italian sausage**
- **2 large onions, chopped**
- **1/2 teaspoon crushed red pepper flakes, divided**
- **1/4 cup olive oil**
- **2 teaspoons minced fresh rosemary**
- **1 1/2 teaspoons salt**
- **1 teaspoon Worcestershire sauce**
- **1 teaspoon pepper**
- **1 medium butternut squash (about 4 pounds), peeled and cut into 1-inch cubes**
- **1 medium acorn squash, peeled and cut into 1-inch cubes**
- **2 cups (8 ounces) crumbled feta cheese**
- **2 small sweet red peppers, chopped**

1. Preheat oven to 375°. In a large skillet, cook the sausage, onions and 1/4 teaspoon pepper flakes over medium heat 8-10 minutes or until sausage is no longer pink and onions are tender, breaking up sausage into crumbles; drain.

2. In a large bowl, combine the oil, minced rosemary, salt, Worcestershire sauce, pepper and remaining pepper flakes. Add butternut and acorn squash, cheese, red peppers and sausage mixture; toss to coat.

3. Transfer to an ungreased shallow roasting pan. Cover and bake 35 minutes. Uncover; bake 10-15 minutes longer or until squash is tender.

TOP TIP

Preparing Winter Squash

To prepare winter squash for use in recipes, place it on a cutting board and carefully cut with a heavy butcher knife. Or, for easiest cutting, partially cook the squash first. Pierce a whole squash several times and microwave on high for 2-3 minutes or bake at 375° for 10-15 minutes. Cut squash in half; remove and discard the seeds. Use as halves or lay each half flat side down and cut slices 1/2 inch thick, discarding the ends. If desired, remove the outer shell from the strips with a sharp paring knife, then cube or mash the flesh as needed.

We love squash, and sausage and feta are flavors my family definitely loves. Don't waste the seeds—roast them just like pumpkin seeds. Toasty for a cold winter's night!
—KELLEYEE FROM TASTEOFHOME.COM

HOLIDAY PORK ROAST WITH GINGER GRAVY

This special dish is perfect for Christmas or New Year's Eve. A mouthwatering ginger gravy and tender vegetables complement the herbed roast.
—MARY ANN DELL PHOENIXVILLE, PA

PREP: 30 MIN.
BAKE: 1 HOUR 40 MIN. + STANDING
MAKES: 16 SERVINGS

- **1 boneless whole pork loin roast (5 pounds)**
- **1 tablespoon minced fresh gingerroot**
- **2 garlic cloves, minced**
- **1 teaspoon rubbed sage**
- **¼ teaspoon salt**
- **⅓ cup apple jelly**
- **½ teaspoon hot pepper sauce**
- **2 medium carrots, sliced**
- **2 medium onions, sliced**
- **1½ cups water, divided**
- **1 teaspoon browning sauce, optional**

1. Place pork roast on a rack in a shallow roasting pan. Combine the ginger, garlic, sage and salt; rub over meat. Bake, uncovered, at 350° for 1 hour.
2. Combine jelly and pepper sauce; brush over roast. Arrange carrots and onions around roast. Pour ½ cup water into pan. Bake 40-50 minutes longer or until a thermometer reads 145°. Remove roast to a serving platter; let stand for 10 minutes before slicing.
3. Skim fat from pan drippings. Transfer drippings and vegetables to a food processor; cover and process until smooth. Pour into a small saucepan. Add remaining water and if desired browning sauce; heat through. Slice roast; serve with gravy.

GARLIC-HERB PARMESAN ROLLS

Fresh-baked yeast rolls are always a hit at holiday dinners. To make it easy on the cook, start them in the bread machine. I arrange them in a tree shape for the yuletide season, but you can also make them in a 13x9-inch baking pan.
—LORRI REINHARDT BIG BEND, WI

PREP: 20 MIN. • **BAKE:** 20 MIN. + COOLING
MAKES: 16 SERVINGS

- **1 cup water (70° to 80°)**
- **2 tablespoons butter, softened**
- **1 large egg, lightly beaten**
- **3 tablespoons sugar**
- **2 teaspoons dried minced garlic**
- **1 teaspoon Italian seasoning**
- **1 teaspoon salt**
- **2¼ cups bread flour**
- **1 cup whole wheat flour**
- **1 package (¼ ounce) active dry yeast**

TOPPING

- **1 tablespoon butter, melted**
- **1 tablespoon grated Parmesan cheese**
- **1 teaspoon Italian seasoning**
- **½ teaspoon coarse salt**

1. In bread machine pan, place the first 10 ingredients in order suggested by manufacturer. Select dough setting (check dough after 5 minutes of mixing; add 1 to 2 tablespoons of water or flour if needed).
2. When cycle is completed, turn dough onto a lightly floured surface; divide into 16 balls. Line a baking sheet with foil and grease the foil. Center one roll near the top of prepared baking sheet. Arrange rolls snugly into four additional rows, adding one more roll for each row, forming a tree.
3. Center remaining ball under tree for trunk. Cover and let rolls rise until doubled, about 1 hour.
4. Brush rolls with butter. Combine cheese and Italian seasoning and sprinkle over rolls. Sprinkle with salt. Bake at 350° for 20-25 minutes or until golden brown. Serve warm.

CRANBERRY-WHITE CHOCOLATE COOKIES

These classics are among my favorite Christmas cookies. I prepare a few batches early in the season, then freeze them to pull out as needed. The tartness of the berries perfectly balances the sweet white chocolate.

—SHERRY CONLEY NOEL, NS

PREP: 25 MIN.
BAKE: 10 MIN./BATCH + COOLING
MAKES: ABOUT 7 DOZEN

- **1 cup butter, softened**
- **¾ cup sugar**
- **¾ cup packed brown sugar**
- **2 large eggs**
- **⅓ cup cranberry juice**
- **1 teaspoon vanilla extract**
- **3 cups all-purpose flour**
- **2 teaspoons baking powder**
- **½ teaspoon salt**
- **2 cups dried cranberries**
- **2 cups vanilla or white chips**

GLAZE

- **2 cups vanilla or white chips**
- **2 tablespoons plus 1½ teaspoons shortening**

1. In a large bowl, cream butter and sugars until light and fluffy. Beat in the eggs, cranberry juice and vanilla. Combine the flour, baking powder and salt; gradually add to creamed mixture and mix well. Fold in the cranberries and vanilla chips.

2. Drop by rounded teaspoonfuls 2 in. apart onto greased baking sheets. Bake at 350° for 10-12 minutes or until the edges begin to brown. Cool for 2 minutes before removing cookies to wire racks to cool completely.

3. For glaze, microwave vanilla chips and shortening at 70% power until melted; stir until smooth. Drizzle over the cookies.

CHRISTMAS MICE COOKIES

Add some whimsy to a Christmas cookie tray with these little cuties that taste like truffles. We always make a few extra batches to share with friends and neighbors.

—DEBORAH ZABOR FORT ERIE, ON

PREP: 30 MIN. + CHILLING • **MAKES:** 1½ DOZEN

- **⅔ cup semisweet chocolate chips**
- **2 cups chocolate wafer crumbs, divided**
- **⅓ cup sour cream**
- **36 red nonpareils**
- **¼ cup sliced almonds**
- **18 pieces black shoestring licorice (2 inches each)**

1. In a microwave, melt chocolate chips; stir until smooth. Stir in 1 cup wafer crumbs and sour cream. Refrigerate, covered, 1 hour or until firm enough to shape.

2. Place remaining wafer crumbs in a shallow bowl. For each mouse, roll about 1 tablespoon crumb mixture into a ball; taper one end to resemble a mouse. Roll in wafer crumbs to coat. Attach nonpareils for eyes, sliced almonds for ears and licorice pieces for tails. Store in an airtight container in the refrigerator.

(5) INGREDIENTS

TRAIL MIX COOKIE CUPS

My granddaughter helped create these cookie cups by using ingredients from my pantry and fridge. We used trail mix to jazz them up for the holidays.

PAMELA SHANK PARKERSBURG, WV

PREP: 15 MIN. • **BAKE:** 15 MIN. + COOLING • **MAKES:** 2 DOZEN

- **1 tube (16½ ounces) refrigerated peanut butter cookie dough**
- **½ cup creamy peanut butter**
- **½ cup Nutella**
- **1½ cups trail mix**

1. Preheat oven to 350°. Shape cookie dough into 1¼-in. balls; press evenly onto bottom and up sides of 24 greased mini-muffin cups.

2. Bake 12-14 minutes or until golden brown. With the back of measuring teaspoon, make an indentation in each cup. Cool in pans 15 minutes. Remove to wire racks to cool completely.

3. Spoon 1 teaspoon each peanut butter and Nutella into each cookie. Top with 1 tablespoon trail mix.

MINTY WREATHS

These keep in a tightly sealed container in the freezer for three weeks, so don't eat them all at once!

—SAMANTHA HARTZELL WASHINGTON, IL

PREP: 35 MIN. + FREEZING • **BAKE:** 10 MIN./BATCH • **MAKES:** 5 DOZEN

- **¾ cup butter, softened**
- **1 cup sugar**
- **⅓ cup 2% milk**
- **¾ teaspoon peppermint extract**
- **½ teaspoon vanilla extract**
- **2 cups all-purpose flour**
- **⅓ cup baking cocoa**
- **¼ cup cornstarch**
- **½ teaspoon salt**
- **1 pound dark chocolate or white candy coating, melted**
- **Assorted sprinkles**

1. In a large bowl, cream butter and sugar until light and fluffy. Beat in milk and extracts. Combine flour, cocoa, cornstarch and salt; gradually add to creamed mixture and mix well.

2. Shape into two 1½-in. diameter rolls; wrap each in plastic wrap. Freeze 2 hours or until firm.

3. Preheat oven to 375°. Unwrap and cut into ¼-in. slices. Place 1 in. apart on parchment paper-lined baking sheets.

4. Bake 10-12 minutes or until set. Remove to wire racks to cool completely.

5. Dip cookies in candy coating; allow excess to drip off. Place on waxed paper. Decorate as desired with sprinkles to resemble wreaths; let stand until set.

FROSTED ANISE COOKIES

I love anise flavoring, and my nana loved sugar cookies, so I put them together. They have a soft, from-scratch texture.
—RACHELE ANGELONI NORTH PROVIDENCE, RI

PREP: 30 MIN. • **BAKE:** 10 MIN./BATCH + COOLING
MAKES: 3½ DOZEN

- **1 cup butter, softened**
- **1½ cups sugar**
- **1 large egg**
- **1 teaspoon anise extract**
- **2¾ cups all-purpose flour**
- **1 teaspoon baking soda**
- **½ teaspoon baking powder**
- **1 can (16 ounces) vanilla frosting**
- **Holiday sprinkles**

1. Cream butter and sugar in a large bowl until light and fluffy. Beat in egg and extract. Combine the flour, baking soda and baking powder; gradually add to creamed mixture and mix well.
2. Drop by tablespoonfuls 2 in. apart onto ungreased baking sheets. Bake at 375° for 9-11 minutes or until golden brown. Remove to wire racks to cool completely.
3. Spread cookies with frosting and decorate with sprinkles. Let stand until set. Store in an airtight container.
TO MAKE AHEAD *Package cookies in an airtight container, separating layers with waxed paper, and freeze for up to 1 month.*

“Yummy! People who normally don't like anise flavor even liked these. I also tried them with almond flavor in place of the anise (and in the frosting as well) and they were equally tasty!”
—AMANDALEEANN FROM TASTEOFHOME.COM

RED VELVET CANDY CANE FUDGE

My favorite kind of cake, red velvet, inspired me to create this fudge. If you want a different shape, spoon the candy mixture into paper-lined mini muffin cups instead of spreading it in a pan.
—CRYSTAL SCHLUETER NORTHGLENN, CO

PREP: 25 MIN. + CHILLING • **MAKES:** 3¾ POUNDS

- **1 teaspoon butter**
- **2 packages (12 ounces each) white baking chips, divided**
- **⅔ cup semisweet chocolate chips**
- **3 teaspoons shortening, divided**
- **1 can (14 ounces) sweetened condensed milk**
- **1½ teaspoons red paste food coloring**
- **4 cups confectioners' sugar, divided**
- **6 ounces cream cheese, softened**
- **1 teaspoon vanilla extract**
- **¼ teaspoon peppermint extract**
- **3 tablespoons crushed peppermint candies**

1. Line a 13x9-in. pan with foil; grease foil with butter.
2. In a large microwave-safe bowl, combine 3¼ cups white baking chips, chocolate chips and 2 teaspoons shortening. Microwave, uncovered, on high 1 minute; stir. Microwave at additional 15-second intervals, stirring until smooth. Stir in milk and food coloring; gradually add 1 cup confectioners' sugar. Spread into prepared pan.
3. In another large microwave-safe bowl, melt remaining white baking chips and shortening; stir until smooth. Beat in cream cheese and extracts. Gradually beat in remaining confectioners' sugar until smooth. Spread mixture over red layer; sprinkle with crushed candies. Refrigerate 2 hours or until fudge is firm.
4. Using foil, lift fudge out of pan. Remove foil; cut fudge into 1-in. squares. Store between layers of waxed paper in an airtight container.

GENERAL INDEX

APPETIZERS
(ALSO SEE DIPS & SPREADS; SNACKS)

APPLES

APRICOTS

ASPARAGUS

AVOCADO

BACON & PANCETTA

BANANAS

BARS & BROWNIES

BEANS & LENTILS

BEEF & CORNED BEEF
(ALSO SEE GROUND BEEF)

Artichoke & Spinach Dip Pizza, 11

Potato Minestrone, 57

Creamy Frozen Fruit Cups, 26

CARROTS
(CONTINUED)

CASSEROLES

Lasagna Casserole, 110

CAULIFLOWER

CELERY

CHEESE (ALSO SEE CREAM CHEESE)

CHEESECAKES

CHERRIES

CHICKEN

Party Crab Puffs, 16

CHILI

CHILIES

CHOCOLATE
(ALSO SEE WHITE CHOCOLATE)

COCONUT

COFFEE CAKES

CONDIMENTS

COOKIES

CORN

CRANBERRIES

CREAM CHEESE

Oat Dinner Rolls, 161

CREAM CHEESE
(CONTINUED)

CUCUMBERS

DELI MEAT

DESSERTS
(ALSO SEE BARS & BROWNIES; CAKES & CUPCAKES; CANDIES & CONFECTIONS; CHEESECAKES; COOKIES; PIES & TARTS)

DIPS & SPREADS

EGGS

FISH & SEAFOOD

FRUIT
(ALSO SEE SPECIFIC KINDS)

GARLIC

GINGER

GREEN BEANS

GRILLED RECIPES

GROUND BEEF

Crustless Spinach Quiche, 36

Cajun Cabbage, 67

NUTS
(CONTINUED)

OATS & GRANOLA

OLIVES

ONIONS

ORANGES

PASTA & NOODLES

Mango-Pineapple Chicken Tacos, 134

PEANUT BUTTER

PEAS

PEPPERS

PIES & TARTS

PINEAPPLE

Baked Spaghetti, 113

Cranberry Sweet Potato Muffins, 159

Vietnamese Pork Lettuce Wraps, 10

SALADS

SANDWICHES & WRAPS

SAUSAGE, PEPPERONI & SALAMI

SCONES

SIDE DISHES

SLOW COOKER RECIPES

SNACKS

Cherry Almond Mousse Pie, 165

Caramelized Ham & Swiss Buns, 56

ALPHABETICAL INDEX

A

B

C

Pork Loin with Raspberry Sauce, 94

D

E

State Fair Subs, 59

F

G

H

I

J

K

L

M

N

Spicy Applesauce, 70

O

White Chocolate-Strawberry Tiramisu, 177

Ingredient Substitutions

WHEN YOU NEED:	IN THIS AMOUNT:	SUBSTITUTE:
Baking Powder	1 teaspoon	½ teaspoon cream of tartar plus ¼ teaspoon baking soda
Broth	1 cup	1 cup hot water plus 1 teaspoon bouillon granules or 1 bouillon cube
Buttermilk	1 cup	1 tablespoon lemon juice or white vinegar plus enough milk to measure 1 cup (let stand 5 minutes), or 1 cup plain yogurt
Cajun Seasoning	1 teaspoon	¼ teaspoon cayenne pepper, ½ teaspoon dried thyme, ¼ teaspoon dried basil and 1 minced garlic clove
Chocolate	1 ounce	3 tablespoons baking cocoa plus 1 tablespoon shortening or canola oil
Chocolate, Semisweet	1 ounce	1 ounce unsweetened chocolate plus 1 tablespoon sugar, or 3 tablespoons semisweet chocolate chips
Corn Syrup, Dark	1 cup	¾ cup light corn syrup plus ¼ cup molasses
Corn Syrup, Light	1 cup	1 cup sugar plus ¼ cup water
Cornstarch	1 tablespoon	2 tablespoons all-purpose flour (for thickening)
Cracker Crumbs	1 cup	1 cup dry bread crumbs
Cream, Half-and-Half	1 cup	1 tablespoon melted butter plus enough whole milk to measure 1 cup
Egg, Large	1 whole	2 large egg whites or 2 large egg yolks or ¼ cup egg substitute
Flour, Cake	1 cup	1 cup minus 2 tablespoons (⅞ cup) all-purpose flour
Flour, Self-Rising	1 cup	1½ teaspoons baking powder, ½ teaspoon salt and enough all-purpose flour to measure 1 cup
Garlic, Fresh	1 clove	⅛ teaspoon garlic powder
Gingerroot, Fresh	1 teaspoon	¼ teaspoon ground ginger
Honey	1 cup	1¼ cups sugar plus ¼ cup water
Lemon Juice	1 teaspoon	¼ teaspoon cider vinegar
Lemon Peel	1 teaspoon	½ teaspoon lemon extract
Milk, Whole	1 cup	½ cup evaporated milk plus ½ cup water, or 1 cup water plus ⅓ cup nonfat dry milk powder
Molasses	1 cup	1 cup honey
Mustard, Prepared	1 tablespoon	½ teaspoon ground mustard plus 2 teaspoons cider or white vinegar
Onion	1 small onion (⅓ cup chopped)	1 teaspoon onion powder or 1 tablespoon dried minced onion
Poultry Seasoning	1 teaspoon	¾ teaspoon rubbed sage plus ¼ teaspoon dried thyme
Sour Cream	1 cup	1 cup plain yogurt
Sugar	1 cup	1 cup packed brown sugar or 2 cups sifted confectioners' sugar
Tomato Juice	1 cup	½ cup tomato sauce plus ½ cup water
Tomato Sauce	2 cups	¾ cup tomato paste plus 1 cup water

Get Cooking with a Well-Stocked Kitchen

In a perfect world, you would plan weekly or even monthly menus and have all the ingredients on hand to make each night's dinner. The reality, however, is that you likely haven't thought about dinner until you've walked through the door.

With a reasonably stocked pantry, refrigerator and freezer, you'll still be able to serve a satisfying meal in short order. Consider these tips:

QUICK-COOKING MEATS—such as boneless chicken breasts, chicken thighs, pork tenderloin, pork chops, ground meats, Italian sausage, sirloin and flank steaks, fish fillets and shrimp—should be stocked in the freezer. Wrap them individually (except shrimp), so you can remove only the amount you need. For the quickest defrosting, wrap meats for freezing in small, thin packages.

FROZEN VEGETABLES packaged in plastic bags are a real time-saver. Simply pour out the amount needed. No preparation is required!

PASTAS, RICE, RICE MIXES AND COUSCOUS are great staples to have in the pantry—and they generally have a long shelf life. Remember, thinner pastas, such as angel hair, cook faster than thicker pastas. Fresh (refrigerated) pasta cooks faster than dried.

DAIRY PRODUCTS like milk, sour cream, cheeses (shredded, cubed or crumbled), eggs, yogurt, butter and margarine are perishable, so check the use-by date on packages and replace as needed.

CONDIMENTS such as ketchup, mustard, mayonnaise, salad dressings, salsa, taco sauce, soy sauce, stir-fry sauce, lemon juice, etc., add flavor to many dishes. Personalize the list to suit your family's needs.

FRESH FRUIT AND VEGETABLES can make a satisfying predinner snack. Oranges and apples are not as perishable as bananas. Ready-to-use salad greens are perfect for an instant salad.

DRIED HERBS, SPICES, VINEGARS and seasoning mixes add lots of flavor and keep for months.

PASTA SAUCES, OLIVES, BEANS, broths, canned tomatoes, canned vegetables, and canned or dried soups are ideal to have on hand for a quick meal—and many of these items are common recipe ingredients..

GET YOUR FAMILY INTO THE HABIT of posting a grocery list. When an item is used up or is almost gone, just add it to your list for the next shopping trip. This way you won't run completely out of an item, and you'll also save time when writing your grocery list.

Make the Most of Your Time Every Night

With recipes in hand and your kitchen stocked, you're well on your way to a relaxing family meal. Here are some pointers to help you get dinner on the table fast:

PREHEAT THE OVEN OR GRILL before starting on the recipe.

PULL OUT ALL THE INGREDIENTS, mixing tools and cooking tools before beginning any prep work.

USE CONVENIENCE ITEMS whenever possible, such as prechopped garlic, onion and peppers, shredded or cubed cheese, seasoning mixes, jarred sauces, etc.

MULTITASK! While the meat is simmering for a main dish, toss a salad, cook a side dish or start on dessert.

ENCOURAGE HELPERS. Have younger children set the table. Older ones can help with ingredient preparation or even assemble simple recipes themselves.

TAKE CARE OF TWO MEALS IN ONE NIGHT by planning main dish leftovers or making a double batch of favorite sides.

Tricks to Tame Hunger When It Strikes

Are the kids begging for a before-supper snack? Calm their rumbling tummies with some nutritious, not-too-filling noshes.

START WITH A SMALL TOSSED SALAD. Try a ready-to-serve salad mix and add their favorite salad dressing and a little protein, like cubed cheese or julienned slices of deli meat.

CUT UP AN APPLE and smear a little peanut butter on each slice. Or offer other fruits such as seedless grapes, cantaloupe, oranges or bananas. For variety, give kids vanilla yogurt or reduced-fat ranch dressing as a dipper for the fruit, or combine a little reduced-fat sour cream with a sprinkling of brown sugar. Too tired to cut up the fruit? A fruit snack cup will do the trick, too.

DURING THE COLD MONTHS, serve up a small mug of soup with a few oyster crackers to hit the spot.

RAW VEGGIES such as carrots, cucumbers, mushrooms, broccoli and cauliflower are tasty treats, especially when served with a little hummus for dipping. Many of these vegetables can be purchased precut.

GIVE KIDS A SMALL SERVING of cheese and crackers. Look for sliced cheese and cut the slices into smaller squares to fit the crackers. Choose a cracker that's made from whole wheat, such as an all-natural, seven-grain cracker.